STATESMANSHIP ON THE BENCH

STATESMANSHIP ON THE BENCH

The Judicial Career of SIR ADETOKUNBO ADEMOLA (CJN), 1939 – 1972

by
Akin Alao

Africa World Press, Inc.

P.O. Box 1892
Trenton, NJ 08607

P.O. Box 48
Asmara, ERITREA

Africa World Press, Inc.

P.O. Box 1892
Trenton, NJ 08607

P.O. Box 48
Asmara, ERITREA

First Printing 2007

Book and Cover design: Saverance Publishing Services

Library of Congress Cataloging-in-Publication Data

Alao, Akin.

Statesmanship on the bench : the judicial career of Sir Adetokunbo Ademola (CJN), 1939-1972 / Akin Alao.

p. cm.

Includes bibliographical references and index.

ISBN 1-59221-570-X ((hb)) -- ISBN 1-59221-571-8 ((pb))

1. Ademola, Adetokunbo, Sir, 1906- 2. Judges--Nigeria--Biography. 3. Statesmen--Nigeria--Biography. 4. Separation of powers--Nigeria. 5. Judicial process--Nigeria. 6. Nigeria. Supreme Court. I. Ademola, Adetokunbo, Sir, 1906- II. Title.

KTA110.A34A43 2007
347.669'014092--dc22
[B]

2007006920

Table of Contents

Foreword by Toyin Falola

This book carefully intermeshes the instrumentalities of law with the personality of a preeminent judge to expose the intricacies of the interactions between the state and its citizens, between the ambitions of rival politicians and electoral laws, between regions in a fragmented federal system, and between the colonial and post-colonial chaotic order. One significant window to the understanding of this complicated web of law and society is the activities of the country's first chief justice, Sir Adetokunbo Ademola. Dr. Alao acknowledges the authoritative status of this highly distinguished judge, his demonstrated ability to negotiate the complexities of the constitution, the controversies he generated in decisions relating to politicians' quests for power, and his robust interpretive revolution in dealing with regionalism and access to federal power.

A fascinating picture of the judiciary and the colonial state emerges—the creation and articulation of a new body of law based on the British system; the altered conceptions of traditional laws; the privileging of a new generation of Western-educated lawyers (of which Sir Ademola was a powerful member) who nurtured an establishment-oriented nature of judging; and the impact of modernism in adjudicating cases.

Sir Ademola and the law, which can be regarded as Siamese twins, were experimenting with a modernist epistemology, arguably responding to the ambiguities of modernity. To be clear, I mean the very modernity of the colonial state itself, which signaled the very wide angle of the vision that informs the writing of this book. As new legal orientations revealed their textures and colors, anchored to the hanger of politics in the closet and thicket of federalism, I can see the emergence of a complicated and treacherous legal and political landscape. Sir Ademola was an astute reader of these phenomena, and he himself contributed to the emerging perceptions that the Nigerian universe would both be orderly and chaotic, and that no one, not even the talented judge, would be capable of controlling the events. The men created the laws, events determined interpretations, and politics shaped their execution. The able judge, as we can tell in the various gestures offered by Dr. Alao, was both an agent and a victim: an agent of law, a victim of time. But he was certainly a master of both.

This book will surely generate considerable interest, not simply because of the astute analysis of the career of this influential judge, more so because of the applications of a careful methodology that attempts a holistic presentation, in rich chapters, of the law and judiciary, politics and the state, the bar and the bench. I see an innate congeniality in Dr. Alao's treatment which allows us to interpret and make sense of the fabric of law, the difficulty of human nature, and contradictory empirical data.

In Justice Ademola's world, we see how politics precedes modernism and how there is a cultural mix between modernism and the political order. Dr. Alao creates a movement—of law in relation to time; time in relation to power; and power in relation to conflict. This is a movement that unfolds an elegant book that is distinctly progressive, articulate in its acceptance of change, optimistic about the relevance of law, and respectful in seeing Justice Ademola and other legal elite as possessing a vision that we can harness to create a functional society.

Toyin Falola
University of Texas Distinguished Professor
Fellow of the Historical Society of Nigeria
Fellow of the Nigerian Academy of Letters
The Nelson Mandela Professor of African Studies At Large
The Frances Higgintbotham Nalle Centennial Professor in History

Preface

This career biography of the first indigenous Chief Justice of Nigeria is intended to provide useful insights into three critical areas in Nigeria's legal history. In the chapters following, this book will examine the interrelationship of the executive and the judiciary under different political structures between 1939 and 1972, and understand the role, relevance, impact, and limitations of the judiciary in Nigeria. It will then critically examine the activities of Sir Adetokunbo Ademola as a jurist and his contributions to judicial administration and the rule of law in Nigeria.

Existing literature on Nigeria's social and intellectual history points to a concern to re-engage and re-evaluate the process of state and institutional building in Nigeria. In spite of the remarkable pioneering efforts of the first generation of Nigerian scholars, recent developments warrant an incisive discourse on the role of the judiciary in state building. It should however be remarked that this effort is not a commissioned biography. It is intended as an academic and objective examination of the judicial career and contributions of Sir Adetokunbo Ademola to the judiciary in its relationship with the executive arm and within the context of the principles of judicial independence and separation of powers. It is also an attempt to understand the judiciary, its tradition, powers and limitations through a critical analysis of the numerous judgements (reported and unreported) and quasi-judicial activities of Sir Adetokunbo Ademola as a judicial officer.

The bench in Nigeria is constitutionally empowered to resolve justiciable disputes and answer questions involving the interpretations of the law. The judiciary grapples with such questions as to whether particular branches of government have met their obligations, whether they have appropriately exercised their powers, and whether they have utilized discretion strictly within the limits of their jurisdiction. This role is both pivotal and paradoxical. As an arm of government, the judiciary is part of the machinery for the establishment of order, law, and good government. It must also at the same time protect individual rights and freedoms against possible government encroachment.

The judicial activities of Sir Adetokunbo Ademola as a Magistrate (1939 – 1949), judge (1949-1955), Chief Justice of the Western Region (1955 – 1958) and Chief Justice of Nigeria (1958 – 1972) shall be assessed to understand the role of the judge in Nigeria with a view to appraising how the judiciary as a paramount agency of social control contributed to the establishment of a stable federation, defense of the fundamental rights of citizens against state excesses in the guise of public policy, the maintenance of the rule of the law and the resolution of conflicts in inter personal relations.

Sir Adetokunbo Ademola's activities on the bench are intended to be a reference point in the examination of the relevance and impact of the judiciary under his leadership with respect to common law in Nigeria, customary law, human rights of citizens and civil liberties, as well as criminal law and legal procedure. As noted by the eminent German jurist Friendrich Von Savigny, law and history have many meeting points. A nation's history is partly reflected in its laws and in the activities of the officers of the law who administer and manage the legal process. This book therefore intends to understand the theory and practice of judicial administration in colonial and postcolonial federal state.

Law, as a means of conduct in a community or society has been variously defined. The mosaic, sometimes-fluid conceptions of law have consequently led to the different perception of its functions. To perform the function of securing justice, resolving social conflicts, ordering the society, lubricating the machinery of social interrelationship, protecting individual and corporate interests and controlling social relations, law has a number of agencies. Law derives its meaning and relevance in organic social relations, where it is necessary to preserve order, redress harm and protect basic freedoms.

The first of these agencies of the law is the judiciary, which gives effect to the spirit and essence of the law by interpreting it correctly to achieve the desired objective. The judiciary and other agencies of law co-jointly determine the adequacy, relevance and importance of law as a means of social control and social justice.

The judicial career of Sir Adetokunbo Ademola demonstrates how a judicial personality could play a central role in the historical development of a country's judicial system. Adegboyega Adetokunbo Ademola was born on February 1, 1906[1] at Abeokuta to the royal family of Sir Ladapo Ademola II. He started school at the Roman Catholic Mission School, Itesi, Abeokuta in 1911 where he proved to be "a very playful boy who would not exert himself.[2] According to Oba Ladapo Ademola, Adetokunbo Ademola was an obedient child who would not want to be rebuked twice for the same offence.[3] At eight years, Adetokunbo Ademola enrolled at the Holy Cross Primary School, Lagos and after the completion of primary school education, he was admitted into St. Gregory's Grammar School[4] from where he transferred to the newly established King's College in 1920; the year his father became the Alake of Abeokuta.[5]

By this time, the depth of the colonial government's interest in providing secondary school education in Nigeria was difficult, if not entirely impossible to determine.[6] Indeed by the 1920's, the colonial authorities in Lagos were becoming increasingly interested in the control of secondary schools than in any other level or aspect of education.[7] The obvious and pressing need for clerks to service the colonial administrative set up and the commercial houses did swing the attention of government to secondary school education. This was indeed responsible for government's greater financial support for schools during the period 1919 – 1929. Henry Carr, the first African Inspector of

Schools, even advocated the establishment of a model secondary school by the colonial government.[8] It would then seem that this opinion formed the basis of the idea behind the establishment of the King's College, Lagos by the colonial government.[9]

In 1925, Adetokunbo Ademola passed out of King's College, Lagos and having also been successful at the Senior Clerical Examination; he was eminently qualified to take up a full time appointment in the colonial civil service. He was consequently appointed a clerk in the Chief Secretary's office at the Nigerian Secretariat,, Lagos.[10] For two years Adetokunbo Ademola served as clerk in the general administration branch where he was a records officer, during which period he consummated an ambition for further studies in the United Kingdom. The comfortable and elitist background coupled with the exigencies of the time and a well-placed ambition to have a more secure career must have provided the necessary impetus for a burning desire to train abroad. According to Adenekan Ademola,[11] the legal and public careers of two of Adetokunbo Ademola's maternal uncles, Sir Adeyemo Alakija and Hon. Olayinka Alakija, substantially influenced his choice of a career. It is believed that at a very early age, Adetokunbo Ademola had the opportunity of being exposed to the career and exploits of these two influential gentlemen. Sir Adeyemo Alakija was reputed among various communities in Nigeria. He was equally particularly interested in prison reforms and in the welfare of ex-prisoners and ex-servicemen.

Adetokunbo Ademola lived with Sir Adeyemo Alakija and had unfettered access to his library, which was made up of books on law, literature, poetry, government and social welfare.[12] Another equally important influence on Adetokunbo Ademola in making a decision to study law was the legal exploit of the early generation of Nigerian lawyers, who not only showed extra-ordinary brilliance, but also added colour to the practice of law in Nigeria. The oratory, flamboyance and erudition of the first generation of qualified lawyers in Nigeria made the legal profession noble and fascinating. There are shreds of evidence to support the suggestion that the proximity of the home in which

Adetokunbo Ademola was reared to the Broad Street made him appreciate and fancy these legal luminaries.[13] The Broad Street, Lagos had the law chambers of Egerton Shyngle[14], Montacute Thompson,[15] Sapara Willaims,[16] Kitoyi Ajasa,[17] E. J. Alex Taylor, [18] and Eric O. More.[19] Adetokunbo Ademola was aware of the exploit in law of this class of Nigerian barristers and the respect they commanded among Lagosians in particular and the people of the southern protectorate in general. Eric Moore and Egerton Shyngle played very active roles in cases involving the colonial secretary of Southern Nigeria on the issues of native land tenure and customary law.[20]

Possibly, the combination of these two factors positively influenced Adetokunbo Ademola's decision to study law in England. Adenekan Ademola however believed that more than any other factor, the enormous and overwhelming influence of the personality and public career of Sir Adeyemo Alakija were in main, responsible for Adetokunbo Ademola's preference to study law.[21] This position becomes further strengthened if set against the fact that Adetokunbo Ademola's choice to study law was in defiance of his father's plan for him to qualify as a medical practitioner.[22]

As noted by Adewoye, the legal profession was not only fascinating and attractive to the innocent minds of young school leavers, it was also lucrative, relevant to the needs of the time and generally accepted by the society. In those days, members of the Bar belonged to a different class in society and they formed its crème.[23] In 1927, Adetokunbo Ademola went to the United Kingdom to study law. Having passed the prescribed qualifying examination, he eventually secured a place at Selwyn College, Cambridge University in 1928. According to Folarin Coker, it may be difficult to describe Adetokunbo Ademola as an outstanding scholar at Cambridge. He was conveniently an average student preparing for a successful legal practice after school. The quality of the legal education he received at Cambridge and the exposure to a broad spectrum of Western style education and values both within and outside Cambridge prepared him for a career in law.[24] As would be shown in later discussions, the orientation of Adetokunbo Ademola as a lawyer and a public person, his perception of social reality and perhaps his philosophical preferences smacked of strong imprints of English tradition and values. This book proceeds on the premise that Adetokunbo Ademola's perception of law, its functions, relevance and scope could best be understood if set against the background of his training in the United Kingdom and his preferred personal disposition to English standards of practice, values and traditions.

On the authority of Folarin Coker,[25] Adetokunbo Ademola was one of those who applied for admission to the Utter Bar and on the 21st day of Trinity Term 1934, the Master Treasurer admitted "those students of this Honorable and Learned Society whose proposal for call to the Degree of the Utter Bar have been authorized by Parliament.[26] As noted by Coker, the call to Bar was both the simplest ceremony in the inheritance of the English law and the most decisive event in the life of every barrister.[27]

Adetokunbo Ademola had his first appointment or articleship in the chambers of Messer Austin Farligh and Co.[28] He used the opportunity to learn the ropes as it were in legal practice. He soon got involved in a form of activism and was actually a front liner in the campaign for the condemnation of racism and the British attitude towards Africa.[29] As a pupil Attorney in the office of A.C.V. Prior, who was then the Attorney General of Nigeria, Adetokunbo Ademola, identified with a Literary and Debating Society or Study Circle that was put together by some educated Nigerians who wanted a forum to meet and discuss essentially Nigerian matters. The membership of the circle included some prominent young Lagosians including, H. A. Subair, R. A. Coker, Olatunji Caxton Martins, Adetokunbo Ademola and Samuel Akisanya. The group sponsored essay writing, lectures, debates and book reviews[30]. In 1935, it arranged a public debate at Glover Memorial Hall to discuss Indirect Rule in Nigeria.

Adetokunbo Ademola had a somewhat brief involvement with party politics when he joined the Nigerian Youth Movement. The Movement, according to J.S. Coleman, was the only pan-Nigerian political association during that period of Nigerian political history.[32] The other existing associations were, trade unions, literary societies, ethnic or clan unions or localized political parities like the Nigerian Democratic Party of Herbert Macaulay. The Nigerian Youth Movement was founded in 1936 as a dynamic progressive and nationalistic political association to protest British colonialism and imperialism in Nigeria and to press for political independence. Membership of the N.Y.M. cut across the country and the professions.[33] While the NYM was active in Nigerian public life, it served as the most articulate forum for nationalist agitation in the inter-war period.

In 1938, the N.Y.M destroyed the seeming invincibility of the N.D.P. by sweeping the pools at the Nigerian Legislative Council election. Adetokunbo Ademola was not a candidate; he however, played a prominent role as an active member of the selection committee of the N.Y.M. He participated fully in the campaigns and even represented the party on poll's day at the Glover Memorial Hall where the names of successful candidates were announced. After the 1938 election, Adetokunbo Ademola resigned his membership of the N.Y.M. He left not only party politics, but also private legal practice. He subsequently took up appointment in the colonial judicial department as a magistrate in April 1939.[34]

Notes

1. NAI/C.S.O./26/28525 Vol. IV, Nigerian Staff List, April 1949.
2. Folarin Coker, *Sir Adetokunbo Ademola* (Lagos: Daily Times of Nigeria, 1972), P. 24
3. *Ibid.*
4. *Ibid.*
5. Oral interview: Hon. Justice Adenekan Ademola 69 years, Retired Justice of the Federal Court of /Appeal, Retired Director of Studies, Nigeria Judiciary Institute Lagos, 14-15 February 1995.
6. A Fajana, *Education in Nigeria 1842 – 1939: An Historical Analysis* (Ibadan: Longman Nigeria Ltd., 1978), p. 176
7. *Ibid.*

8. *Ibid.*
9. *Ibid.*
10. Folarin Coker... p. 28
11. Interview with Adenekan Ademola, February 14, 1995.
12. Folarin Coker ... p. 28
13. *Ibid.*
14. For details see "The Late Hon J. Egerton Shyngle: A Sketch by a Blue Bag" *Nigeria Daily Times* 16 June 1926
15. Omoniyi Adewoye, "Self-Taught Attorneys in Lagos 1865 – 1913", *Journal of the Historical Society of Nigeria* vol. V. No. 1, 1969.
16. Sapara Williams was the first qualified Nigerian Lawyer. For details, see Omoniyi Adewoye" Sapara Williams: Lawyer and Public Servant". *Journal of the Historical Society of Nigeria*, Vol. 6 No. 1, 1971.
17. Sir Kitoyi Ajasa was the first Lawyer to be knighted by the British Monarch. Together with Sapara Williams, J. Egerton Shyngle formed the backbone of legal practice in Lagos for a time.
18. E. J. Alex Taylor was known as the cock of the Bar who enrolled as a barrister of the Supreme Court in 1905. He had a very successful practice and later became the leader of the Nigerian Bar.
19. Eric Moore enrolled as a barrister of the Supreme Court in 1903
20. Folarin Coker... p. 32
21. Oral interview: Justice Adenekan Ademola 15 February 1995
22. *Ibid.*
23. Omoniyi Adewoye, *The Judicial System in Southern Nigeria 1854 – 1954: Law and Justice in a Dependency* (London: Longman Group Ltd., 1977), pp. 116-177.
24. Folarin Coker... p. 32
25. *Ibid.*, p. 35
26. *Ibid.*
27. *Ibid.*, p. 36
28. *Ibid.*
29. For details of his activities, see J. S. Coleman *Nigeria: Background to Nationalism* (Berkeley: University of California Press, 1958), pp. 208-209.
30. *Ibid.*, p. 216.
31. Nigeria Daily Telegraph March 20, 1935

32. For details of Nigerian political parties and nationalism, see J. S. Coleman *Nigeria: Background to Nationalism* (Berkley: University of California Press, 1963) and R. Sklar, *Nigerian Political Parties* (Princeton: Princeton University Press, 1963).
33. J. S. Coleman, *Nigeria: Background to Nationalism*... p 218.
34. Folarin Coker ... p. 40.

Acknowledgements

I appreciate with gratitude the pivotal role of Professor Omoniyi Adewoye, who first fired my interest in the field of legal history and who eventually supervised the study of which this book is a product. Dr. Ademola Popoola deserves special mention for his readiness to correct errors of interpretation and putting the work in shape. For solid conceptual framework credit must be given to Dr. Jare Oladosu and to Dr. Kemi Rotimi for a more elegant presentation. I am also grateful to Professors Femi Omosini, Richard Olaniyan, Biodun Adediran Akin Olorunfemi and Sola Akinrinade, all senior colleagues at Ife, for making the workplace conducive for research. Tayo and Kemi Adesina provided accommodation and comfort for me at Ibadan as often as I called on them.

I equally appreciate the contributions of the following people who in their own little ways encouraged me to publish this book in its present form: Barrister Ibukun Babajide, Prof. Kayode Alao, Dr. Gboyega Ajayi, my siblings, Mrs.E.O. Ogungbemi, Dr. (Mrs.) Irene Durosaro, Mr. Segun Alao and of course Titilayo Olubunmi Alao (of blessed memory). My wife, Iretioluwa and our children Damilola and Tinuola provided a most conducive atmosphere for academic work at home. I thank the staffs of the National Archives, Ibadan, Obafemi Awolowo University, Ile-Ife. University of Ibadan Library, IFRA Library and the Supreme Court Library and Archive, Lagos. Hon. Justice Adenekan Ademola of the National Judicial Institute, Mr. Justice Desalu former Registrar of the Supreme Court of Nigeria and of course, Hon. Justice Emmanuel Fakayode also provided useful source materials for which I am very grateful. Barrister S.B. Ajayi facilitated my visit to and use of the library facilities at Chief S.P. Ajibade's Chambers in Ibadan. I am grateful to Mr. Omotayo of the same chambers.

Finally, I wish to acknowledge with thanks, the sustained interest of the doyen of African Studies, Professor Toyin Falola in legal history as a field of academic study and in the publication of this book.

Akin Alao
Ile-Ife

Chapter 1

Introduction

> *It is in the courts and not in the legislature that our citizens primarily feel the keen cutting edge of the law. If they have respect for the work of the courts, their respect for law will survive the shortcomings of every other branch of government, but if they lose their respect for the work of courts, their respect for law and order will varnish with it to the great detriment of society.*
>
> Arthur Vanderbilt, *The Challenge of Law Reform* (Princeton: Princeton University Press, 1995), p. 4

This chapter provides a theoretical framework for the book and discusses the key concepts of government, separation of powers, the independence of the judiciary and the judicial process to provide a background for the discussion of the interrelationship of the executive and the judiciary in Nigeria using the chequered judicial career of Adetokunbo Ademola as reference.

The concept of government in the modern sense is based on the tripod of the executive, legislative and the judiciary with varying degrees of interrelationship, overlaps, and inter-penetration. The end for which men institute a regulatory body over their affairs is however at the level of theory and ideology.[1] This end for which government is established depends on the intellectual, philosophical, and perhaps ideological persuasion of the inquirer on the one hand, and the society's stage of development on the other. Leading thinkers and philosophers of the enlightenment age such as Thomas Hobbes, John Locke, Voltaire, Montesquieu, and Rousseau were concerned with politics during the widespread political upheavals of the 16th and 18th centuries in Europe. The age of monarchical absolutism when powerful European monarchs ruled with strict authority provoked the development and promotion of ideas of freedom and liberty among the intellectual elite and philosophers.[2] Indeed the historical antecedents of the doctrine of separation of powers could be traced to the political writings of Locke, Rousseau and Montesquieu. Locke lived in England during the late 17th century and had a more optimistic view of human nature. He believed in individual natural rights and that people were born into the world free and equal. He contended that a man had rights to life, liberty and the ownership of property. To him, the duty of government was the protection of the natural rights of man. The French Philosopher Rousseau had great faith in the common people and argued in favour of equality of all. He also described the ideal society based on his personal reflections on human nature in *The Social Contract*. For Rousseau, a social contract is an agreement among the people living together in a given society. In Rousseau's ideal society, the members of a community would agree among themselves to give up part of their freedom for the good of the group as a whole. The decisions of the majority or the general will would apply to everyone. The major problem in Rousseau's position borders on whom and how would society determine what he called the general will.

The modern conception of the principle of separation of power owes its origin to the thoughts of Montesquieu who showed a remarkable concern for the preservation of political liberty. He was a French noble and judge who spent nearly twenty years comparing various forms of government from antiquity to his own age. In 1748, he published his findings in a seminar work titled *De l'Espirit des Lois.* This work established Montesquieu as one of the founders of political science as an academic discipline on the systematic study of government. In the continuing need to protect the individual against despotism and oppression, Montesquieu opined that power must not be concentrated in the hands of a few individuals[3] or a group. He believed that unless power was made to check power, it would be abused. The guarantee against the possible misuse of power was found in establishing mutual checks among legislative, executive and judicial arms of government. This doctrine recognized the inherent danger of an absolute union of these functions in one person or body. This should not however be misinterpreted to mean the respective allocation of powers to three distinct organs with no interrelationship among or between them to prevent the abuse of power. Montesquieu believed that individual human beings are motivated by economic interest, and to control those in power; the various classes or economic interests should be mixed among the arms of government to prevent the domination of others by one.

> Political liberty is to be found only when there is no abuse of power, but constant experience shows us that every man invested with power is liable to abuse it, and to carry his authority as far as it will to go.
>
> To prevent this abuse, it is necessary from the nature of things, that one power should be a check to another... when the legislative and executive powers are united in the same person or body... there can be no liberty.... Again, there is no liberty, if the judicial power is not separated from the legislative and executive... There would be an end of everything, if the same exercise all three powers.[4]

In practice, the principle of separation of powers is based on the premise that legislative, judicial and executive powers are separate from and independent of one another. This arrangement is intended to provide a system of checks and balances that limits the powers of the government on the one hand and protects the rights of individuals or what Montesquieu called liberty on the other.[5] Montesquieu's justification for separation powers in government provided a robust intellectual authority for the American constitutionalists. The Americans believed and operated on the premise, that Montesquieu did not subscribe to the contention that each arm of government would have no partial agency in or no control over the acts of each other. According to James Madison in *The Federalists* Number 47,

> Montesquieu's meaning could amount to no more than this, that where the whole power of one arm is exercised by the same hands, which possess the whole power of another arm, the fundamental principles of a free constitution are necessarily subverted.

He went further and concluded that,

> unless these departments be so far connected and blended, as to give to each a constitutional control over the others, the degree of separation, which the maxima requires as essential to a free government, can never in practice be duly maintained.[6]

A balance would be achieved only through a systematic distribution of power among the three branches of government in a manner that would separate judicial, executive and legislative functions, and mix economic interests among the three. The typical American system of checks and balances exemplifies the essence of separation of powers by mixing the functions. For instance, the executive nominates Supreme Court justices and the Senate approves them. However, once the justices sit on the bench, they are free to review the actions of those responsible for their initial appointment to the bench. For instance, the Supreme Court ruled in *U.S.* v. *Nixon*[7] that President Richard M. Nixon must give up some of his tape recordings to the special prosecutor investigating the Watergate scandal. The decision of the court emphasized the principle of separation of powers and the administrative process of checks and balances.

Through judicial review, American judges ascertain the consistency of legislative or executive acts with the court's view of the proper balances between constitutional power and the limits placed on power.[8] In cases of inconsistency, the courts are empowered to declare the acts null and void. On many occasions, the American courts are called upon to look into legislative or executive actions in terms of the degree to which they infringe upon the rights of individuals, groups, states, etc. In delivering judgments, these courts define the rights of individuals within the constitutional system. This was best illustrated in *Marbury, v. Madison* 1803[9]. *Brown of Education*[10] *Martin v. Hunter's Lessee*[11] *and Cohens v. Virginia.*[12] As rightly put by Aihe, Oluyede, [13] and Braiwaite, [14] what the doctrine of separation of powers implies in theory and in practice, is that none of the legislature, the executive and the judiciary should exercise the whole or part of another's power. It does not however exclude influence or control by one over the acts of another.[15] Contemporary usage or understanding of the doctrine of separation of power connotes the division of power among the three key branches of government namely the executive, the legislative and the judiciary. It could equally be understood as the principle of checks and balances that deals with the constitutional mechanism by which each branch of government inter-relates with and defends itself against any encroachment by the other branches of government.

INDEPENDENCE OF THE JUDICIARY

The separation of judicial power from the maze has perhaps three particular implications. It requires that judicial power to decide justiciable disputes between parties must exist as a power separate from and independent of executive and legislative control or influence. The power of adjudication must be vested in the judicial arm, which must be composed of persons different from and independent of those who compose the executive and legislature.[16] The judiciary must also adopt a procedure different from that for execution and law making. The independence of the judiciary is essentially not in the sense that members of the judiciary should not co-operate with the other arms to achieve the common end of carrying into effect the underlying purposes and intent of the constitution. The independence is in the sense that the acts of each of the three basic arms of government shall not be controlled by or subjected directly or indirectly to the coercive influence of either of the other departments.[17]

To ensure and enhance the quality of justice available in the law courts, modern constitutions attempt to grant the judiciary some amount of independence from the other two arms of government. The independence of the judiciary is to ensure that judges perform their judicial duties fearlessly and impartially. Absolute necessity of recourse to law has long been established by democratic constitutions in the resolution of conflicting claims.[18] If this were to be so, the necessary corollary according to Lord Denning is that judges must be independent.[19] They must be free from any influence by those who wield power.[20] In situations of unhealthy relationship among the arms of government and in instances of undue influence, overt or covert on the judiciary, judicial officers cannot be trusted to decide whether or not power is being abused by either of the other two arms of government.[21]

The independence of the judiciary seems for all practical purposes a running battle requiring eternal vigilance. This becomes necessary when one considers Alexander Hamilton's time honoured observation that the judiciary possessed neither the purse nor the sword. The judiciary has no force but merely judgment, and must in all instances ultimately depend on the power of the executive even for the enforcement of its judgment.[22] The position is succinctly presented in *United State v. Lee*, when Justice Samuel Miller observed:

> Dependent as these courts are for the enforcement of their judgments upon officers appointed by the executive and removable at his pleasure, with no patronage and no control of the purse or the sword, their power and influence rest solely upon the public sense of necessity for existence of a tribunal to which all may appeal... and the confidence reposed in the soundness of their decisions and the purity of their motives.[23]

Judges of all judicial traditions, share the same view on the need for an independent judiciary, an institution unfettered or emasculated by the whims and caprices of the other two arms, the press, labour unions or intimidating pressure groups. The extent to which a judicial body is independent could be better understood and appreciated by an examination of the system of judicial administration, the judicial process and methods of appointing and firing judicial officers. While it is possible for the judiciary to claim independence, a content analysis of the judicial pronouncements is capable of exposing judicial performance to more critical assessment and evaluation.[24]

One of the essential pillars of effective political administration is a strong, purposeful, and virile judiciary, one that could serve as bulwark against all forms of irresponsibility. The strongest advocates of effective government would not deny the fact that to safeguard individual liberty, government should be limited by separating judicial from executive and legislative powers.[25] The unfortunate situation of military rule in many third world countries has distorted and confused the whole essence government responsibility to the popular will of the people. Constitutionalism, which is an important pillar of the rule of law, depends more upon how limitations imposed on government by the constitution are interpreted and enforced. Accordingly, the limitations cannot have much meaning or effectiveness unless there is a separate procedure that includes an independent agency and personnel for an authoritative interpretation and enforcement of laws.

In the words of Nwabueze, there is thus, clearly, an obvious and undeniable need for a "machinery separate, in terms of structure and personnel from, and independent of that of the execution of legislation," which could review both executive and legislative activities.[26]

THE JUDICIAL PROCESS

Peltason has observed that the procedure, through which courts arrive at a decision, is a set of inter-related procedures and roles noted for its complexity and intricacies.[27] The judicial process involves the technical procedure for deciding disputes between parties by an authoritative person or persons whose decisions are to be obeyed.[28] In the discharge of their duties, judges make authoritative statements on how the laws are to be applied and such statements are known to have generalized impact on the behaviours or conduct of many people quite different from the parties in the dispute on which decisions are made. It becomes obvious, that the judicial process is both a means of resolving disputes between recognized and specified persons and also a process for making public policies. The latter role makes the judiciary's interaction and inter-relation-ship with the executive profound and co-extensive. An understanding of this relationship will necessarily enhance society's appreciation of the dynamics of the machinery of government.

The orthodox or formalistic theory of the judicial process is grounded on the belief that judges are trained technicians who apply their specialized knowledge to discover answers to legal disputes. The judicial process is thus concerned with merely applying the given rules to the facts of the case. Accordingly, the process is a self-contained world with it own dynamics and totally divorced from the political system. Judges and the laws they apply are presumed to be neutral among competing interests within the political community. The orthodox theory sees the judge as a spokesman for the more enduring values of the society, not merely the wishes of those who are for the moment governing that society.

As noted by Sir Allen Carleton Kemp in his remarks on the English legal system:

> 'Our law has had its political vicissitudes and at certain periods of its history, it has been threatened with degradation into an instrument of government; it might indeed have suffered that, but for the resistance of men like Sir Edward Coke. But today (sic) there is nothing more repellent to Anglo-Saxton legal instinct than the corruption of law by political ideology."[29]

Judicial activism believes that the judge plays a creative role in judicial administration especially in relation to the so-called "hard cases" where there are no settled principles of law as precedents to guide the judge in coming to a sound conclusion. Activism in the judiciary holds that although the courts are bound only to interpret laws and decide only legal questions, in their search for fundamental principles of law on which to rest the weight of their decisions, judges and their courts are empowered beyond the fine letters of the law to the general set of philosophical beliefs which informed the making of the particular law.

This position was eloquently stated by the *Times* of London in a leading article on the performance of the House of Lords in the case of *Express Newspapers. v. McShane and Rossminter.*[30] The paper averred:

> Throughout the history of the English legal system, there have existed two broad strands of judicial approach. There have been those judges who have taken the view that without usurping the functions of Parliament, a judge has the duty to interpret the law as far as he can in a way which accords with social and personal justice, which upholds rather than destroys the civil liberties of the individual, which looks with suspicion and not equanimity on the increasing encroachment of the state and other power groups in the lives of citizens.[a]

On the other hand, a conservative judge sees his judicial task as maintaining the authority of the state and interpreting Acts of Parliament strictly. Such judges support the words of the law in preference to the justice of the case.[32] A conservative judge is always eager to argue and affirm that it is never the duty of the judge to assume the task of parliament through statutory interpretation.[33] Both Lord Denning and Lord Mansfield are regarded as distinguished English judicial activists, while Lord Devlin represented the conservative tradition.[34]

Legal realism is an attempt to understand, appreciate, and accommodate certain realities in judicial administration. The belief is that the law is what the judge says it is. The law is not certain and the facts are not easy to ascertain. The judge therefore, has to make a choice at any given time about which statute to interpret or apply to a set of facts before him. The realists are inclined to regard legal doctrines as justifications for results based on common sense and natural justice. Realism in the administration of justice is interested more in what could be called "judicial legislation" and tends to detest unnecessary formalities and technicalities. The realists are also skeptical and abhorrent of abstractions that they believe are capable of distorting the judge's perception and conceptualization of social reality. The law is considered to be continually in flux and that judicial decisions are more often a reflection of the person of the judge. It is argued that paying constant attention to and showing a correct awareness of the social context of judicial decisions would enhance effective judicial performance. The separation between the law and the interpretation judges give is quite artificial and subject to a number of other factors. Judges are, in a limited sense, lawmakers and not mere law finders.

Realism truly believes that the judge has both professional and political constituencies. At one level, the judge's decision could be a resolution of controversy between individual litigants with potential meaning, consequence, and implication for similarly situated persons in the future. At another level, the decision of the judge could amount to a resolution of competing social issues, extending to an attempted reconciliation of perceived value conflicts in the society.[35] Good examples could be seen in the celebrated welfare cases of the Warren courts in the United States.[36] At this level, a decision of the court especially at the appellate stage has important political, ideological, and sociological implications.

Contemporary theories of jurisprudence recognize the judge's role as mediatory, that is, to balance conflicting interests in the society in order to achieve maximum satisfaction at least cost. This position is an acceptance of the creative role of the judge especially with regard to how judgments are affected or influenced by public policy or other extra legal considerations. In truth, judges are not to refrain totally from deciding political questions, they are however, ethically and professionally required to refrain from deciding political questions too brazenly. Realism believes that judges cannot be uprooted and isolated from contemporary realities. A Judge's perception and understanding of social reality cannot therefore, remain uninfluenced by current and prevailing values in the society. On the other hand, judges by virtue of their professional orientation, ethics, and integrity, are barred from making volatile judicial pronouncements that could be considered both passionate and partisan. The judge ought not to be too concerned with hot or orthodox political issues. It is trite to contend that the effectiveness of a judicial decision is best measured by its ability to transcend mere partisan consideration

In both theory and practice, a judge must be neutral between the parties to a lawsuit and be dedicated to the technicalities of his profession. Though judges choose between alternatives and options, the difference between one judge's choice and another does not always derive from any significant difference in their technical knowledge of the law. In most cases, their differing reactions are attributable to the conflicting values that the case under consideration presents. Accordingly, the realists believed that, to the extent that judges must inevitably choose between competing values, they are bound to have a fair knowledge of the social consequence of their choice. From the foregoing, perhaps it would be pertinent to know the extent that the values of individual judges impinge on the application of rules to specific cases. According to Cardozo,[37] judges cannot help but be influenced by the traditions and values of the society or a section of it in which they have been reared. "The great tides and currents which engulf the rest of men do not turn aside in their course and pass the judges by".[38] In deciding cases therefore, judges especially at the appellate level must make a choice between different public policies that might result from decisions and thus, often between specific values. Judges by the circumstances of their training, orientation, and predisposition are bound to have specific convictions of which set of values are necessary to the good of the society and what policies could accelerate the process of development. It is assumed that the provisions of the constitution, the laws and executive orders that judges interpret and apply are ordinarily ambiguous to the extent of being amenable to two or more reasonable interpretations.

As elegantly stated by Oliver Wendell Holmes in 1881,

> The felt necessities of the time, the prevalent moral and political theories, intuitions of public policy avowed or unconscious, even the prejudices which judges share with their fellow-men have had a good deal more to do than the syllogism in determining the rules by which men should be governed.[39]

The realists believe that the judge is most creative where general principles of jurisprudence are patently ambiguous, where constitutional, statutory or administrative phrases are equally vague. They contend that a judge is likely to be more creative in circumstances of unimpressive precedents, where previously decided cases do not provide useful direction and where history is uncertain. In these circumstances, a judge's personal values cannot but have significant impact on his decisions. Indeed a judge's very perception of his alternatives or even his realization that in fact alternatives are open, will inevitably be heavily influenced by his values. This position is premised on the compelling socio-scientific assumption that "a person sees what is significant with significance defined in terms of his relationship to what he is looking at."[40]

The values of a judge may influence him consciously or unconsciously. And since his values affect his perception, he may not be aware of their immediate impact. A judge who is aware of his values may consciously work to see them achieved in judicial decisions and in public policy. The vagueness of many legal rules and the complicated nature of the factual situations are capable of helping judges make choices. This should not however be misconstrued to imply a license. As rightly said by Cardozo, the judge "is not a knight errant roaming at will in pursuit of his own idea of beauty or of goodness."[41] A judge cannot always give free rein to his values in decision-making unless such values are widely accepted in the community or that they represent the preferred values of the power elite who exercise effective political power. The judge is constrained from giving free rein to his values and ambitions.[42] The first institutional constrain is the need to convince other members of the bench of the ground for taking a particular decision or a position. This becomes important in a system of appellate adjudication of collegiate arrangement. The appellate courts in Nigeria are usually made up of a panel of not less than three judges. According to Fatai Williams, the justices of the Supreme Court of Nigeria during his own time engaged in robust arguments and sharp disagreements that seemed to defy reconciliation.[43] A court with this type of arrangement and intellectual orientation would not allow the personal value preferences of just a member to always dominate its decision. The personal values of judges are also undermined by the fact that the judge is only empowered to make judicial orders. It is the duty of the executive arm to execute judicial decisions and treat them as public policy.

While it is possible for the judge to colour his decisions by his values, he still needs the concurrence of the executive before this could be translated to greater heights as public policy. Judicial decisions are open to the political checks of the executive and the legislature and to the court of public opinion. The judge is constantly reminded of the fact that his decisions have no more than moral force until they are backed up by executive force. The fundamental problem in linking values and decisions are obviously one of methodology. There is a need to discover the values of a judge and to assess their impact on his decision. As rightly observed by Fatai Williams, a judge must learn to suppress his private feelings on every aspect of a case. "On the whole, judges must and do lay aside our private views in discharging our judicial function."[44] The discourse above, has shown that judges appear to make laws but with some limitations on their law making power. Some of these limitations are intellectual. For instance a judge has an obligation to give adequate reasons for his position. There are also some institutional requirements that would force the court to defer to the power of another branch of government. There is always a need to avoid involvement in hotly partisan issues. The limitation could also be psychological, which could be a need to recognize the role of individual biases and prejudices in judicial decision-making.

A close examination and careful perusal of court decisions in Nigeria would suggest that no particular theory of jurisprudence could be said to have had a pervading and overwhelming influence on the character of judicial administration. It is however obvious that the Nigerian bench of the Adetokunbo Ademola era had a strong imprint of English legal and judicial heritage. Recent events and developments in the courts and in the political process have shown that judges in Nigeria are willing to understand, borrow and adapt certain beneficial features of other judicial traditions.

Through the court system and especially by the quality of its judgments, the judiciary could enhance the capability of government to achieve the goals of public policy. On the other side of the divide, the court is also an active participant in the process of distributing rights, duties, costs, benefits, rewards and punishments amongst members of the society through the resolution of conflicting claims. It is worthy to note that the courts perform their functions within a framework of rule, procedure, and traditions that in some cases may impinge on the province of either the executive or the legislature. It is obvious that the functions of the three arms of government are not so rigidly departmentalized or kept in watertight compartments. Where the three arms of governments are differentiated, there are bound to be continuous process of interaction, infraction and accommodation of one by the other. The machinery of government is better lubricated, when an arm enhances the quality of each of the others in achieving set goals and objectives. The relationship between the arms of government is therefore multi-dimensional in many respects depending on the degree of altruism and the extent to which such relationships promote or retard the activities of government. When the relationship enhances the quality of governance, then it is beneficial and accepted, but when it retards progress it becomes counter productive, diversionary, and negative.

The judiciary and its personnel provide a viable area for study in government and administration in view of the crucial role the courts have played in the evolution of the Nigerian State. The courts in both original and appellate jurisdictions and under different political dispensations have been relied upon to decide major issues of state policy and public interest. The Federal Supreme Court and its successor, the Supreme Court of Nigeria between 1954 and 1966 became involved in matters of grave constitutional and political importance, matters that threatened the survival of the state system and the relationship of the State with individual members of the polity. This could be seen in areas of protecting the fundamental rights of the individual against breach by the state and in conflicts between the federal government and the regional or state governments. Based on the judicial career of Sir Adetokunbo Ademola, the first indigenous Chief Justice of the Supreme Court of Nigeria, the book is an expansive evaluation of the interrelationship of the executive and the judiciary. This examination is situated within the context of significant historical development of the period between 1939 and 1972. Efforts have been made to discuss some significant events to put in correct historical perspective, the role of Adetokunbo Ademola in the inter-relationship of the executive and the judiciary.

The judicial career of Sir Adetokunbo Ademola spanned the period of colonial rule during which the judiciary could be appropriately regarded as a department in the executive set up. *Terrel* v. *Secretary of State for the Colonies.*[44] the *locus classicus* on the position of the colonial judge affirmed that the judge held offices at the pleasure of the British Crown, and colonial judges were essentially members of the colonial legal service. The colonial judicial officer was first and foremost a civil servant whose schedule of duties and conditions of service were determined by the Governor. As rightly observed by Nwabueze, the colonial judiciary was part of the colonial civil service or perhaps the special branch then known as the colonial legal service.[45] To this extent, a judicial appointment was considered a career job, which rested essentially on a system of promotion from either the magistracy or from other positions in the judicial or legal department. The Governor was the head of both the government and the executive arm. He appointed judges with the approval of the Secretary of State for the Colonies in London.[46]

In essence, the judiciary had to rely on the executive even on matters relating to the welfare of judicial officers. As noted by Roberts Wray,[47] an appointment into the colonial department was synonymous, except in the definition of official duties, to a career of an administrative civil servant. The colonial judicial officer was at best an administrator carrying out the professional duties of interpreting the letters of the law in the resolution of civil and criminal law suits. The colonial service procedure required the Governor to submit annual reports to the Colonial Office at Westminster in London on the judicial performance of the Chief Justice in order to streamline and harmonize the system of colonial administration. The Chief Justice was also to submit to the Governor similar reports on each of the judges under him. In spite of the administrative advantages of the regulation, it would seem that the system was put in place, primarily, to safeguard the power, political and economic interest of the colonial master. The governor or any of his subordinate officials compounded the situation when judges had to arbitrate in cases involving the interest of the state. The regulation also emphasized the subordinate position of the colonial judicial officer. As noted by Adewoye, the subordinate status of the colonial judiciary was intended to strengthen the basis of the authority of the executive arm in order to ensure the paramount character of the Governor who was the Crown's local representative.

The structure of the judiciary under colonial rule, the method of appointing judicial officers, the tenure of office of judges, the subordinate relationship of the judiciary to the executive and the judicial behaviour of judges in varying degrees of combination tended to make the colonial judiciary a willing agency in safeguarding the interest of the colonial power.

Accordingly, Adewoye rightly observed "it would appear that colonial courts consciously or unconsciously tended to make themselves amenable to safeguarding the interests of the colonial power."[48] Nwabueze believes that in practice, judicial officers under the colonial system enjoyed maximum security of tenure and complete independence from interference by the executive largely as a result of two major factors. In the first instance, the colonial executive had a tradition of respect for the independence of the judiciary. Again, the colonial executive was essentially an administrative machinery controlled by officials who had no personal political stakes in the government of the country and are therefore less likely to be interested in bending the judiciary to their own political desires.[49] It would however seem that the colonial executive was dedicated to the cause of the British Empire in Nigeria to the extent that it could and actually influenced the judiciary in order to promote the power and mercantile interests of Britian.[50] It was evident that the colonial executive was particularly interested in the activities of the various levels of adjudication. The maintenance of peace, law and order and the provision of excellent and conducive atmosphere for the promotion of trade and commerce became the major obsessions of the colonial executive.

Ayandele[51] was right when he noted that the British did not set out to build a Nigerian nation and they never intended to prepare the people for any future leadership role. Rodney's exposition of colonialism presents a critical analysis of the colonial experience and confirms our position that the colonial process distorted and perverted Nigerian value system in order to promote the cause of imprialism.[52] The Judiciary was not spared, as Nigerian legal practitioners reared in the British common law tradition were specifically encouraged to acquire British habits, tastes, and thought patterns through a system of cultural indoctrination.

Writing from a vantage position as a political officer and who had enough contact with the system of judicial administration even after the 1933 reforms, Crocker believed that the law was administered by barristers whose findings were subject to higher administrative review, and whose career advancement depended on their having as few reversals of their decisions as possible.[53] The magistrates and judges therefore "naturally tended to follow the dotted lines of the letters of the law in order to ensure their promotion."[54] At that level, legal accuracy, knowledge and formality became more cherished than justice."[55]

In considering the dilemma of the colonial judge, Adewoye has argued that, while it is true that there were cases decided purely on merit and in accordance with the law, majority, if not all of such cases, were suits in which the fundamental issues of power, authority, prestige, and major economic interests of the colonial regime were not being questioned.[56] In order to ensure the survival of Britain's hegemonic control and domination of colonial Nigeria, the methods of recruiting judicial officers emphasized the need to appoint magistrates and judges who by training and socialization, had imbibed the English value system and who could be predicted, trusted and controlled.[57] The strict supervision and administrative control of the judicial activities of magistrates and judges, the insecurity of tenure and the absolute reliance on the executive arm for funding, defined the inter-relationship of the executive and the judiciary under colonial rule.

The above describes the character of the Nigerian judiciary, which was carried into the post independence era. As this book will demonstrate, the appointment of Adetokunbo Ademola as the first indigenous Chief Justice of the Supreme Court of Nigeria, did not, in any major sense, change the direction of the judicial system. The outlook of the courts, specially in constitutional matters, remained a reflection of the preferences of the political and power elite. It was obvious that the leadership of the court lacked the intellectual and ideological premise to develop an assertive and definite judicial tradition.

Notes

1. George H. Sabine and Thomas L. Thorson. *A. History of Political Thought* (Illinois: Dryden Press, 1973), pp. 3-18.
2. Peter Stearns Donal Schwartz and Barry Beyer(eds), *World History: Traditional and New Directories* (New York: Addison Wesley Publishing Company, 1989). Pp. 435-436
3. *Encyclopedia of the Social Sciences* Vols. 7&8. 1968
4. *Ibid.*
5. George H. Sabine and Thomas L. Thorson. *A History of Political Thought...* p. 514.
6. Alexander Hamilton, James Madison, and John Jay. *The Federalist Papers* New York: Mentor Inc., 1961).
7. *U.S.* v.*Nixon,418 U.S.* 683 (1974) For details of the events leading up to and surrounding the case, see Archibald Cox, *The Court and the Constitution* (New Delhi: Asian Books Pvt Ltd. 1989).
8. Alexnder Hamilton, James Madison and John Jay, *The Federalist Papers* (New York: Mentor Inc. 1961), pp. 302-303.
9. *Marbury. V. Madison* 1 crunch 137 (1803)
10. *Brown V. Board of Education* 349 U.S 294 (1955)
11. *Martin V. Hunter's Lesse* 7 crunch 603 (1813)
12. *Cohens V. Virginia* 6 wheat 264 (1821)
13. D.O. Aihe and P.O Oluyede, *Case and Materials on Constitutional Law in Nigeria* (London: Oxford University Press, 1979).
14. Tunji Braitwaite, *The Jurisprudene of the Living Oracles* (Benin City: Ethiope Publishing Corportion, 1987).
15. M.J.C Vile, *Constitutionalism and the Separation of Powers* (London: Oxford University Press, 1981), p. 13.
16. John C. Donovan, *Democracy at the Crossroads,* (New York: Holt Rinehart and Winston Inc. 1978), p. 27. The British tradition where, the Lord Chancellor is head of the House of Commons, head of the House of Lords and member of the cabinet is a notable exception.
17. Lord Denning. *What Next in the Law* (London: Butterworths, 1982), p. 310.
18. See Section 33 Nigerian Constitution 1979 especially Section 33 Sub Section 1.
19. Lord Denning,*What Next in the Law...* p. 310

20. *Ibid.*
21. *Ibid.*
22. *United States v. Lee* (1882) 106 U.S. 196 at p. 223.
23. *Ibid.*
24. For details of the peculiar Nigerian situation, see among other works. Atanda Fatai Williams, *Faces, Cases and Places.* (London: Butterworths, 1983), pp. 100-109... J.D. Ojo "The Independence of the Judiciary in Nigerian, 1960-1981" (mimeograph, September 1995).
25. B.O. Nwabueze, *Idea and Facts in Constitution Making* (Ibadan; Spectrum Books 1992), p. 190
26. *Ibid.*
27. Encyclopedia of the Social Sciences, 19 s.v. "The Judicial Process". By J.W. Petalson.
28. *Ibid.*
29. Allen Carleton Kemp, *Law in the Making* (Oxford: Clarendon Press, 1964), p. 56
30. A Leaky Umbrella" *London Times,* 18 December 1979.
31. *Ibid.*
32. Lord Denning, *The Closing Chapters* (London: Butterworths, 1983), p. 188.
33. *Ibid.*
34. See for instance his avowed position in, *Lord Devlin. The Judge* (Oxford: Oxford University Press, 1978).
35. Edward White, *The American Judicial Tradition...* pp. 372-374
36. For details, see Archibald Cox. *The Warren Court: Constitutional Decision as an Instrument of Reform* (Boston: Hughton Mifflin Company 1968).
37. B.N. Cardozo, *The Nature of the Judicial Process* (New Haven: Yale University Press, 1960), p. 168. Benjamin Cardozo, according to Felix Frankfurter, is deemed probably the greatest intellect in the history of the English speaking judiciary. See Felix Frankfurter, "John Marshall and the Judicial Function" *Harvard Law Review,* vol. 69. No 2 ec. 1955 at p. 217.
38. *Ibid.*
39. Oliver Wendell Holmes, *The Common Law,* (Cambridge Masachusetts: Harvard University Press, 1963), p. 5.

40. Hadley Cantril, "Percetion and Interpersonal Relations", *American Journal of Psychiatry, 114, (1957) p. 121.*
41. B.N. Cardozo, *The Nature of the Judicial Process* ... p. 141.
42. Fatayi Williams, *Faces, Cases and Places* ... p. 95.
43. *Ibid,* p. 96.
44. *Terrell* v. *Secretary of State for the Colonies* (1953) 3 W.L., p. 331
45. B.O. Nwabueze, *Merchinery of Justice in Nigeria,* (London: Butterworths African Law Series 1963), p. 282.
46. *Ibid.*
47. For details, see Robert Wray, *The Judicial Tradition in Africa* (London: Butterworths, 1983).
48. Omoniyi Adewoye. *The Judicial System in Southern Nigeria* ... p. 77.
49. B.O. Nwabueze, *Machinery of Justice in Nigeria...* p. 283.
50. *Ibid.*
51. E.A. Ayandele *The Educated Elite in the Nigerian Society* (Ibadan: Ibadan University Press, 1974), p. 98.
52. Walter Rodney *How Europe Underdeveloped Africa* (Dar Es-Salam: Tanzania Publishing House Ltd., 1972).
53. W.R. Crocker *Nigeria: A Critique of British Colonial Administration* (London: George Allen & Unwin Ltd. 1936), p. 232.
54. *Ibid.*
55. *Ibid.* p. 233.
56. Omoniyi Adewoye, *The Judicial System...* p. 78.
57. *Ibid.* pp. 99-100.

Chapter 2

The Colonial Experience

> *....In a commercial class society, law is a weapon in the hands of the economically (hence politically) dominant class.[1] Whenever it is convenient for the dominant class, law may serve as an instrument of legal control, legal justice or legal change, and not social change, social control and social justice.[2]*

Before the advent of British commercial and political interests, customary laws governed Nigerian societies and communities at various levels of political sophistication. The machinery for the administration or these customary laws consisted entirely of customary tribunals of institutions. In 1849, a British consulate for the Bights of Benin and Biafra with headquarters at Fernando Po was established in response to the representation of some British traders who were dissatisfied with the quality of justice available at the indigenous tribunals.[3] The consular courts and their obvious inadequacies paved the way for the introduction of properly constituted British courts. According to Adewoye, the expansion of English law in much of Southern Nigeria was compelled by both administrative and economic requirements of the British.[4] The survival of the British enterprise in Nigeria depended on the ability of the local administration to exercise undisputed power in the settlement of disputes and to punish what it regarded "as deviant patterns of behaviour".[5] British legal system was also considered appropriate for use in the introduction, retention and protection of the exploitative British fiscal and financial policies in Nigeria.[6]

After the annexation of Lagos in 1861, a number of courts, based on the British pattern of judicial administration were established between that year and 1872.[7] These included: The Court (1863), the Commercial Court (1863), the Petty Debt Court (1863), the Vice-Admiralty Court (1863), the Court of Requests (1871) and the Court of Divorce and Matrimonial Causes (1872)[8]. All these courts except the Vice-Admiralty Court were abolished in 1876 and replaced by a single Supreme Court, which had a superior and unlimited jurisdiction. The Supreme Court, as constituted in the Southern Protectorate, had similar jurisdiction as the High Court of Justice in England.[9]

The annexation of Lagos paved the way for a systematic and steady extension of British political and economic interest to other parts of Southern Nigeria, west of the lower Niger. By 1901, a British protectorate had been established over the whole of the landmass, reaching as far as Benin and including virtually the whole of Yorubaland. An earlier treaty concluded in 1893 by the government of Egbaland and the British Crown and contained in the Egba Jurisdiction Ordinance No. 14 of 1904 guaranteed the independence of Egbaland.[10]

Southern Nigeria had the Supreme Court, which consisted of a Chief Justice and a small number of puisne judges. The Supreme Court in spite of its limitations with respect to the small number of its staff was charged with a jurisdiction covering the whole of Southern Nigeria.

The exclusion of Yorubaland from the jurisdiction of English style courts before 1915 caused a lot of displeasure to the British administration in Lagos.[11] The extension of the trade frontier from the coast inland led to steady influx of British traders into the Yoruba homeland. Ostensibly, the argument was that the British government became alive to its responsibilities of protecting the lives and economic interests of its British subjects and thus, the intervention. It would however seem that Britain was particularly interested in using the instrumentality of law to pacify and maintain a conducive atmosphere necessary for the growth and development of trade all over Yorubaland.

By the Egba (Jurisdiction of Supreme Court) Ordinance 1904, the Supreme Court of Lagos was empowered to exercise jurisdiction over the whole of Egbaland in accordance with the provisions of the Supreme Court Ordinance of 1876.[12] The jurisdiction granted the court was to be exercised over non-natives in Egbaland. The jurisdiction could however be stretched in some instances such as in civil disputes between a native and a non-native and in criminal cases such as murder and manslaughter. Despite this provision, a dubious caveat that "nothing in this treaty, shall be deemed to take away the powers and jurisdiction of the native courts of Egbaland over matters between and affecting natives of Egbaland only", exposed the over riding concern of the British administration which was to ensure a peaceful atmosphere. A situation of relative peace was to be established, ensured, and sustained in order to facilitate the wholesome control of the economy of Yorubaland by British traders.

The circumstances that led to the suggestion that the Alake should re-consider the treaty of 1893, which guaranteed the independence of Egbaland would obviously strengthen the position above. Lord Lugard had advised the Alake in 1913 that he was not prepared to use British military force to sustain in power a government he had no control over.[13] The Alake was apparently either cajoled or intimidated to sign a new agreement in 1914, placing Egbaland without reservation under the British.[14]

The same strategy was employed against Oyo, Ife, Ibadan and Ijebu-Ode[15] when existing ordinances defining their relationship with the British were repealed by the Jurisdiction of Courts Extension (Protectorate) Ordinance 1915.[16] The 1915 Ordinance extended the jurisdiction of the Supreme Court, Provincial Courts and Native Courts established by law to the whole of Yorubaland. In effect by 1915 the period of partial independence of Yorubaland from the jurisdiction of British Courts had come to an end.[17]

In 1893, the administration of the Oil Rivers Protectorate was organized and by 1900 the British government imposed complete jurisdiction over the Protectorate.[18] Accordingly, the new political edifice known as the Protectorate of Southern Nigeria had visible executive, administrative and judicial structures and institutions to meet the exigencies of colonial administration.[19] The newly appointed High Commissioner established a Supreme Court and Statutory Native Courts to replace the former arrangements of the Consular Courts, Courts of Equity and the Courts of the Royal Niger Company.[20]

The British occupation of the Northern part of present day Nigeria culminated in the establishment of the Protectorate of Northern Nigeria in 1900.[21] The High Commissioner by the Protectorate Courts Proclamation of 1900[22] established Supreme Court, Provincial Courts and Cantonment Courts. The Native Courts Proclamation of 1900 established statutory native courts to regularize the existing judicial arrangements of the Emirs.[23] The jurisdiction, constitution, law of the courts, and other enumerated powers of the British courts necessarily made the administration of Justice in Nigeria an effective instrument in the maintenance of the peace through administrative control and legal justice.

Lugard's judicial measures were an extension of what was sometimes called political or administrative justice. Lugard claimed the advantage of convenience for this system in that it brought a simple and speedy British court almost to the doorstep of the people, just as it was cost effective.[24] Lugard was, from the onset, determined to be the ultimate controller of all departments in his administration and therefore his over lordship of the Northern Protectorate was absolute. British judges who served in the North were in the final analysis considered the administrative agents of the Governor, forced to apply the Lugardian philosophy and administer justice to enhance the vision of Lugard for Nigeria. Judges were discouraged from seeing the chief justice as their professional leader and thereby obliterating the separation of power between the executive and the judiciary and also destroying the independence of the judiciary.

One of the major structural adjustments of the amalgamation of 1914 was the introduction of the judicial system of the Northern Protectorate to the other parts of the country. These measures were to Lugard, one of the major and earth breaking policies of his administration, one that gratified him in the exercise of supreme power. In his words, "if I did nothing else during my term in Nigeria, but effect this great reform, I should feel I had not worked without result."[25]

As chief justice of the Northern Protectorate, Sir Edwin Speed supported the idea of introducing the judicial system of Northern Nigeria into the Southern Provinces. Pursuant to this, an Ordinance was issued that established a three-tier court system. The chief justice and four other junior judges constituted the Supreme Court. It had a jurisdiction limited to the colony and some other designated places that were considered vital to British commercial interests. The Supreme Court also functioned as a court of appeal for cases coming from the divisional courts. It is however curious that the jurisdiction of the Supreme Court was final only in criminal cases. In civil cases, appeal could be made to the Privy Council in London as if to emphasise the dependency of Nigeria on the British legal system.

The 1914 reforms equally provided for the division of the Supreme Court into divisional courts; one each for provinces east and west of the Niger. Station magistrates were made commissioners of the Supreme Court and were by that appointment, empowered to try cases in which the claims did not exceed £50 or criminal cases where the penalty was not more than six months imprisonment or a fine of £50 or twelve strokes of the cane. The provincial courts had jurisdiction over all Nigerians and non-Nigerians except within certain specified limits of the Supreme Court. The Resident who was the most senior political official in each province served as the president of the provincial court, while the district officers were commissioners. The provincial courts were restricted to penalties not exceeding £100 fine, five years imprisonment, and corporal punishments.

One major inadequacy of the provincial court system was that legal practitioners were not allowed to appear before the court. There was however a proviso that the chief justice might, in some rare cases, allow legal representation. Legal practitioners were barred from the provincial courts because Lugard and his close associates and fellow travellers believed that lawyers were exploiting the ignorance of litigants to extort money from them. C.L. Temple believed that the uneducated Nigerians obviously preferred the political officer as judge because the fine letters of the law would not hedge him down. Exploitation of litigants was very prevalent in the Southern Provinces where it was more or less a scandal. Lawyers and moneylenders actively encouraged their clients to pursue cases with the least merit, just to bleed them. It would seem that Lugard believed that unsuspecting Nigerians would be better protected by administrative officers who were encouraged to be paternalistic in dealing with the people. Representation by counsel trained in the niceties of English law was assumed too sophisticated for the masses of the people. A litigant was however allowed appeal to the Supreme Court where a trained lawyer could represent him. In the opinion of R. L. Buell, this option was least appealing to the people.

The obvious imperfections and inadequacies of the 1914 judicial arrangement were roundly condemned by an articulate cross section of the elite in Nigeria.[26] The reorganization fell short of expectations because Sir Edwin Speed, who was charged with the responsibility of drafting the necessary instrument, was circumscribed by circumstances beyond his personal control. Despite due consultation with Hon. Justice Willoughby Osborne who was Chief Justice of Southern Nigeria (1906 to 1913), Sir Edwin was satisfied with the evolution of a system that would be applicable to the whole country and which would have minimal impact on the existing and imperfect system "except in rare instances where it would conflict with the interest of good government".[27]

Willoughby Osborne, C.J. of Southern Nigeria had a strained relationship as head of the judiciary with the executive branch.[28] He maintained that the Chief Justice was the head of the Judicial Department, hence he urged the Governor to have due consultation with him before making appointments affecting the staff in the Judicial Department.[29]

The Chief Justice also attempted to make the judiciary independent of the executive. In spite of the complaints of the Chief Justice on undue executive interference in purely judicial matters such as the transfer of judicial officers to the Legal Department by the Governor[30], the Colonial Office up-held the Governor's right over the appointment of judicial officers. The Governor was however directed that "as a matter of propriety, and for the better conduct of business, the chief justice should be consulted whenever it is possible to do so".[31] By 1914 and thereafter, the judiciary was organized to provide judicial back up to colonial executive and administrative control of the Nigerian State.

Before, the introduction of the 1933 reforms, the judicial system emphasized executive justice. The courts, especially the provincial courts, which gave the Resident in charge of a Province practically unlimited powers[32] appeared to have administered justice with a view to promoting the sacred interested of Britain in Nigeria. As noted by Adewoye: "in the colonial history of Nigeria, perhaps no other colonial measure aroused so much opposition and protest as the judicial reorganization of 1914."[33]

Protests against the reorganization were articulated and organized by the press, the Bar Association in Lagos and Calabar and some concerned individual lawyers. Active protest clubs were formed to vehemently and courageously protest the reforms, which were believed to be conservatively retrogressive, oppressive and outlandish. The reforms were also criticized by political associations in Nigeria as a part of a concerted and consciously laid down scheme, designed for the purpose of preventing any interference with and all opposition against the colonial government in Nigeria.[34]

With the benefit of hindsight, obviously the protests against the 1914 judicial reforms were genuine, considering the fact that the criticisms were meant to highlight areas that were capable of affecting the quality of justice obtainable in the Nigerian courts; even the credibility of the judiciary. The so-called reforms had indeed the consequence of disproportionately increasing powers exercisable by political administrative officers in exclusively judicial matters. It meant an over concentration of power in the hands of the executive to the detriment of the people who were at the receiving end of executive justice. As noted by Margery Perham, although for a different argument, Lugard's judicial measures were an example of political or administrative justice. This was at the expense of social or professional justice. The constitution of the Nigerian judiciary up to 1914 was as imperfect as it was no more than an administrative tribunal. In the words of the chief justice, Sir Edwin Speed what existed then could not be described as a system of justice.[35]

Because of the criticisms of the 1914 reforms, the judicial reforms that were introduced in 1933 embodied a lot of compromises. Despite the obvious limitations of earlier reforms, British colonial officers in Nigeria still believed that the provincial court system was suitable for the majority of Nigerians. The Supreme Court was believed to be obstructionist and capable of encouraging exploitation of the illiterate population by crafty lawyers.[36]

The period of 1931-1935 marked a turning point in the history of the judiciary in Nigeria and in its relationship with the executive.[37] Sir Donald Cameron embarked on a comprehensive reorganization of the judiciary and succeeded in achieving what amounted to "a complete reversal of the principles hitherto governing the administration of justice in Nigeria".[38]

The 1933 reforms could be summarized as:

1. The inauguration of a system of Native Courts of Appeal and a consequent limitation of the powers of certain Native Courts.

2. The abolition of the Provincial Courts and the substitution for these of a High Court for the Protectorate, under which were series of Magistrate Courts.
3. The admission of legal practitioners to practice in both the High Courts and the Magistrate Courts.
4. The subordination of tall types of Courts, (the Native Courts to the High Courts) to the over-all jurisdiction of the Supreme Court.
5. The establishment of a system of appeals from the Supreme Court and the High Courts of Nigeria to the West African Court of Appeal.[39]

The epoch making reforms were delivered by four main ordinances: (a) The Native Courts Ordinance No. 44 of 1933 (b) The Protectorate Courts Ordinance No. 45 of 1933 (c) The Supreme Court (Amendment) Ordinance No. 46 of 1933 and (d) The West African Court of Appeal Ordinance No. 47 of 1933. The entire ordinance became effective as from April 1, 1934.[40] For the purpose of this book, the Protectorate Courts Ordinance No. 45 of 1933 deserves special attention and examination. The Ordinance was instrumental to the establishment of the Magistrate Courts, which provided the first tuft for the judicial activities of Sir Adetokunbo Ademola in 1939.

The Protectorate Courts Ordinance No. 45 established two new types of Courts to replace the provincial courts. The High Court consisted of the Chief Justice (as the Chief Judge), judges and assistant judges. A Resident might be given the powers of a judge in respect of any particular cause or matter within his province.[41] According to Elias, the jurisdiction of the High Court was coextensive with that of the Supreme Court.[42] It should however be noted that, the High Court had no jurisdiction in (a) probate, divorce and matrimonial cases; (b) admiralty and, (c) proceedings arising under certain ordinances. The Court had no original jurisdiction in land cases, but could entertain such cases as appeal cases from the Native Courts.[43]

The same Ordinance at section 7, established courts of summary jurisdiction called Magistrate Courts. Each Magistrate Court was presided over by a single Magistrate. Magistrate Courts were of three grades with varying degrees of jurisdiction or competence.

According to the Attorney General in 1943, the original jurisdiction in civil cases was

(a) Grade 1 Magistrate had jurisdiction in (i) all personal actions in contract and tort and (ii) all suits between landlord and tenant, if the amount involved was not more than £100.
(b) Grade II & III Magistrates were limited to cases involving not more than £100 and £25 respectively.

In criminal matters, a Grade 1 Magistrate had power of summary trial of persons charged with crimes punishable either by fine not exceeding £200 or by imprisonment not exceeding 2 years or by both. He could receive and inquire into all charges of indictable offences and of making suitable orders there on. Grades II and III Magistrates had all the powers of Grade 1 Magistrate except that they were limited to cases involving not more than £100 fine or 12 months imprisonment and £25 fine or 3 months imprisonment respectively.[44] Grade I Magistrate Courts were to be manned by lawyers described as: "whole time, fully qualified barristers of the judicial department".[45]

A careful consideration of the jurisdiction, staff and administrative role of Magistrate Courts, especially Grade 1 Magistrate Courts will confirm the relevance and centrality of the courts so judicial administration, maintenance of peace and good government in the protectorate. In the first instance, a Magistrate Court was competent to take appeals from Native Courts and could transfer cases from a Native Court either to itself or to another Native Court, in accordance with the provisions of any ordinance establishing the particular Native Court. A Magistrate Court could reserve questions of law in civil cases for the opinion of the High Court, just as it could promote reconciliation in civil matters. The law administered by a Magistrate Court was the common Law, the doctrines of equity and the statues of general application that were in force in Britain on 1st January, 1900.

To emphasize the importance of the Magistrate Courts under the new judicial scheme of things, and perhaps to enhance the quality of legal representation and justice, the ordinance provided for the employment of legal practitioners. Legal Practitioners were allowed in all civil and criminal cases before a Magistrate Court or High Court.[46] However, in cases of appeals from Native Courts, a legal practitioner was allowed only in land cases involving £200 or more,[47] or where the property lay in one of the fifteen places in Eastern Nigeria, which were mentioned, in the second schedule of the Ordinance.[48]

Legal representation in land cases coming as appeals was however short-circuited. Such legal representation, according to Elias, must be preceded by a written application stating the question of law involved in the appeal. The presiding judge (if the High Court) or Magistrate could decide whether or not to permit the legal practitioner to appear in the case. Despite obvious attempts to make justice less executive ridden, the 1933 reforms still allowed the District Officer in certain cases, an amount of clout in the courts which could affect the quality of justice.[49] For example, the ordinance allowed the District Officer a right not only to appear in all criminal appeals from the Native Courts, but also to show cause why such appeals should or should not be allowed. The administrative role and executive powers of the District Officers and their relationship with the Resident and High Commissioners necessarily made the District Officers powerful even before Magistrates.

As important as the Magistrate Courts were to judicial administration during this period, the Courts had the problem of acute shortage of personnel. As noted by Adewoye, there were only thirteen professionally qualified magistrates in Nigeria in 1940.[50] The bulk of those who served, as magistrates were Administrative Officers who had limited knowledge of the law and whom Crocker described as hedge barristers.[51] He described some of the Administrative Officers as purveyors of executive tyranny and oppression and as men who were unsure of themselves, chronically and inevitably concerned with promotion.[52]

The colonial government in Nigeria in the inter war years was obviously reluctant in appointing Africans into high and sensitive judicial office as the Magistracy. The dearth of African and professionally qualified personnel to serve as magistrates and judges became a matter of grave concern not only to the Chief Justice in Nigeria, but also to the Colonial Office in London. This problem was compounded by three major factors. The British Government in Nigeria, was still of the opinion that, in spite of the major reform brought about by the 1933 ordinance, the executive branch through the activities of Administrative Officers serving as Magistrates, were better than professionally qualified lawyers.[53] As pointed out by Adewoye, "contrary to what has been suggested", the judicial reforms introduced by Sir Donald Cameron, "did not end the era of executive justice, for political officers continued to exercise their influence in judicial matters".[54]

The executive continued to make the discharge of the judicial duties of judges and magistrates, unnecessarily burdensome and loathsome. In 1945, when the Chief Justice embarked on the annual tour of Judicial Divisions and Magisterial Districts in the Western Provinces between 30th September and 4th October,[55] he regretted that the executive arm of government failed to provide suitable quarters and courtroom facilities for Magistrates. He observed that the arrangement was a negation of how best to ensure justice.[56] In the words of Sir John Verity;

> ...It is not in the best interests of the administration of justice either that the magistrate should be dependent upon a private landlord for accommodation, or that there should be competition between the magistrate and other officers for the use of government quarters."[57]

On the issue of courtroom facilities, the Chief Justice lamented that he:

> was in certain instances most unfavourably impressed with the existing Courts, Chambers and Registry accommodation, more particularly in regard to the Magistrate Courts at Abeokuta, Ife and Sapele.[58]

The colonial executive was responsible for quite as number of the problems associated with the judiciary during the period of colonial rule. While it was desirous of the judiciary to dispense justice rooted in the confidence of the subject people, the incessant intervention of the executive in the process of judicial administration and its control of the purse were potent enough to frustrate the judiciary. The actions and sometimes in-action of the executive destroyed the confidence of the people in the ability of the court to dispense justice and as such many of them went away thinking that the judge was biased or incompetent.[59]

Government intervention and activities in the daily administration of the courts made it difficult for the judiciary to have complete and unfettered rein in the administration of justice. The relationship between the colonial legal department that was responsible for the appointment, promotion and matters affecting court personnel and the judicial department tragically emasculated the judiciary. The office of the Attorney General was supervisory over that of the Chief Justice. On many occasions, the Governor acting on the advice of the Attorney General, by passed the Chief Justice in recommending applicants for purely and essentially judicial appointments to the Colonial Office in London.[60] In 1935, J.A. Maybin as Officer Administering the Government in Nigeria acting under the advice of his Attorney General wrote what could at best be described as an indictment of the Chief Justice. He recalled the Chief Justice's notice to earlier correspondence, which complained of "lack of precision in the routine system followed in the offices of the Chief Registrar and Police Magistrate of the Saint Anna Court". He regretted that further instances of defects in office routine had been brought to his notice and cited two instances:

(a) That the Chief Registrar gave no specific allocation for stationery to the Police Magistrate of Ebute Metta

(b) That the Police Magistrate kept no record of stationery received or issued.[61]

He concluded by stating equivocally that;

> Precision in estimating, inventing and accounting is essential and it would appear that the trouble in these cases arose largely from defects in the system in those offices, which would appear to require examination.[62]

It would seem that the executive especially after the 1933 reforms felt threatened by the enhanced status of the newly created High Court and Magistrate Courts. The rationale given by Sir Donald Cameron for the abolition of the executive ridden Provincial Court system was considered specious and unconvincing. The colonial administrative officers believed that the Governor did not take the Service into confidence before the introduction of the reforms.[63] They wondered why the Governor, "a man of exceptional ability and character" should have ignored so completely the argument that the reforms would introduce unnecessary "legalism and lawyers into the administration of justice in colonial Nigeria". It would be recalled that Sir Donald Cameron presented a most coherent speech to the Legislative Council in March 19333 justifying the reforms. The salience of his argument is quotes *in extenso* in order to underscore the major reason for the reforms.

> If the judgement of the Court is to be the judgement of an officer experienced in the art of sifting and weighing evidence and is to be based solely on the evidence which has been laid before him in the case, it does not matter a great deal to me what he is called... But, if the decision of the Court may properly be swayed by non-judicial consideration within the knowledge of the Administrative Officer, and is therefore not to be based solely on the evidence which has been led, then... the court has ceased to be a judicial tribunal and the officer has ceased to be a

> judicial officer. Change the system of law, if you will, and punish the people by administrative measures by Administrative Officers exercising a kind of parental correction because the people are primitive; but remember always, pray, if you do so, you will thereby be depriving the natives of the protection of any judicial court and any judicial system of law.[64]

The colonial executive before and after Sir Donald Cameroon believed that the Provincial Court system was an experiment of great originality and significance. They believed that the Provincial Courts provided, the opportunity for Administrative Officers to undertake judicial functions and this had certain advantages for the colonial enterprise. The administration was therefore very bitter against Sir Donald Cameron, what the stood for, and the reforms he introduced especially the High Court and Magistrate Courts. The Provincial Court System "was abandoned at the instance of the Governor" whose experience was entirely secretariat, a law officer in England (apparently Grattian Bushe) and a handful of officials in the colonial office, and it was abandoned without discussion". The statement above represents the feelings and the disgust the colonial administrators had for the Magistrate Court system.

The non-availability of competent and professionally qualified men to serve as judges and magistrates in the colonial judiciary also compounded the problem of the judiciary. In October 1945, the Governor Sir Arthur Richards requested the Chief Justice to recommend names of barristers who could be appointed as Magistrates[65] to fill existing vacancies. The Chief Justice delayed in replying in order to afford himself enough time to meet and discuss with members of the Nigerian Bar who could be approached.[66] His observation, which he subsequently conveyed to the Governor, was that, members of the Bar were not prepared to be appointed magistrates at the present rate of pay. Such appointment would have meant a loss of a considerable income.[67] It was regrettable for the Chief Justice to note that "only members of the Bar who were prepared to take magisterial posts were those who had very little practice due to incompetence, or those who were too old to be of any use".[68]

The situation of a serious dearth of African and professionally qualified personnel provided the executive, the opportunity to embark on the appointment of Administrative Officers as magistrates. The better-placed protectorate of Southern Nigeria which had qualified barristers more than the Northern Protectorate, even had to appoint one hundred and ten Administrative Officers as magistrates. This class of magistrates continued to dispense justice not with respect to law, but to administrative expediency as it used to be under the Provincial Court arrangement, albeit, with some minor limitations.[69]

Adegboyega Adetokunbo Ademola was appointed Magistrate at Warri in the Warri Province of the Southern Protectorate. This appointment was after the departure of Sir Donald Cameron, the hard working and assertive Governor, the man who attempted to re-conceptualise and radicalise the judicial process in colonial Nigeria, and the man who was severely criticized by administrative officers who felt threatened by the 1933 judicial reforms. In 1938 as in other times, vacancies were declared for magistrates of the Protectorate Courts.[70] More vacancies existed following the withdrawal of the candidacy of M.H.C. Gill, the transfer of Mr. R.O. Sinclair to Northern Rhodes and the appointment of Mr. G.T. Lowry to the establishment of police magistrates.[71] Two of the five existing vacancies were filled with the appointment of Messrs F.S. Pretheroe and C.W. Reece.[72] The Acting Lieutenant Governor W.E. Hunt was not aware of any local candidate to recommend to the Secretary of State for the Colonies. He therefore requested the Colonial Office in London to take necessary steps to fill the three existing vacancies at an early date. [73]

By a confidential memo to the Colonial Office, the Lieutenant Governor showed his desire to recommend African candidates for one of the remaining magisterial posts.[74] On January 27, 1939 Governor B.H. Bourdillon sent in Mr. F.E. Olude Euba's application for consideration as magistrate by the Colonial Office.[75] However, the appointment of Adegboyega Adetokunbo

Ademola as magistrate had been made in the Judicial Department in April 1939[76] before the appointment of Mr. Euba was made in November 1940.

Before his appointment as Magistrate, and between 1934 and 1938, Adetokunbo Ademola had served the colonial government in various capacities as Pupil Attorney in the office of the Attorney General of the colonial government in Nigeria, and in the judicial department where he understudied presiding magistrates in the Magistrate Courts. He later transferred to the Unified Nigerian Administrative Service and was posted to the secretariat of the Eastern Provinces in Enugu.[77] His schedule of duties included matters broadly related to the administration of the Native Courts Ordinance No. 44 of 1933 and the review of the system of tax collection.

The institutional frustration of being an African in the service of a colonial and foreign government forced Adetokunbo Ademola out of the unified Nigerian Administrative Service. He had a brief spell in party politics and practiced as a legal practitioner in divisional Courts across Southern Nigeria, especially Lagos, Benin, Ijebu-Ode and Warri Province.[78] It is however, unfortunate that there are no records of the legal philosophy, erudition and brilliance of Adetokunbo Ademola as a legal practitioner during this early period.

By a curious twist of events, Adetokunbo Ademola returned to the Colonial Judicial Department in 1939 at a time other African lawyers were little interested in taking any appointment with the colonial government considering the meagre salary and the differential salary scales between European and African employees. The appointment of Adetokunbo Ademola as Magistrate was subject to the conditions laid down generally in the Colonial Regulations and General Orders (Nos. 155-164). The letter of appointment expressly stated that he would be liable for transfer to any legal appointment of similar status and emoluments in another department anywhere within the Colony and Protectorate of Nigerian including the Cameroon, which was under British Mandate. The appointment however, was not in the Unified Colonial Legal Service.[79]

The appointment of Adetokunbo Ademola as Magistrate and his subsequent assumption of duty as Magistrate Full Powers in Warri were a part of the process of appointing qualified Africans into essentially European posts. The British colonial government in Nigeria had its secretariat situated in Lagos with the Governor at the head. The whole country was administratively divided into three groups of provinces namely, Northern, Western and Eastern groups of provinces, with headquarters at Kaduna, Ibadan and Enugu respectively. Each group of provinces had a Chief Commissioner as head who was also responsible to the Governor in Lagos. Each province within the group of provinces was under a Resident who was directly responsible to the Chief Commissioner. Every province in turn had one or more divisions, each under a District Officer with an Assistant District Officer, depending on the size of the division. The District Officers and Assistant District Officers were responsible to the Resident.[80]

Warri Province was one of the six provinces in the Western Group of Provinces with headquarters in Ibadan. The province was divided into four divisions to facilitates and enhance administrative efficiency. In 1939 the Resident Warri Province was Major R.L. Bowen,[81] while L.L. Cantle and S.L. Knight were District Officers in the Jekri-Sobo Division assisted him.[82] R.L. Bowen was a meticulous officer who showed a remarkable understanding of colonial administration in Southern Nigeria, where paramount rulership, the cornerstone of Indirect Rule was not hitherto prevalent. R.L. Bowen, in spite of the existence and enormous influence of pre-colonial civil administrative machinery of the people in the Warri Province, was able to popularise the Native Authority Councils. He also managed the strained relationship between the Itsekiri and the Urhobo to the admiration of his superiors in Ibadan and Lagos.[83] The Resident was particularly interested in maintaining peace in his province, while also ensuring that good measure of law and order prevailed. The instruments of colonial administration including the judiciary and the police became veritable instruments in the hands of R.L. Bowen.[84]

As noted above, in spite of the 1933 reforms and the subsequent attempt to put an end to executive justice, Administrative Officers did large proportion of magisterial work. With the imminence of war in 1938 and its eventual outbreak in 19i39, a number of Administrative Officers were absorbed into the armed forces.[85] Those who could not be absorbed were called upon to execute numerous additional functions to promote the British war effort. This situation exposed the need to recruit full time qualified Africans to serve as magistrates in the protectorate courts.[86] Additionally, His Excellency the Governor of Nigeria considered it advisable as far as possible "to divorce the judiciary from the executive and administration".[87] This was the mood of the colonial government when Adetokunbo Ademola was appointed magistrate in 1939.

Shortly before Adetokunbo Ademola assumed duties as Magistrate in the Warri Province in 1939, Messrs H.B. Cox. Acting Magistrate and F.S. Protheroe Magistrate, had held regular sessions at Warri and Sapele.[88] The headquarters of the Magistrate was however moved in 1938 from Benin to Warri to underscore the relative importance of Warri as a commercial nerve centre.[89] The large number of cases attended to in the province made it imperative for Administrative Officers to devote the better part of their time to judicial work. The period also witnessed an escalation in the number of cases to be heard especially at Warri and Sapele. Litigation became very expensive and the lawyer's fee often exorbitant. The fee for the defence of a simple case of trespass was as high as £50, while the total fees paid by both sides were over £80.[90] In spite of the fees, the courts continued to be popular and as noted by the *Southern Nigeria Defender*;[91]

> The people of Warri are widely known for their case making propensities. They being blind to reason hardly forgive each other and always choose to settle their differences in the courts.[92]

Warri was also known for widespread criminal involvement. This was however one of the social ills caused by uncontrolled rural-urban migration during this period. Discussing the important problem of criminal tendencies in the Warri Province, a public affairs commentator who had a good knowledge of the people, expressed his shock when he noticed the heavy calendar of cases before the High Court and the Magistrate Court in Warri. The cases comprised mainly crimes of first order namely; murder in cold blood, kidnapping, stealing with violence, house breaking and burglary.[93]

The executive as represented by the Resident Warri Province, attempted to use the courts and the police to maintain law and order, and to provide a conductive atmosphere for the promotion of trade especially during the period of war. The extent to which the administration attempted to use the courts to ensure peace and good administration on the one hand, and the willingness of the courts to be so used on the other, defined the nature, scope and intent of the interrelationship between the executive and the judiciary during this time.

By the end of 1939, arrangements for the prosecution of criminal cases could be described as satisfactory.[94] Most of the criminal cases from the Urhobo division were sent for hearing at Warri. Messrs F.S. Protheroe and A.A. Ademola both Magistrates Full Powers held court sessions at Warri and Sapele. At Burutu, the Collector of Customs continued to act as magistrate with limited powers. The phenomenal decrease in criminal cases in the township of Warri was according to the Resident, due to a much stricter enforcement of township regulations involving minor offences.[95] In spite of intensified police activities, illicit distillation of gin, which was a major irritation to European trade in liquor, was still prevalent throughout the Province in 1939-1940. The colonial authorities found it difficult to detect the sites of local distilleries because distillations were carried out so easily in the remote and inaccessible villages. The District Officers remained helpless and many of them even confessed their inability to solve the problem and bring the culprits to face the wrath of the law.

The Magistrate Courts under Adetokunbo Ademola could not impose stricter sanctions that could serve as deterrents, despite the fact that the District Officers advocated stiffer penalties. Mr. B.J.A. Mathews, the District Officer for Aboh Division said:

> It is unlikely that a conviction at the present time has (sic) any deterrent effect whatever, as the offender must be given the option of a fine and the fine itself must be one which it is within his means to pay.[96]

L.L. Cantle District Officer, Jekri-Sobo Division was more dejected by the situation when the remarked:

> The Superintendent of Police reports that the small fines inflicted in the magistrate court have no deterrent effect whatever. Advice to Councils and people is not only ignored but smiled at.[97]

However, despite the insinuation of the District Officers to the effect that the Magistrates' seemingly soft penalties for illicit distillation of local gin were responsible for the continued perpetration of the crime, the Resident R.L. Bowen was more objective in his assessment when he said:

> As regards illicit distillation, I fear that this will always remain with this province and as the increase in duty on spirits continues to rise, there is little hope that this traffic will show any real decline".[98]

The Magistrate Courts in the Warri Province continued to play their role in the dispensation of justice by ensuring the resolution of conflicts in civil suits and in criminal cases. The colonial administration defined and supervised the type of relationship that existed between the colonial executive set up and judiciary. The continued use of Administrative Officers as Magistrates in purely judicial functions and the inability of such officers to separate what was essentially judicial from administrative blurred the executive perception of what separation of powers should be.

The Chief Commissioner Western Group of Provinces, G.C.W. Whitley attested to the cordial working relationship that existed between the executive and the bench on which Adetokunbo Ademola sat in 1939. In his remarks to the Governor he stated *inter alia*:

> As I said in Legislative Council, I should welcome the appointment of another full time African Magistrate in the Western Provinces. Ademola in the Warri – Benin Circuit has completely justified his appointment.[99]

Throughout the year 1940, Adetokunbo Ademola held his usual court sessions in Warri. The much-expected inter-ethnic land cases that had been a source of strained relationship between the Itsekiri and the Urhobo did not come up for adjudication either in the high court presided over by Mr. Justice Jackson, Assistant Judge or in the Magistrate Court. The only case that threatened communal peace was the local dispute between Akugbene; a Western Ijaw society and Okuamana Urhobo society.[100] The reference of the case to the court for adjudication did not allow the communities to resort to measures that could lead to a breakdown of law and order. One remarkable thing in colonial Warri province was the readiness of the people to use the law courts for the settlement of conflicting claims, especially claims to land.[101] The Chief Commissioner believed that the increase in the work of the courts especially in their civil work confirmed the financial solvency of the people in Warri Province in spite of the war.[102]

The colonial administration in the Province continued to ensure that the administration of justice at all levels was not contrary to the ultimate objective of keeping the province safe for commerce. The Second World War underscored the relative importance of Nigeria. Nigeria played a prominent role in the allied war effort by her contribution of material and men.[103] The fall of France and the closing of the Mediterranean were two major reasons for the recognition of Nigeria's strategic location in Africa. The country provided the main line of communication by air to the Middle East and the Far East. As a result of her strategic location in the allied war plan and her men and material resources, colonial Nigeria assumed temporary importance in the British scheme of things.[104]

Warri Province was of considerable economic importance, considering the volume of trade that was carried out at the ports of Burutu and Forcados.[105] To attend to the numerous civil and criminal cases in 1943, Mr. Justice Olumuyiwa Jibowu, Mr. Justice Graham Callow and Mr. Adetokunbo Ademola devised an efficient and effective procedure in the discharge of their judicial functions.[106] The new approach required the magistrate to travel through the divisions and in the course of his travels deal with all civil cases and all criminal cases that could be dealt with on the spot.[107] The system was a modest attempt on the part of the judiciary to draw a line, however thin, between the executive and the judiciary. It was a bold attempt, considering the predilections of the colonial executive, to see the judiciary as subordinate part of administration at all times. The local colonial executive saw the courts as an agency of maintaining the law and not for the dispensation of justice. The courts were encouraged and assisted to use the fine letters of the law to back up and add strength to administrative policies. Justice could be available only in cases where it would promote and sustain peace, law and order.

Adetokunbo Ademola having been reared in the British legal tradition and based on his administrative experience and exposure was able to maintain a good working relationship with the local colonial executive. He was assisted in this regard by two major factors. In the first instance, the jurisdiction of the Magistrate Court as defined by the 1933 judicial reforms, did not allow him to entertain cases that could bring him in collision course with the executive.[108] The years of baptism as magistrate were filled with law and order cases that unlike constitutional cases required no more than the application of the law as stated. Secondly, the Magistrate had a cordial personal relationship with the local executive especially Major R.L. Bowen, Resident Warri Province, L.L. Cantle and S.L. Knight both District Officers for Jekri-Sobo Division. These European officials were convinced of

Adetokunbo Ademola's sincerity, loyalty to the colonial administration and dedication to duty.

The relationship between the executive and the judiciary in the Warri Province received a boost in 1942, when another Nigerian judicial officer was posted as Assistant Judge to the Province. On July 27, 1942 Mr. Justice Olumuyiwa Jibowu was posted to Warri to relieve Mr. Justice Jackson who left the Province. The personality, achievements, and competence of Olumuyiwa Jibowu were more than enough to give him a respectable standing, even among European colonial officers. On April 21, 1942 the Secretary of State for the Colonies conveyed the approval of the British Government to the Governor. The appointment took effect as from April 20, 1942 on a salary, which was three quarters of what a European holder of the same office would earn.[109] The elevation of Mr. Justice Olumuyiwa Jibowu to the higher bench was considered a rare feat for an African.[110] Colonialism emphasized race inequality and believed that African intellectuals, regardless of their high academic qualifications, sterling qualities and impeccable character, could not go beyond a particular stage in the civil service.[111] Mr. Clement Malone of Antigua as Chief Justice of the Leeward and Windward Islands in the West Indies[112] was the first judicial officer of African descent to preside over a British Supreme Court. Mr. Justice Olumuyiwa Jibowu became known for his candour, perfect understanding of the law and sternness. According to the Acting Resident Warri Province, Justice Jibowu's stern sentences were responsible for the noticeable drop in the number of burglaries in the township.[113]

It would seem therefore, that the relationship that existed between the courts and the colonial administration remained mutually beneficial within the scope of colonial practice. Colonial administration still looked down on African officers and in spite of the stature of Mr. Justice Olumuyiwa Jibowu, racism could not be ruled out in the British colonial attitude toward him. For instance African judges and magistrates suffered denigration in the hands of colonial Administrative Officers who could not fathom the elevation of Africans to essentially and exclusively

European positions.[114] The African judge presiding over a colonial court was more or less an agent of policy implementation and not necessarily of policy interpretation. The African judicial officer compelled by the circumstances of his appointment was duty bound to carry out the specific policy instructions of the colonial administration. Judicial review of executive action was not a course of action ever contemplated by the colonial judiciary. The restrictions imposed on the magistrates and judges made it difficult for some of them to establish excellent working relationship with the local administration in their provinces.

The new Supreme Court and Magistrate Courts Ordinances were put in the statute book in May 1943.[115] The purpose of the Supreme Court Ordinance was *inter alia*:

i. to merge the High Court of the Protectorate into the Supreme Court and create a Supreme Court of Nigeria with unlimited jurisdiction throughout Nigeria; and
ii. to make all judges puisne judges and thus abolish the present invidious and anomalous distinction between Puisne Judges or Judges and Assistant Judges.[116]

The purpose of the Magistrate Courts Ordinance was to abolish the distinction between the Supreme Court for the colony and Magistrate Courts for the protectorate, and in their stead, to constitute Magistrate Courts throughout Nigeria. However, despite the provisions of the new ordinances and the attempts to refine the process and machinery of justice in colonial Nigeria, colonial administrators still believed in the supremacy of the executive over the judiciary. The creation of Native Authorities in Southern Nigeria and the attendant over bearing importance of the Resident, District Officers and even Assistant District Officers necessarily undermined the independence of the judiciary. British colonial officials in Southern Nigeria left no stone unturned in their attempt to introduce the Native Authority system, sustain it and make it relevant to the administration of their colonial possession in Southern Nigeria.

Within this context, and as a result of the emergence of a new wave of nationalism, some African judicial officers believed that the colonial administration was not capable of maintaining an honest relationship between the administration and the judiciary. The judiciary was still considered an accomplice of the executive in the maintenance of law and order, creation of a conductive atmosphere for the development of commerce and the promotion of unequal economic relationship between the colony and Britain. According to the Southern Nigeria Defender,[117] Mr Adeleke Adedoyin Magistrate Full Powers at Ikot Ekpene resigned his appointment as Magistrate under the colonial government, largely as a result of the inability of the colonial administration to distinguish between the maintenance of law and order and the administration of justice.[118] While he was magistrate, Adeleke Adedoyin was very impressive and was known for his sound judgment and fairness. He became involved in the nationalism of the Second World War period and could no longer tolerate British attitude to justice in colonial Nigeria.[119] Before his resignation, he had a number of disagreements with British Colonial officials in his area of jurisdiction.

African Magistrates and judges who could manage a relationship with the colonial administration, continued on the bench. Adetokunbo Ademola had no cause to re-examine his appointment and he settled down to business in the Magistrate Court Warri, having satisfied himself that even within the restrictions and restraints on judicial activism, there could still exist a working relationship between the bench and the executive. The appointment of Adetokunbo Ademola as Magistrate could not have been without the influence of his father, Sir Ladapo Ademola who was then the Alake.[120] His judicial appointment was to be jealously protected and particular care must be taken to ensure that the existing cordial relationship between his father and mentor on the one hand, and the colonial administration on the other was not ruptured. The most appealing option to Adetokunbo Ademola was to be strictly guided on all sides by rules of law made according to British standards, values and ideals. A strict adherence to the rules of the law enabled him to support British commercial enterprise and sustain a relationship of commercial dependence on Britain, which reflected the exploitative structural integration of the colonial economy. Structural integration obviously became a coercive measure that ensured the incorporation of the colony's economy into the periphery of the international capitalist system.

At a rather simplistic level of discussion, the strict adherence of Adetokunbo Ademola to rules and his support for public policy ensured his acceptance by colonial government. Between 1939 and 1945, he was able to establish himself as a competent Magistrate who by his training in the best tradition of English legal education and circumstances could administer justice according to law to the admiration and commendation of his superior colonial officers.

Warri Province continued to be of particular interest to the colonial administration. The Resident would not allow the possibility of a breakdown of law and order, just as the Chief Commissioner confessed his desire and wish for the maintenance of peace and concord among the ethnic groups in the province, especially between the Itsekiri and the Urhobo.[121] Adetokunbo Ademola's duties as magistrate made him a strong factor in the maintenance of law and order. He committed himself to the task and by the time he was appointed judge, he had served in virtually all the divisions within the province.[122] It would seem that, Adetokunbo Ademola enjoyed his appointment as magistrate and also his relationship with the local colonial administration. For instance in 1940, he informed the Chief Justice Sir Donald Kingdom of his preparedness and willingness to cover areas outside of his own circuit in order to expedite the process of judicial administration.[123]

Adetokunbo Ademola was committed to using the court to enforce compliance with rules and regulations among members of the society. The Police Force in Warri enforced the Township Regulation with a view to reducing the incidence of crime to the barest minimum. Adetokunbo Ademola complemented the efforts of the Police by imposing maximum penalty allowed for violation of township regulations and other such offences. Before he became Magistrate in Warri, his predecessor in office Mr. F.S. Protheroe had been accused of imposing "small fines which had no deterrent effect whatever".[124] During this time, the Police had considerable difficult in combating the menace of urban crime when confronted with legal quibbles often raised in the magistrate court by the defence. The colonial executive in fact believed that regard for legal finesse served as a handicap when dealing with crime especially in the Urhobo area.[125]

The court presided over by Adetokunbo Ademola was known for its firmness and pro colonial administration attitude. The judicial performance of Mr. Justice Olumuyiwa Jibowu, which had been noted earlier, encouraged Adetokunbo to re state a belief in the ability of the courts of law to ensure the maintenance of law and order. An examination of the performances of Adetokunbo Ademola in the variety of cases that came before him will provide insight into the judicial attitude of the magistrate and also indicate the relationship that existed between the executive and the judiciary even at the local level of the Warri Province.

On January 12, 1944 Joseph Olokoba, a man who had nine previous convictions for criminal involvements and activities, was sentenced to 12 months imprisonment.[126] His conviction was for picking the sum of 11s Od from the pocket of one Mallam Tsalhatu Idi in the Ogbe Ijaw market. The magistrate believed that the convict was a hardened criminal and therefore ruled that, even after the completion of his term of imprisonment, Olokoba should be under Police watch and supervision for another 12 months.[127] Adetokunbo Ademola also sentenced a woman, Mrs. Konuko Ikere to either pay a fine of 30s or go behind the bars for seven days because she allowed her child to walk about in the market and committing nuisance outside a public toilet in the premises of the market.[128] The prosecution had alleged that the woman was negligent and paid no regard to the township regulation that forbade minors from aimless wandering and nuisance. The sentence was intended to serve as deterrent to other market women who could be similarly placed. Again, it was an attempt to reiterate the fact that, the court and the administration work hand in hand to ensure the maintenance of law and order even at the level of public hygiene and sanitation.

In the same court, the Magistrate on Friday January 14, 1944 frowned at the criminal involvement of Tom Enebeli who was a foreman in one of the cranes of the United Africa Company Wharf at Burutu. He was sentenced to 3 months imprisonment with hard labour for receiving 11 glasses, 4 bottles of Santal Oto perfume and 1 tin of yeast, stolen from his employers.[129] The sentence could not have been otherwise considering the place of the United African Company in the British economy during and after the war. Colonial administration in Warri showed considerable concern for the commercial interest of the company especially at the Wharf in Burutu. Efforts were intensified by the Police to prevent port theft and other related crimes. The courts were encouraged to pass maximum sentence on criminals involved in felony against the interest, not only of the United African Company, but also of other commercial houses. In another case, a United Africa Company stationery Depot store man, Aaron Ezemeku was sentenced to 2 months imprisonment with hard labour for stealing a coat and a pair of glasses valued at £4.5s.[130] It would be noted that the Warri Province became known for thefts and burglaries during the war years, and the courts were called upon to deal harshly with those involved. Such crimes called for stiffer penalties and the courts did not fail in their duties to clamp down heavily on criminals arraigned before them.

Adetokunbo Ademola also dealt with cases bordering on profiteering however minor. For instance a woman, Madam Oritsemajogba was fined 10s or 7 days imprisonment for unlawful gain of 6d on the sale of a tuber of yam.[131] Before delivering judgement, the magistrate warned not only the woman standing trial before him, but all traders that, as profiteering on yams was increasing, he would give no option of fines to future offenders.[132]

The colonial administration had been involved in the sale of yam tubers at controlled prices to the public. The exigencies of war had affected the availability of yam tubers since yam was part of the food items for Nigerian soldiers involved in the Second World War. Many traders had capitalized on the scarcity of yam to profiteer, making it necessary for the colonial administration to regulate the sale of yam. Violation of the trade regulation was therefore made a subject to be dealt with by the Magistrate Court.

Adetokunbo Ademola also used his court to assist the colonial administration in enforcing its policy on the allocation of stalls in designated markets.[133] The Maclver new market was purposely built for those women who could not obtain stalls at the Ogbe-Ijaw market.[134] According to the instructions of the Local Authority, no woman was to be allowed to sell her foodstuffs in the open space at the Ogbe Ijaw market. However, contrary to this instruction, some eleven women were caught violating the regulation. They did not apply to the administration for allocation of stalls. They were consequently brought before the magistrate, who on 27 April 1944 sentenced them to either pay a fine of One shilling each or five days imprisonment for selling their foodstuffs at illegal spots where no stall had been allocated to them.[135]

Another case, which attested to the relationship between the local administration and the judiciary in the Warri Province, was the case of Chief Edema Arubi in 1944. Since the establishment of the Native Authority system in the Warri Province, Edema Arubi had been particularly interested in the working and operation of the system. He had raised a number of objections against the composition, membership and *modus operandi* of the system. He had even petitioned the entire hierarchy of British colonial administration not only in Nigeria, but also at the Colonial Office, London.[136] He could be regarded a thorn in the flesh of the local colonial administration. His activities as a public letter writer, an unrelenting petitioner and above all, his enormous influence on the Olu of Itsekiri made him an irritant to the local colonial administration.[137]

For example Major Bowen had Edema Arubi in mind when he said in his annual report for 1941 that:

> There is little improvement in the Itsekiri Council which is still overshadowed by the arrogant personality of the Olu. Some of the Council (sic) appear to be keen on improving the Administration, but they do not appear to be strong enough to overcome the influence of the place seekers around the Olu who so continuously advise him in the wrong direction with such fulsome flattery that he can think of nothing but his personal prestige and aggrandizement...[138]

No doubt, the colonial administration had been looking for an opportunity to clip the wings of Edema Arubi as it were. An opportunity presented itself in October 1944 when Edema Arubi was involved in an otherwise flimsy case with one of his clients. Preliminary investigations started on October 17, 1944 before Adetokunbo Ademola in the sensational charge of perverting the course of justice brought by the Police against Edema Arubi.[139] According to the Southern *Nigeria Defender*, Edema Arubi was formerly of the Accountant General's office Lagos. On his retirement, he set up the Civil Illiterates Defence Service and became a well-known letter writer, who had a number of clients on various subjects and matters.[140]

A.C. Willoughby, the Chief Inspector of Police, Warri Province conducted the prosecution of the charge of extortion preferred against Edema Arubi.[141] After a careful review of both the prosecution and the defence, Adetokunbo Ademola declared Edema Arubi guilty on three counts for offences under the Illiterate Protection Ordinance.

As expected, in his allocutus before the sentences was passed, Edema Arubi said he believed that the Police had taken undue advantage of his. He referred to a former Superintendent of Police, Mr. Armstrong who he alleged had said in an open court during one of the cases, that the police in Warri had written his name in their black book.[142] Having been found guilty, the magistrate proceeded to sentence Edema Arubi to a fine of £5 of one-month imprisonment on each of the three counts on which he was found guilty. The sentences were however, to run concurrently.[143]

The circumstances of the case, the prosecution and the judgement would confirm that the colonial administration trusted the judiciary to deal with all forms of opposition to the whole of British enterprise in colonial Nigeria. The sentence, although light should be seen in the light of an attempt by the colonial administration to underscore the point that, it was capable of dealing decisively with any opposition to its preferred course of action and administrative style. The social and political clout of Edema Arubi not withstanding, he was convicted and sentenced to teach a particular lesson.

Perhaps, it is necessary at this stage to recognize and appreciate the fact that, the relationship that existed between the colonial administration and the judiciary with particular regard to the magistracy of Adetokunbo Ademola in the Warri Province was not one sided. The British colonial officials including the Resident became personally involved in the affairs of the court. The personal preference of the magistrate in his private capacity made him identify with the labour union in Warri. He was respected by all categories of workers irrespective of status in the colonial civil service.[144] As an African holding a responsible post of Magistrate, which hitherto was essentially reserved for Europeans, he commanded the respect and won the admiration of the leadership, rank and file of the labour union especially at Warri.

In May 1944, Adetokunbo Ademola was invited as the distinguished Chairman at a civil reception organized by the Nigeria Civil Service Union Warri for the retiring Mr. E.O. Way. The colonial administration confirmed the cordial inter-relationship of the executive and the judiciary by the presence of Major R.L. Bowen (Resident Warri Province). Messrs L.L. Cantle (Senior District Officer) and P.R. Foulkes Roberts (Local Authority) at the ceremony.[145] The judicial activities of Adetokunbo Ademola as Magistrate in the Warri Province continued until 1946 and by that time, he had been able to establish himself as a competent magistrate, who understood and who could protect British colonial interests in Nigeria.

As magistrate, Adetokunbo Ademola was not directly responsible to the Resident, but to the Governor through the Chief Justice. The nature of colonial rule and subjugation, coupled with colonial administrative style made it virtually impossible not to have a relationship with the Resident who could be regarded as the on the spot representative of the executive at the local level. The Resident was administratively required to oversee and to make reports on every government department in his province. He submitted comprehensive reports to the Chief Commissioner on the activities of government, reactions of subject people to government activities and on social and economic developments in his province annually. In a sense, the Resident was the general overseer; the Chief Executive Officer charged with the onerous responsibility of ensuring the success of the British enterprise in its totality in any particular province.

As part of a general scheme, the Magistrate Court Warri was considered appropriate for use in promoting the interest of the colonial administration in Warri during this time. The relationship between the executive and the judiciary assumed a new dimension, when it was realized by the local colonial administration that the issue of lease on crown lands could be handled by the judiciary in favour of the administration.[146] The old Warri second-class township was held on a long lease by the colonial government. The lease was administered first by a Station Magistrate and later by a Local Authority who was assisted by an Advisory Board.[147] The leases however became controversial in certain instances to the extent that the Local Authority had to seek the official intervention of the Resident and the Commissioner of Lands at the Colonial Secretariat in Lagos.[148]

Of particular relevance to our understanding of the interrelationship between the executive and the judiciary in the Warri Province was the case that the administration referred to as illegal occupation of crown lands. On February 16, 1945, E.W. Mylius was compelled to bring to the notice of the Commissioner of Lands, Lagos certain illegalities, which arose in connection with, plot number 3 Block IV in Alder's Town, Warri. According to the Resident, the plot in question was demised under Deed 39 of Volume V. registered as No. 41 at page 41 in volume 215 of the Land Registry in the office of the Commissioner of Lands, to one Madam Ereden.[149] By the time the Resident was writing, one Madam Diana Shute occupied the plot.[150] The original occupant to whom the plot was demised was living as a concubine of one Jacob Odafiokpo at the time of her death.[151] The Resident deposed that, after her death, Jacob Odafiokpo made an illegal assignment of the plot to one Madam Ajamuoghan Etie, the mother of Diana Shute who was considered the rightful owner of the plot of land after the death of the former. Other interested parties contested this.[152] The local colonial administration was confronted with the dilemma and therefore requested the Commissioner's advice as to how best to legalize Madam Diana Shute's claims to the plot of land. The Resident concluded his letter by acknowledging the prevalence of similar illegal assignments in Warri Township and believed that they would be resolved.[153]

The Commissioner of Land, Lagos replied the Resident's letter on February 28, 1945 and acknowledged the difficulty posed by the problem.[154] He believed there was no easy solution, but proposed three possible courses of action, viz;

a. to arrange for an assignment to the occupant;
b. to arrange for a surrender and then issue a new lease to the occupant; and
c. to obtain an order of forfeiture and issue a new lease to the occupant.

The Resident having obtained the understanding of the Commissioner proceeded to institute an action in the name of the Commissioner of Lands against Madam Diana Shute for the forfeiture of the plot of land in question under section 16 Cap 84 of the Crown Land Act.[155] The Magistrate Court under Adetokunbo Ademola considered the case and on August 1, 1945 gave judgement in favour of the colonial administration to the effect that, the lease was forfeited[156] and the Commissioner of Land was to take possession of the plot of land.[157] The court also awarded six shillings as cost against the defendant.[158] This approach describes how the colonial executive used the courts to promote the interest of British Administration in Nigeria.

According to Coker, the period 1939-1945 was essentially years of faith in the ability of Adetokunbo Ademola to perform the duties of his appointment as Magistrate, Full Powers.[159] The period was understandably and essentially a learning stage and obviously the experiences stood him in good stead in his judicial performance later in his career as judge on the higher bench.

Notes

1. E.O. Esiemokhai, *The Colonial Legal Heritage in Nigeria*. (Akure: Fagbamigbe Publishers, 1986), p. 2.
2. *Ibid.*
3. B.O. Nwabueze, *Machinery of Justice in Nigeria*. (London: Butterworths & Co. Ltd), p. 46.
4. Omoniyi Adewoye, *The Judicial System in Southern Nigeria 1854-1954: Law and Justice in a Dependency.* (London: Longman Group Ltd), p. 18.
5. *Ibid.*
6. *Ibid.*
7. B.O. Nwabueze, *The Machinery of Justice of Nigeria...*, p. 47.
8. *Ibid.*
9. *Ibid.*
10. *Ibid.*
11. T.O. Elias, *Groundwork of Nigeria Law,* (London: Butterworths & Co. Ltd. 1962), p. 103.
12. *Ibid.*
13. *Ibid.*
14. *Ibid,* p. 50.
15. *Ibid.*
16. *Ibid*, pp. 50-51.
17. *Ibid*, p. 51.

18. *Ibid*, p. 56.
19. *Ibid.*
20. *Ibid*, p. 57.
21. T.O. Elias *Groundwork of Nigeria Law...*, p. 110.
22 *Ibid.*
23. *Ibid*, The Native Courts Proclamation No. 5, of 1900.
24. Margery Perham, *Lugard: The Years of Authority 1898 – 1945* (London: Collins Clear Press, 1 960), p. 429
25 Lugard to Lady Lugard 17 March 1914 cited in Mergery Perham... p.431
26. For an elaborate discussion of the judicial reorganization of 1914, see Omoniyi Adewoye *The Judicial System in Southern Nigeria,* pp. 147-149.
27. T.O. Elias, *Groundwork of Nigeria Law...* p. 123.
28. T.N. Tamuno, *The Evolution of the Nigerian State: The Southern Phase 1898 – 1914*. (London: Longman Group Ltd., 1972), p. 153.
29. *Ibid.*
30. *Ibid*, p. 153.
31. C.O. 520/92, C. of 28 June, 1910 to Officer Administering the Government of Southern Nigeria cited in T.N. Tamuno. *The Evolution of the Nigerian State...* p. 154.
32 For details see, T.O. Elias, *Groundwork of Nigeria Law* on the judicial reorganization of 1914.
33. Omoniyi Adewoye, *The Judicial System in Southern Nigeria...* p. 147.
34. *Times of Nigeria*, 5 May, 1914.
35. See Memorandum prepared by Chief Justice Sir Edwin Speed. Report on Amalgamation, pp. 77- 82, in Margery Perham *Lugard: The Years of Authority, 1898 – 1945* (London: Collins Clear Type Press, 1960) p. 429
36. Omoniyi Adewoye *The Judicial System in Southern Nigeria....* p. 222.
37. T.O., Elias, *Groundwork of Nigeria Law...* p. 137.
38. C.O. 583/183 Judicial System in the Protectorate of Nigeria" Minute by A Fidden, 11 May, 1932 cited in Omoniyi Adewoye, *The Judicial System in Southern Nigeria...* p. 222.

39. For detailed discussion of the reforms as contained in the enabling ordinances, see T.O. Elias, *The Nigeria Legal System*. (London: Butterworths and Co. Ltd., 1963), pp. 140-151.
40. T.O. Elias, *Groundwork of Nigerian Law*... p. 142.
41. *Ibid.*
42. *Ibid.*
43. *Ibid.*
44. T.O. Elias, *Groundwork of Nigerian Law*... p. 159.
45. N.A.I.C.S.O. 26/28525 Vol. V. p. 659.
46. T.O. Elias, *Groundwork of Nigerian Law* ... p. 143.
47. *Surukatu & Anor, v. Dende & Ors.* (1914), 7 WACA 50.
48. The enumerated places where Degema, Calabar, Buguma, Bakana, Onitsha, Warri, Sapele, Koko, Forcados, Burukutu, Bonny, Opobo, Port Harcourt, Aba and Enugu.
49. Omoniyi Adewoye *The Judicial System in Southern Nigeria*... p. 229.
50. *Ibid*, p. 233.
51. W.R. Crocker *Nigeria: A Critique of British Colonial Administration*... p. 232.
52. *Ibid.*
53. N.A.I. CSO/26/29257 Vol. Xl "Administrative Officers with Magisterial Powers". CSO 26/29257 Vol. 1-5 "Administrative Officers with Judicial Powers".
54. Omoniyi Adewoye, *The Judicial System in Southern Nigeria*... p. 241.
55. N.A.I. CSO 26/29590 Vol. VI Inspection Notes by the Chief Justice, p. 17.
56. *Ibid*, p. 18.
57. *Ibid.*
58. *Ibid.*
59. See the views of Delvin J. in R.v. *Barnsley Licensing Justice, ex parte Barnsley and District Licensed Victuallers Association* cited by de Smith. *The Judicial Review of Administrative Action*... pp. 220-224.
60. N.A.I. CSO/26/28525 Vol. II & III Protectorate Court: Appointment of Judges and Assistant Judges.
61. N.A.I. CSO/26/30390 Maybin to the Chief Justice, 1935.

62. *Ibid*, p. 2.
63. W.R. Crocker, *Nigeria: A Critique of British Colonial Administration...* p. 231.
64. Address of the Governor to the Legislative Council, March 1933.
65. N.A.I. CSO/26/2860/85, The Governor to the Chief Justice of Nigeria.
66. *Ibid.*
67. *Ibid.*
68. *Ibid.* The Chief Justice would have preferred more competent and dynamic lawyers to take up magisterial appointments.
69. Omoniyi Adewoye *The Judicial System in Southern Nigeria...* p. 234.
70. N.A.I. CSO/2825 Appointment of judges and Assistant Judges Protectorate Courts p. 528.
71. *Ibid.*
72. *Ibid.*
73. *Ibid.*
74. *Ibid.*
75. *Ibid.*
76. N.A.I CSO 28525 Vol. V. Appointment of Magistrates Protectorate Courts p. 607.
77. Folarin Coker *Sir Adetokunbo Ademola* (Lagos: Daily Times of Nigeria, 1972), p. 38. It would seem that the decision to take a judicial appointment was heavily influenced by the preference of his wife who preferred a less volatile career for her husband.
78. *Ibid.*
79. N.A.I. CSO. 28525 Vol. V. Appointment of Magistrate Protectorate Courts. Order 29, specified the other entitlement of the newly appointed magistrates including, salary annual increment rate, annual leave, accommodation and furniture.
80. Onigu Otite, *Autonomy and Dependence: The Urhobo Kingdom of Okpe in Modern Nigerian* (Evanston, Illinois: Northwestern University Press, 1973), p. 90.
81 NAI CSO 26/2/11857 Vol. XVI Warri Province Annual Reports 1939-1940 p. 14.
82. *Ibid.*

83. *Ibid.*
84. *Ibid.*
85. His Excellency Sir Arthur Richard Maiden Speech to the Legislative Council, 1944.
86. *Ibid.*
87. *Ibid.*
88. NAI CSO/26/2/11857 Vol. XV Warri Province Annual Report 1938 paragraph 41.
89. *Ibid.*
90. *Ibid.*
91. *Southern Nigeria Defender*, 6 February 1944 Professional Confussionists in Warri, p. 3.
92. *Ibid.*, p. 3.
93. *Ibid.* Warri had a total of 328 civil and 779 criminal cases in 1938 alone. For details, 1938 Annual Report Warri Province p. 15.
94. NAI CSO 26/2/11857 Vol. XVI Warri Province Annual Report 1939 – 1940.
95. *Ibid.*
96. NAI CSO 26/2/11857 Vol. XVI Warri Province Annual Report, 1939.
97. *Ibid.*
98. *Ibid.*
99. *Ibid.*
100. *Ibid.*
101. *Ibid.*
102. *Ibid.*
103. *Ibid.*
104. *Ibid.*
105. NAI CSO/26/211857 Vol. XVIII Warri Province Annual Report 1941 Onwards, pp. 40-42.
106. NAI CSO/26/2/11857 Vol. XXIV Warri Province Annual Report 1943, p. 9.
107. *Ibid.* Paragraph 37.
108. For details of the 1933 judicial reforms see Omoniyi Adewoye, *The Judicial System in Southern Nigeria...* pp. 221-248. B.O. Nwabueze, *Machinery of Justice in Nigeria...* pp. 77-79, also T.O. Elias, *Groundwork of Nigerian Law...* pp. 137-148.

109. NAI CSO 26/2/28525/Vol. 1 p. 3.
110. *Ibid.*
111. *Ibid.*
112. *Southern Nigeria Defender*, March 1, 1944.
113. *Ibid.*
114. During a legislative session in 1944 and on the floor of the Legislative Council Lagos. Hon. Akerele was so enraged by the continued disaffection of the colonial Attorney General toward Africans in the legal and judicial departments.
115. *Southern Nigeria Defender* January 4, 1944.
116. *Ibid.*
117. *Southern Nigeria Defender* October 7, 1944.
118. *Ibid.*
119. *Ibid.*
120. Folarin Coker, *Sir Adetokunbo Ademola*... p. 30.
121. NAI CSO 26/2/11857 Vol. XX Warri Province Annual Report 1945.
122. Folarin Coker, *Sir Adetokunbo Ademola*... p. 48-50.
123. Report on the Chief Judge's inspection of the Court of the Magistrate (Full Powers), Warri on the 8th October 1940 p. 94.
124. NAI CSO/26/2/11857 Vol. XV 1938 Warri Province Annual Report paragraph 47.
125. NAICSO/26/11857 Vol. XV 1938 Warri Province Annual Report paragraph 47.
126. *Southern Nigeria Defender*, January 12, 1944.
127. *Ibid.*
128. *Southern Nigeria Defender*, January 13, 1944.
129. *Ibid.*
130. *Southern Nigeria Defender*, September 7, 1944.
131. *Southern Nigeria Defender*, August 31, 1944.
132. *Ibid.*
133. *Southern Nigeria Defender*, April 27, 1944.
134. *Ibid.*
135. *Ibid.*
136. Omoniyi Adewoye, *The Judicial System in Southern Nigeria*..., p. 192.
137. *Ibid.*

138. NAI CSO/26/2/11857. Vol. XXIII, 1941.
139. *Southern Nigeria Defender*, October 18, 1944.
140. For details of his courage and tenacity of purpose, see Omoniyi Adewoye, *The Judicial System in Southern Nigeria...*, p. 192.
141. *Southern Nigeria Defender*, October 18, 1944.
142. *Ibid.*
143. *Ibid.*
144. *Southern Nigeria Defender*, May 6, 1974.
145. *Ibid.*
146. NAI/WP/236/101 Illegal Occupation of Crown Lands, E.N. Mylius to the Commissioner of Lands.
147 C.O. Omoneukarin, "Reminiscences of the Old Warri Province" (Warri Unpublished Manuscript, 1946).
148. NAI/WP/236/10 Illegal Occupation of Crown Lands.
149. *Ibid.*
150. *Ibid.*
151. *Ibid.*
152. *Ibid.*
153. *Ibid.*
154. *Ibid.*
155. /WP/236/20, Local Authority to President Warri Province.
156. Suit No. W/134/45.
157. *Ibid.*
158. *Ibid.*
159. Folarin Coker, *Sir Adetokunbo Ademola...*, pp. 48-49.

Chapter 3

The Development of a Judicial Behaviour 1946 - 1954

On most matters of private law, it may be more important that the law be settled than that it be settled correctly. Therefore, governing most matters of private law by the idea of men long dead is usually not only satisfactory, but may sometimes be affirmatively desirable. But on the problem of public law, which at any given time are especially difficult, creating law that will benefit living people is far more important than the law be settled. Therefore, on most matters of public law being governed by the ideas of men long dead is unsatisfactory and may even be abominable.

Davis 'Judge Made Law in England" *Colombia Law Review* pp.201, 205.

In January 1946, Adetokunbo Ademola was redeployed to Lagos as magistrate at St. Anna Court where he stayed for one year. He was relieved at Warri on January 8 by Mr. Ikushika Roberts[1] who had a limited circuit to cover since the magistrate at Onitsha covered the Asaba division of Benin Province.[2]

At St. Anna Court Adetokunbo Ademola continued to hold sessions punctually and regularly. It seemed Adetokunbo Ademola had lost interest in partisan politics and the new wave of nationalism of the post Second World War era. 1946 was remarkable for the emergence of a more radical and more intellectual attitude to nationalism.[3] The post war attitude of the British government that was quite contrary to the spirit and essence of the Atlantic charter provoked reaction from an articulate cross section of the country.[4] There was also the development of better political awareness among Nigerians,[5] during which time the relevance of the British Empire in Nigeria became a source of concern and a subject of endless debates.[6] The judicial reforms of 1943 had started to yield dividends and specifically, the magistrate courts became a beehive of judicial activities just as the magistrate courts assumed a new significance in the administration of justice.[7] The abolition of the protectorate courts emphasized the relative important position of the magistrate courts.[8] The reforms also compelled the magistrates to be more deeply involved in and concerned about the quality of the judgments they gave. In 1945, the judicial immunities of magistrates were removed as civil and criminal actions could be instituted against any magistrate in another court. This was intended to be a safeguard against arbitrary exercise, or possible abuse of judicial powers.[9]

The executive also sought to control the exercise of judicial discretion by the magistrates. In January 1945, an Executive Bill was presented to the Legislative Council, which was the first of the additional Bills that were being proposed to implement the judicial reforms.[10] Several Ordinances relating to the reform were enacted in March 1943, but they had not been brought into force by 1945.[11] The Magistrate Court (Civil Procedure) Ordinance, 1945 was proposed to cover the whole of the practice and procedure in magistrate courts concerning actions for the recovery of debts and demands, and in actions for damages and for other causes within the civil jurisdiction of Magistrate Courts.[12] The Ordinance that the executive sponsored solely had almost no input from the Chief Justice.[13] The Governor only informed the Chief Justice of the existence of the Bill. The Attorney General had even printed the draft before the office of the Chief Justice knew about its existence.[14] On January 11, 1945, His Excellency Arthur F. Richards sent a copy of a Bill for an Ordinance entitled "The Magistrates' Courts (Civil Procedure) Ordinance, 1945", with an explanatory memorandum prepared by the Attorney General to the Chief Justice.[15] The Governor wanted that the Bill be published in the Gazette of 25th of January and therefore requested that the Chief Justice should forward his comments on the Bill to him, not later than 22 January. The request left the Chief Justice with only eleven days to write his comments on such an important Bill on his department.[16] The Bill set out the procedure in magistrate courts in great detail and comprehensively too. The Attorney General believed that, if a magistrate would learn the Ordinance, he would have no difficulty in knowing what to do in practically any eventuality. The forms which were applicable to the various parts of the procedure before him were shown in the margin against each particular provision in the Ordinance.[17]

In the words of the G.L. Howe, the Attorney General:

> It is hoped that this Bill comprehensive as it is, will be of the utmost assistance to magistrates, especially those who may be placed in difficulties through being either unable to obtain assistance or who are situated in out-of-the-way places and may be unable to have access to the recognized textbooks and reports of decided cases.[18]

The process of drafting the Bill and more importantly the intent and content of the Magistrates (Civil Procedure) Ordinance, 1945 have two major implications for the on going discourse on the interrelationship of the executive and the judiciary in colonial Nigeria. In the first instance, the executive believed that the judiciary could be presented with a *fait accompli.* The Governor was not prepared to entertain the arguments of the Chief Justice expressed on an earlier occasion, of the judicial convenience of inputting certain legislation into the Rules of Court.[19]

In submitting the Bill for the belated consideration of the Chief Justice, the Governor said *inter-alia*:

> I am not unaware of the view that your Honour has expressed on a previous occasion that legislation of this nature can more conveniently by embodied in Rules of Court than in an Ordinance, and this is shared by most judges and magistrates.[20]

However in a show of executive arrogance which became the hallmark of the relationship between the executive and the judiciary, the Governor, concluded;

> The question was considered by my predecessor in Executive Council which advised that the proposed Ordinance will be of great assistance to magistrates. Sir Bernard Bourdillon concurred in the advice tendered and I am not disposed to vary the decision taken on that occasion".[21]

The executive therefore had its way and the Attorney General in the following words disparagingly dismissed the little amendment proposed by the Chief Registrar on behalf of the Chief Justice:

> I am far from convinced that any necessity exists for the proposed amendment. As I understand 74/75 herein, the difficulty arises from what appears to be the inability of a magistrate Grade I to fix in advance the times of the sitting of his Court in out districts.... Nothing is more essential for a successful judicial system than the knowledge that a court will be held at a certain time, and I must urge that every attempt be made so to do before 'ad hoc' legislation is considered.[22]

The Attorney General believed that the amendment proposed by the Chief Registrar which the former preferred to call 'ad hoc' legislation could upset the system approved and enacted in the reform Ordinances.[23] He said that Government should be given facts to prove that the system so approved was not practicable, despite efforts to make it work, before that system was changed.[24]

The other implication of the Magistrate' Courts (Civil Procedure) Ordinance, 1945 for the judiciary, was the undisguised effort to force the magistrate courts to operate within a straight jacket. The Ordinance was based on the County Courts Acts of England, and the forms were nearly all taken from the County Court Rule.[25] The magistrates were drenched by alien judicial interpretations of the provisions of the ordinance. They were not allowed the use of discretion to deal with local situations. The ordinance confirmed the desperation of the executive to use the Magistrate Courts as instruments for the subversion and distortion of Nigerian legal and judicial values and substituting them with English legal values, which "were complex and esoteric."

This describes the situation that was prevailing in 1946 when Adetokunbo Ademola sat at St. Anna Court I Lagos. As Police Magistrate, he entertained a good number of cases that were prosecuted by the Police in defense of the interest of the state or government.[26] His judicial performance showed a preference to technicalities of procedural law.[27]

In the inter-relationship with the executive, he became overtly supportive of the administration, just as the British orientation of his legal education compelled a narrow construction of the role of the judiciary in government. As noted de Smith, the English orientation in the 1950's was in favour of judicial self-restraint.[28] He believed that the courts found it difficult to be persuaded that the executive had acted *ultra vires*. Being a product of this tradition, Adetokunbo Ademola was rather restrained in his judicial attitude to causes affecting the interest of the executive. Although his court insisted on compliance with statutory requirements as to form and procedure, his judgements on issues of policy showed a remarkable deference to the opinion being advanced by the executive. This attitude could be seen in almost all the first generation Nigerian judicial officers.

Adetokunbo Ademola in 1946 at St. Anna Court I, had a somewhat predictable reaction to the variety of cases that came to his court. Where the Police Prosecutor could establish the guilt of the accused, he gave maximum sentence. For example on January 22, 1946, Adetokunbo Ademola sentenced Freeman Francis Wellington Eiriki on three counts of forgery and stealing.[29] The prosecutor stated that from the months of September 1945, to January 1946 being a clerk under the United Africa Company, the accused had intent to defraud. It was alleged that Eiriki made false entry in pay slips number 6121, 13298, 11312,

11310, 11326, 13238 and 13284 belonging to his employers. They also accused him of stealing £38, forging the UAC pay slips and knowingly and unlawfully altering the pay slips. Adetokunbo Ademola discharged the accused on the fourth count but sentenced him on the remaining three counts to six months imprisonment.

In cases, where the prosecutor failed to do a thorough investigation, and by that creating a doubt in the minds of reasonable people, Adetokunbo Ademola did not fail to discharge the accused if it would not adversely affect the economy or law and order interest of the colonial state. According to Adetokunbo Ademola, "the true test of fair hearing . . . is the impression of a reasonable person . . . Whether from his observation, justice has been done in the case."[30] For instance, the long standing case of official corruption preferred against one Samuel Adeleye, a registration clerk at the Labour Office, Oko-Awo in Lagos,[31] was determined in accordance with this judicial attitude.

Monday, January 14, 1946, Adetokunbo Ademola heard a case, which involved a government official. Frederick Olomo who was a nurse at the African Hospital was charged on three counts.[32]

(1) That on January 11, 1946, he had in his possession a poison (Fourteen tablets of M & B 693 and Seven tablets of M & B 760) with intent to use them for an illegal purpose.
(2) That during the month of November 1945, in a manner too rash and negligent and likely to cause harm, gave a medical or surgical treatment to one Sule Anjolaiya by giving him an Atropine Sulphate injection into the skin or tissue of the body.
(3) That, he during the month of November 1945, not being registered or licensed under the Medical Practitioners and Dentists Ordinance No. 20334 practiced medicine by giving Atropine Sulphate injection to one Sule Anjolaiya.[33]

The accused understandably pleaded not guilty and since the prosecuting officer, Inspector Christopher Anokwu did not oppose bail, the court granted the request for bail to the accused on the sum of £50 and one surety in the same amount.[34] As bad as the case was on the face of it for the defense, Adetokunbo Ademola eventually discharged and acquitted the accused when evidence was produced that, the deceased did not suffer an immediate death after receiving the injection. In fact, he got better and died later. The benefit of doubt was in favour of the accused that the deceased probably died by other causes apart from the injections administered on him by the accused.[35]

This instant case has perhaps two important implications for this discourse. In the first instance, the prosecution lost the case, as a result of negligence and carelessness on the part of the Criminal Investigation Department of the Police Force. It confirms what Justice Adenekan Ademola called the poverty, naivety and gross inadequacy of the C.I.D.[36] He believed that the judiciary faced a lot of problems during colonial rule largely as a result of the bankruptcy of ideas and primitiveness of techniques employed by the C.I.D. in the conduct of criminal investigations.[37] The executive controlled the police and it was not properly equipped and managed to serve as a useful preliminary agency of administering and promoting justice.[38] The second implication is that, the performance of Adetokunbo Ademola in the case portrays a new judicial attitude which confronted otherwise sensational cases with calm and presence of mind with a view to bringing the spirit of the law to agree with the letters of the law.[39] According to Justice E. O. Fakayode, Adetokunbo Ademola would not decide one way or the other, until he had satisfied himself that there was an agreement between the spirit and letters of the law in any particular case.[40]

The Acting Judge at Opobo, Mr. Justice C.N.S Pollard was due to proceed on his annual leave in September 1947.[41] The Chief Justice was convinced of the efficiency, loyalty and dedication of Adetokunbo Ademola and therefore requested the Governor to approve his transfer to, Opobo[42] The Governor approved and Adetokunbo Ademola was appointed an "Acting Judge to Opobo and try the cases there and at Abak".[43] By this, the British administration both in London and in Lagos confirmed its interest in the career mobility of Adetokunbo Ademola even in 1947. His father, Sir Ladapo Ademola who as a prince played a very prominent role in the Egba United Government was noted for his strength of character.[44] He became a remarkable personality even before he became the Alake. He also established a very strong network of friendship with a number of well-placed British colonial officials including Sir William McGregor and the influential Margery Perham.[45] The appointment of his son as Acting Judge in 1947 and subsequent involvement in extra-judicial but related duties could therefore be understood. E.O. Fakayode believed that Adetokunbo Ademola was favoured by the colonial administration in his career on the bench for perhaps three important reasons.[46] In the first place, he was able to convince the British administration of his hard work and loyalty at a very early stage in his career.[47] Secondly, he was fortunate not have had similarly committed African colleagues to compete with for favours with the administration. Finally the goodwill his father commanded among European administrators in Nigeria gave him added advantage.

The so-called Leopard murder cases of 1947 in the Eastern Provinces provided another opportunity for Adetokunbo Ademola to re-establish how the courts in colonial situations could serve as agency of control. The cases that he handled were essentially law and order cases[48] and he did not shy away from administering justice with a view to promoting the mercantile interest of Britain in the strategic towns of the Niger Delta. In the words of Esiemokhai, the colonial legal system used law as an instrument of "legal control, legal justice or legal change, but not as an instrument of social change, social control and social justice.[49]

In 1948, the colonial government decided to revise the Supreme Court Legislation and the Rules of Court. It was believed that the existing Supreme Court Legislation and Rules of Court had to be revised in order to accommodate the changing realities of the post war era. Justice Charles Abbot who was then Judge at Enugu, Mr. Manyo-Plange, a Senior Crown Counsel from the Office of the Attorney General and Adetokunbo Ademola,

Magistrate St Anna Court, Lagos were appointed into a special committee.[50] The specific term of reference was "to, examine the existing Supreme Court Legislation and Rules of Court and recommend changes as necessary"[51]

In 1948, Adetokunbo Ademola was appointed an arbitrator in Warri. His long stay in Warri as a judge coupled with his involvement in the resolution of conflicts arising from the sale of crown lands in Warri were enough to put him in a good stead to understand the intention and the preferred course of action by the colonial government.[52] In 1947, the colonial administration in Warri in accordance with the terms of the leases, revised upwards rents payable on a number of crown plots.[53] The upward review led to a number of complaints and petitions, which queried the purpose, and intents of the review. Government did not intend to impose itself openly on the people, it therefore appointed an arbitrator to look into the merit of each case and make a declaration.[54] Adetokunbo Ademola as arbitrator gave decisions in favour of the crown on all the petitions and complaints. By the end of the year, the Resident Warri Province R. Wilkes reported that over £1000 were collected as arrears into the coffers of the colonial government due largely to compliance with the decisions of the arbitrator.[55] The performance of Adetokunbo Ademola was not unnoticed and he subsequently became a toast of the colonial government in Lagos.[56]

By a consistent commitment to protecting British colonial interests, Adetokunbo Ademola continued to enjoy the goodwill of many colonial administrators. The relationship between his court and the executive became mutually beneficial to the two parties. In February 1946, Mr. Justice F.S. Protheroe of the High Court at Warri proceeded on leave, and there was a strong need to provide a relief judge.[57] Adetokunbo Ademola was appointed to act as judge and throughout his tenure in office until 2 December, 1949, he performed the duties of his high office to the admiration and commendation of the colonial administration.[58] While commenting on the 1949 Annual Report of the Warri Province, the Chief Commissioner, Western Provinces directed that a letter of appreciation be sent to the Chief Registrar for the information of the Chief Justice.[59] The letter attested to the dedication and hard work of Adetokunbo Ademola during the year under review.[60] The period 1946-1949 coincided with the end of an era of administrocracy in colonial Nigeria. According to Nicolson, the atmosphere was clouded with a general dissatisfaction within the colonial public service.[61] There was also the emergence of an elite of several thousands of Nigerians clamouring for constitutional advance, for career opportunities, for economic development, for "democracy", freedom, "independence", "self government", "socialism" and "progress".[62] As noted earlier, the era equally opened up career upward mobility for Adetokunbo Ademola in the colonial service. His mentor and benefactor Sir Adeyemo Alakija continued to pave the way for his nephew.[63] Adeyemo Alakija was a contemporary at the Bar of Sir Henley Coussey of the Gold Coast. Mr. Alakija was called to the English Bar in the same year as Sir Henley in 1913.[64] Adeyemo Alakija had a flourishing and lucrative legal practice and it was even speculated that Adeyemo Alakija might probably "take silk" i.e become a Queen's Counsel. Unlike his friend Sir Henley Coussey who subsequently became the President of the West African Court of Appeal, Adeyemo Alakija for some personal reasons did not sit on the bench. He however, encouraged Adetokunbo Ademola to go through all the rungs of the judicial ladder. The purpose of the on-going discourse is to reiterate the fact that, Sir Adeyemo Alakija was well known to the British government in Nigeria and the colonial office in London. He was therefore in a position of eminent advantage to protect and promote the interests of Adetokunbo Ademola within the colonial set up.[65] Adeyemo Alakija was a nominated member of the Legislative council in Lagos, representing Egba Division from February 1934 to 1938. He was later elected the third member for Lagos in the Legislative Council in 1938. It would be recalled that Adetokunbo Ademola played a very significant role at this election, which destroyed the seeming invincibility of the National Democratic Party of Herbert Macaulay in Lagos politics.[66] Adeyemo Alakija remained in the legislative council until 1940. As a member of the legislative council, he was very outspoken on reforms within the colonial set up. For example in a parliamentary debate on March 7, 1939, he delivered a long address in which he strongly urged the promotion of many more Africans to European posts in the Civil Service.[67] He equally advocated better opportunities of public service for Nigerian lawyers.[68] This was perhaps an attempt to use the floor of the legislative council to prepare a conducive atmosphere for the career of this nephew on the bench. There is ample evidence to support the contention that Adeyemo Alakija had a very strong influence over the colonial administrators in Nigeria. He was once, with Ernest Ikoli, appointed to serve as the only two Africans on the Advisory Committee on Economic Development and Social Welfare.[69] The committee was set up by Governor Bourdillon to "consider, coordinate and make recommendations to the Government regarding the economic and social welfare development schemes in Nigeria with particular reference to finding employment for demobilized Nigeria soldiers".[70] In 1926, it had been established that Adeyemo Alakija was too friendly with the European colonial administration. He however felt that his apparent rapprochement with the British was to construct a

> bridge connecting the two sections, to understand the white man's view and interpret it to my countryman and to interpret to Europeans the needs and aspirations of my countrymen.... many an African individually, and many a native cause have I assisted by this very association for which I am held up to the hatred and obloquy of my own people.[71]

As rightly pointed out by Ayandele, the validity of such assertions and claims by front liners like Adeyemo Alakija, that they identified the true interests of the masses of Nigerian people is still in doubt. Adeyemo Alakija continued to use his clout within the colonial set up to promote personal interests including those of his relations.[72] In 1943, he shared with Stephen Bankole Rhodes the honour of being the first two Africans to be nominated to sit on the Governor's Executive Council. Sir Bernard Bourdillon remembered Adeyemo Alakija for his readiness to see Government point of view, and with a pinch of diplomatic finesse, recognized his equally remarkable preparedness to disagree with the Government when he felt that way.[73]

In recognition of his services to the British Crown, Adeyemo Alakija was made a knight in 1944. It is equally important to allude to the stature of Sir Adeyemo Alakija in the socio-cultural life of Lagos that could endear him to the British. He was in the forefront of the agitation for the recognition of the Lagos white-capped chiefs by the British government.[74] He was conferred with the title of Bariyun of Ake and Baba Isale (grant patron) of Lagos. The first title was in recognition of his services to Abeokuta, while the second was for his record of service in Lagos public life.[75] Sir Adeyemo Alakija was also an influential member of a freemasonry association and he rose to become the Grand Master. The association drew its membership from both the indigenous and foreign societies. Highly placed British administrators and public servants were members of the Lodge House.[76] The public image, clout, personality and wealth of Sir Adeyemo Alakija were gargantuan enough to be employed in the promotion, enhancement and protection of the interests of his nephew Adetokunbo Ademola who had confirmed his acceptance of all that Sir Adeyemo Alakija stood for.

On November 18, 1949,[77] European Superior Police Officers and men of the Nigeria Police detachment led by F.S. Phillip, a Superintendent of Police, killed at least twenty-one and wounded another fifty-one striking miners at the Iva Valley Coal Mine.[78] This marked the climax of various acts of oppression, intimidation and cruelty meted out to the Nigerian labour force by the colonial administration.[79] The macabre display of brute force by British Officers happened at a time when the Nigerian labour organizations were in disarray and quite unprepared for a concerted resistance of European highhandedness and atrocities. The Iva Valley massacre was condemned by a good number of anti-colonialists organizations led by the Zikist National Vanguard, which attempted to capitalize on the widespread condemnation to destabilize British administration in Nigeria.[80] The occasion was used to form the National Emergency Committee made up of mainly Zikist National Vanguard and pro-NCNC labour unions and with a very wide representation throughout Nigeria. Membership of the Committee included K.O. Mbadiwe, Ade Ibikunle-Akitoye, V.J Ekpo, K Jaja Nwachukwu S.O. Masi and Margaret Ekpo.[81]

The National Emergency Committee successfully mobilized the working class with a view to achieving the solidarity of the nationalist movements and the labour unions. It embarked on a campaign to educate the masses about the atrocities of colonial rule and called for greater political awakening among the Nigerian masses. It would seem that the colonial administration quickly realized the political intentions of the National Emergency Committee and therefore decided to show administrative concern to what happened to the Nigerian miners at the Iva-Valley.

It is the intention of this book to go beyond earlier examination[82] of this issue and to argue that the Commission of Inquiry that was set up by the Governor was no more than a face saving device and an attempt to arrest the possible escalation of the crisis into a nationalist agitation for an end to colonial rule and domination. The calculation was that a quasi-judicial resolution of the miners struggle would take the steam off the nationalists clamour for a total redefinition of colonial rule in Nigeria.

By an instrument dated December 3, 1949, and issued as Government Notice No. 1702, the Governor appointed W.J. Fitzgerald (Chairman) S.O. Quashie, Idun, A.A Ademola and R.W. Williams to constitute a commission of inquiry under section 2 of the Commissions of Inquiry Ordinance, 1939 with the following terms of reference:[83]

> to inquire into and report on the recent disorders in Nigeria with special reference to the recent labour troubles at Enugu Colliery and the events which followed.[84]

The membership of the Commission was made up mainly of people with predictable judicial attitude. The only member who was not a judge, was Mr. R.W. Williams who was a labour member of the British Parliament for Wigan and who was once the legal adviser to the National Union of Mine Workers in the United Kingdom.[85] He had a long experience of mining regulations and conditions as well as of trade union negotiations.[86] The little concessions granted the workers union could be attributed to his personal efforts and ideological position as a labour parliamentarian.

The Chairman of the commission, Sir William Fitzgerald was formerly the Chief Justice of Palestine before he became the President of the Lands Tribunal, which was an important judicial office in the United Kingdom. He was appointed to that office by the Lord Chancellor of England. He therefore had every cause to protect British interests in Nigeria. Mr. Justice Quashie Idun was a judge of the Supreme Court in the Gold Coast who had a record of collaboration with the British administration. His detest for militant nationalism could best be assessed, if set against the circumstance that led to his dismissal as Judge of the Ghana High Court Bench by President Kwame Nkrumah. He equally allegedly had the penchant of being too grateful to his benefactors.

Mr. Justice Adetokunbo Ademola, as the only Nigerian member of the Commission, had by 1949 built a reputation of being too sympathetic to and supportive of government positions on critical issues. He had just been appointed a judge of the Supreme Court, a Government Arbitrator, a member of the Committee for the Revision of Supreme Court Laws and Rulers of Court and now, the only Nigerian member of the Fitzgerald Commission of Inquiry. His interconnections, official and unofficial, with government coupled, with his own preferred attitude of a gentleman in the strict English sense and not an agitator, made him quite susceptible to thinly disguised manipulations by the colonial authorities.

The report of the Commission, which was submitted to the Governor in March 1950, showed a criminal disregard of the personal loss of the miners at the Iva Valley mine.[87] The report was rather too broad and spoke in general futuristic terms. The document bore the characteristic double talk diplomatic language of the British. It emphasized constitutional approach to decolonization in Nigeria, reformation of the public service and the reorganization of labour unions.[88] To confirm our earlier position, that the intention in setting up the commission of Inquiry was to douse political agitation for independence, the Fitzgerald report concentrated attention on proposals for the establishment of a Ministry of Labour, Conciliation Boards, a National Tribunal and General Conciliation Machinery. At paragraph 142, it stated:

> The lesson that appears to us to be learnt from Enugu and which stands out from our Enquiry is the paramount necessity in West Africa of isolating industrial disputes from political agitation.[89]

It would seem that the administration used the occasion of the Commission to sweep under the carpet, the specific demands of the miners at Iva Valley. The families of those who lost their lives as a result of the shooting by the police were not considered. The report was silent on what compensations were to be paid to such families and how the wounded could be rehabilitated.[90]

The report of the Commission was prepared at No. 24 Abington Street London SWI starting from January 23, 1950 despite the fact that the hearing of evidence was concluded on Thursday January 5, 1950.[91] Between January 7 and 23, 1950, the Chairman apparently had wide consultation with influential officials of the British Government especially at the Colonial Office, London. The choice of London as the venue for the preparation of the report of events that happened in Nigeria also confirms the possibility of the influence of the Colonial Office on the members of the Commission and by extension on the final report of the Commission.

The concurrence of Adetokunbo Ademola to virtually all the venom poured on the nationalist movements and trade unionism in Nigeria is a signification of his own attitude to the two institutions. By the time he was appointed to serve on that Committee as the only Nigeria member, the Governor was assured of Adetokunbo Ademola's preparedness to protect the interests of British administration in Nigeria against the onslaught of nationalist agitation.

Adetokunbo Ademola was subsequently appointed a puisne judge of the Supreme Court in Tinubu Square, Lagos. In the words of a newly qualified Barrister, who appeared before him during this time, Adetokunbo Ademola was "a kind, courteous, humane judge" whose "displeasure could be quickly stirred against those who had deliberately flouted the law or who willfully caused unnecessary suffering to others"[92] F.R.A. Williams, the first Nigerian Queen's Counsel, described Adetokunbo Ademola as a shining example of a judge who talked very little on the bench and interrupted only when it was absolutely necessary to do so. He always encouraged young, talented and ambitious lawyers by a dignified sympathetic consideration of their presentations.[93] Adetokunbo Ademola also as a new puisne judge sustained the morale and enthusiasm of new counsel by tolerating their inexperience sometimes-specious arguments and little knowledge of the basic elements of law.[94]

In the early 1950's, Adetokunbo Ademola's career on the bench received a fillip when he had the opportunity of sitting in Lagos, Onitsha, Port Harcourt and Ibadan as puisne judge of the Supreme Court. One of the cases that came up before him in Lagos, was *The King* v.. *Emmanuel Oyefolu & Ors.*[95] The facts of the case were that five accused persons were charged with breaking into the shop of the British West Africa Corporation (BEWAC) in Lagos and stealing the sum of £8,000 from the safe, According to the defense counsel, the case against the accused persons was that the cashier conspired with Oyefolu, who was the Chief Accountant's steward among others to procure the check locking keys from the Chief Accountant's flat.[96] The circumstances of the case compelled the defense to make an application to the effect that the court should visit both the shop and the flat. This was to determine the validity of the prosecution's case that the steward had the opportunity to take the Chief Accountant's keys, open the safe in the shop and return them neatly before the Chief

Accountant came out of the bathroom and within a time span of ten to fifteen minutes.[97] The application to visit the *locus in quo* was granted and the court visited the two locations. The judge thereafter convicted the accused persons and sentenced them to five years imprisonment with hard labour.[98] The defense appealed against the decision of Adetokunbo Ademola resting its case on the fact that when Adetokunbo Ademola adjourned to the *locus in quo* it was in the absence of the first accused - Emmanuel Oyefolu. The appeal was allowed and the judgement of the Court of Appeal became the leading case on the procedure to be adopted whenever a court was visiting the *locus in quo.* The procedural error of the judge in this case alerted him on the need for constant vigilance on the technical aspects of the law. The seemingly unimportant oversight of the court swung the benefit of the doubt in favour of the accused and allowed them to escape imprisonment with hard labour.

The post Second World War boom had its implications for economic development and financial transaction in Nigeria especially in the major urban centres of politics and economy. The expansion in business and its attendant implications on inter-personal economic relationship popularized the use of the courts in resolving conflicts among contending parties. The High Courts and the Supreme Court therefore entertained suits that bordered on financial and economic inter-dependence. The colonial administration was equally committed to promoting and establishing healthy commercial climate by the establishment of institutions that were meant to facilitate economic growth and commercial development. The rapid growth in economic inter-relationship also produced its own side effects especially with regards to how the business community raised capital for investment.

One of the readily available sources of capital for investment was by mortgage.[99] The Lagos business community therefore, witnessed a surge in the use of landed property to serve as collateral security for loans urgently required for commercial activities. The colonial government became anxious to protect the interests of both itself and the people who could be unfavourably affected by the activities of dubious speculators. The office of the Commissioner for Lands was strengthened to serve as the last clearing house for the verification of the validity of claims to title on land in any part of the country.[100] The courts were equally expected to resolve conflicting claims to land and to intervene in exposing shady mortgage transactions in order to protect the interests of genuine investors and finance houses.

The first major suit Adetokunbo Ademola decided as a puisne judge in Lagos was one of fraud in sale by a mortgage. In the case of *Viatonu* v. *Odutayo* and *Kuyoro* consolidated with *Kuyoro* v. *Viatonu*, the plaintiff, Viatonu had mortgaged a property at No. 9 Shotelu Street, Lagos to Odutayo, which Odutayo exercising her powers of sale, sold by private treaty to Kuyoro. Viatonu went to court, asking the court to set aside the sale. Kuyoro by another suit wanted the court to give him permission to recover possession of the premises, which Viatonu was still occupying. He also wanted the payment of £50 for Viatonu's continued use and occupation of the premises.[101] The fact of the case was that, when Viatonu received notice of foreclosure, she went to Odutayo the mortgage, who then agreed to grant an extension of two months. Within two weeks, Viatonu tendered the debt in full, but Odutayo said it was too late, because the property had been sold to Kuyoro for £6000. The sinister aspect of the transaction was that the mortgagee, (Odutayo), the auctioner and Kuyoro the purchaser were all partners in the firm of Odulaja and Co, which sold the property as autioners. The judge believed that there was collusion and that the sale could not be said to be fair and *bona fide*.

> It is trite law that equity will protect a mortgage from unreasonable treatment and where a mortgage has been harsh and arbitrary the courts would not fail in their duty and would invoke their equitable jurisdiction[102]

A declaration was thereafter made that the sale and conveyance to Kuyoro were void against Viatonu and in the event of Viatonu redeeming, they must be set aside. In the other suit, the claims for recovery of possession and £50 for use and occupation of the premises initiated by Kuyoro were dismissed.[103]

The position of the court was essentially to protect the interests of unsuspecting mortgagors who could fall into the hands of unscrupulous moneylenders who were only interested in dispossessing their clients.[104]

Adetokunbo Ademola was posted to Port Harcourt in 1950 and one of the important cases he handled was *Amachree & Ors.* v. *Newington*. The case was essentially one involving the District Officer, Degema Division as defendant and some Chiefs of Kalabari as plaintiffs. The colonial administration had an interest in the case because the chiefs sued the District Officer who was only discharging his duties as the chief law and order officer in Degema Division. The drastic steps that he took in maintaining law and order were duly reported to Government through the office of the Resident, Rivers Province.

In order to properly assess the performance of the judge in the determination of this case, perhaps it is necessary to understand the background to the case, since it has not been comprehensively examined in earlier works. The Kalabaris and the Okrikas had conflicting claims to fishing sites, which had almost defiled solutions. The report of a Commission of Enquiry to settle the age-old disputes was not well received by the Kalabaris. The District Officer made an attempt to discuss the report with all the groups in the Rivers area with a view to implementing the recommendations made by the Commissioner. The Kalabaris were unwilling to discuss the report at all and the meeting broke down when the Kalabaris refused to attend any more as from August 1, 1950. On August 5, 1950 an incident happened on the river at a great fishing centre known as Ochokorocho.[105] It would appear that many Okrika fishermen lost their lives. The District Officer believed that the Kalabaris were the perpetrators of the massacre and therefore on August 10 1950 requested the Kalabari Chiefs to give him sixty names of those who were involved in the crime. The chiefs about thirty in all said they knew nothing about the massacre. When the Chiefs would not give the District Officer, the names of people involved, he subsequently detained them in the Reading Room at Buguma. Some of the detainees were released and by August 15, 1950 when they were removed to Kula, only nine most important Chiefs remained in detention.[106] On August 23, the Resident Rivers Province visited them at Kula and reprimanded them for their anti administration conduct in not helping police investigation into the massacre they were subsequently free. On August 28 the Chiefs were again detained at Degema when they refused the District Officer's request for the sixty names of culprits of the crime. After two days of restriction to the Government Rest House, Degema they were allowed to go home.[107] The Kalabari Chiefs sued the District Officer for insult and false imprisonment jointly claiming the sum of £20,000 as damages.[108]

Adetokunbo Ademola determined the case with reference to Supreme Court (Civil Procedure) Rules Order IV, Rule 2 that he believed did not apply in a case like this.[109] In very simple language, the judge explained the law in relation to the facts of the case in question in a manner that, it would be difficult to fault his exposition of the law.

> To my mind, where A, B and C are unlawfully detained, it cannot be said that B and C have jointly with A ground for instituting a suit. Each to my mind has a separate ground depending upon the damage he suffered for instituting a suit. There is not necessarily joint ground upon which they can institute one suit. Whether upon separate grounds A, B and C can sue jointly is the question"[110]

He answered the question in a manner that confirmed his preparedness to be as supportive of the colonial administration as ever:

> I hold the view therefore in this case that the plaintiffs cannot all bring one suit claiming damages generally for damage suffered by each on an alleged false imprisonment"[111]

With respect to the plaintiff's claims on three different alleged detentions on three different dates, the judge believed that the amount claimed in respect of each alleged detention must be stated on the writ. He introduced complications that were extraneous to the case into his discussion and built up a secure ground for rejecting the joint claim for damages.

> The court may find that only in one case of the alleged detentions was the detention unlawful; how then would the court be able to decide how much A of the £20,000 the plaintiffs claim in respect of that one detention found to be unlawful? A broader issue is that the court may find that three of the plaintiffs were unlawfully detained in respect of two detentions, two other unlawfully detained in respect of one detention; three unlawfully detained in respect of the three detentions. How then can the damages be assessed?"[112]

It is interesting to know that this particular case, which involved the dignity of nine most important chiefs in Kalabari, could be so cleverly dismissed on the basis of probability by the judge. It would seem that the court could have been more interested and involved in the determination of what detentions were lawful or unlawful and how best to redeem the already battered public image of the nine Chiefs. As expected, and in consonance to what the judiciary stood for under colonial rule, the appeal of the plaintiffs to the West African Court of Appeal was dismissed on June 2, 1952 on the ground that the suit was wrongly constituted under the law applicable. The Court held that the alleged damage of each plaintiff could only be personal to him and there was no common ground of action. In the opinion of the Court, Order IV, Rule 2 did not permit joiners of causes of action.

The decisions of the courts in this particular case were portrayals of the level of advocacy in Nigeria during this period. Many of the Nigerian lawyers who were in advocacy showed a large dose of limited knowledge of the law. For instance, counsel for the Okrika Chiefs, Dr. Udoh Udoma, despite the fact that, the defendant did not deny any of the facts and allegations regarding the detentions of the Chiefs, concentrated his presentation on the validity of the writ. He allowed the District Officer to get away with his very weak justification for detaining the Chiefs. i.e that unexplained circumstance justified the detention of the Chiefs at the different periods mentioned. The performance of barristers in cases involving government or any if its agents would therefore seem a viable aspect of this study. Many of them allowed a judge who had an attitude that could be described as supportive of Government interest to have a leeway. The judgement confirmed the apprehension of Lord Atkins on the attitude of judge, who on more question of construction when face-to-face in the claims involving the executive, became more executive than the executive.[113]

In *Horvat v. Police*,[114] a case that bordered on the sacredness of the spirit of the law, Adetokunbo Ademola would not leave anybody in doubt as to his understanding of criminal procedure. In the lower court, the prosecution closed its case, the defense was closed, and both sides addressed the court on February 11, 1952.[115] The Magistrate adjourned for a considered judgement to be delivered on February 13, 1952. On that date, when the case was called, the learned Magistrate instead of giving his decision in the matter, recalled the accused into the box and subjected him to severe questioning on his doubts. At the conclusion of this round of questioning, the Magistrate proceeded to give his decision and found the accused guilty on all the counts as charged. The accused appealed to Adetokunbo Ademola's court where it was held that it was wrong on the part of the Magistrate, after the case had been closed and adjourned for judgement, to recall and question the appellant, apparently, in order to clear up his doubts in the case.

> That course deprived the appellant of the chance of the benefit of the doubt in the case put before the court by the prosecution. To my mind, this is against the spirit of the law.[116]

The Supreme Court in Port Harcourt with Adetokunbo Ademola presiding was also called upon in 1952 to introduce sanity into the activities of moneylenders. As noted earlier, the post war economic boom and the rise of highly speculative business led to the emergence of crudely organized mortgaged institutions, finance and trust houses in the major urban centres. The colonial administration was highly suspicious of these moneylenders who were regarded to be closely connected with judicial fraud.[117] According to Adewoye, moneylenders often advanced money to unsuspecting litigants at highly exorbitant rates of interest to pursue often times bad cases.[118] The Moneylenders Ordinance was therefore an attempt to regulate the activities of the practitioners and to protect the interests of their clients. It became the responsibility of the colonial administration to ensure that persons without unlawful intent were allowed to practice and operate as a moneylender.[119] Adetokunbo Ademola's judgement in *Re Marcus O. Ajaero* (Appellant) that "as every year, a new certificate is needed and a new licence, the grant of refusal or a certificate under S.8 (1) of the Moneylenders Ordinance arises afresh, every time an application is made for a certificate"[120] confirmed this. The logic of his argument is summed up succinctly, that a separate certificate was required in respect of every separate licence. Accordingly, a moneylender who got a certificate the preceding year might be refused a certificate if by the time he made the application, enough facts about his person and character could be ascertained to disqualify him as not a fit and proper person to carry out the business of money lending. Application for certificates according to the judge, were to be considered every year, each on its own merit, irrespective of the fact that an applicant previously held a certificate and or licence.[121]

This case was the first Nigerian case on the proper interpretation of the Moneylenders Ordinance, Cap. 136: Sections 6 (1) and 8 (1). The judgement thereafter strengthened the arms of the colonial administration in its effort to sanitize the business, since practicing moneylenders had to show good cause every year why their certificates and licences should be renewed.[122]

The closing days of Adetokunbo Ademola as judge in Port Harcourt in 1952 confirmed his preference for strict construction of statutory provisions in its literal sense. The position of the judge in *Bright* v. *E.D. Lines Ltd & General Manager, Nigerian Railway,* portrayed him as clever judge who was prepared to hide behind the fine letters of the law to shield a negligent government corporation against a harmless private legal entity.[123] The judge capitalized on an apparently pardonable mistake of the plaintiff's lawyer who addressed his notice to the Wharf Superintendent of the Nigerian Railway, Port Harcourt, instead of the General Manager, Nigerian Railway at the Principal Office, Lagos. In spite of the argument that the notice was in order as long as the Railway Administration was aware of the claim, the judge struck out a seemingly legitimate claim of £213-19s-1d when he held that:

> Before an action can be brought against a Railway Administration a notice fulfilling the requirement of S-40 (2) of the Railways Ordinance must be observed in manner prescribed by S.41 on the General Manager at the Principal office of the Railway Administration.[124]

The judge apparently did not consider equity and what the financial implications the plaintiff would have to bear, if he were to serve the notice in Lagos when his usual place of business was Aba. However, when the plaintiff asked for leave of Court to amend the claim to read jointly and severally in order to compel the firm of E.D. Lines Limited bear the claim, the judge declared "I do not think it is equitable to grant such leave and I hereby refuse to grant the application".[125] Adetokunbo Ademola's performance in this case, was an example of how the courts in the era of colonial rule maintained obviously defective statutory provisions. Such statutory provisions were meant to give government commercial corporations dubious advantage and unnecessary legal protection.

In 1953, Adetokunbo Ademola became the judge of the Supreme Court holding at Ibadan. He succeeded Sir Olumuyiwa Jibowu who became deeply involved in cases pending at the

West African Court of Appeal. The opening years of the 1950's opened a floodgate of litigations, which required the courts to interpret certain sections of the 1951 Macpherson Constitution and resolve differences arising therefrom.[126]

As noted by Elias, the 1951 constitution contained a lot of imperfections and lacunae.[127] There was no provision either in the Constitution or in the Adaptation of Laws Order for any re-organization of the courts on the basis of the three Regions. A provision of the amended Interpretation Ordinance made every Ordinance a Public Ordinance and every law a Public Law.[128] Unless the contrary was expressly provided by such Ordinance or Law, each would be judicially taken notice of as such by any court in Nigeria. In this circumstance, although the courts (except Native Courts)[129] remained the concern of the Central Government based in Lagos, the Laws they administered were under the constitution partly regionalist.

The 1951 constitution therefore introduced confusion as to what laws would regulate the activities of individuals in the society at any given time. It was soon found out that three sets of laws; Ordinances of the Central Government; laws by the Regional Governments and Local Customary law of the Province or District could be applied by any of the courts.[130] The constitution was inadequate to the extent that, it did not give the average Nigerian the opportunity to know which law would govern his daily conduct, well in advance of being dragged before the courts.[131]

The case of *Regina v Ilorin Native Court Ex parte Jimoh Aremu and others* (Applicants)[132] was quite related to the inadequacy of the 1951 constitution under reference. Although the case was brought before the Supreme Court under the Native Courts Ordinance, Cap 142 Section 10 (1), the appellants were obviously ignorant and confused about the judicial system under which they would be tried before they were brought before the lower court. The fact of the case was that the appellants were convicted of riot in the Ilorin Area by the Junior Alkali Court of Ilorin applying Moslem Law. They claimed that they belonged to the Yoruba stock of Southern Nigeria settled in the Ilorin Area of the Northern Region and that they should have been tried under the Yoruba native law and custom obtaining in that area.[133] In spite of the ingenious argument of the applicants' counsel that, if there were more than one native law and custom in the area of jurisdiction, they must all be taken into consideration and the native law and custom of the ethnic group concerned shall be administered when a man from that group was on trial for an offence; The Judge however held otherwise.

> ... If there are many tribes (sic) in the area, each with its own Native Law and Custom, the court will administer that Native Law and Custom which is (sic) predominant in the area[134]

The position of Adetokunbo Ademola as Judge on the interpretation of section 10 sub section 1 of the Native Courts Ordinance, showed the seeming ignorance of the judge on the political history of Ilorin. There is conclusive evidence to sustain the argument that Ilorin was founded by the Yoruba and that up till 1825 when Abdul-Salam, the son of Mallam Alimi assassinated Are Afonja, the Yoruba held sway in Ilorin.[135] It was colonial rule that made Ilorin a part of the Northern Region and that arrangement did not remove the fact that a sizeable proportion of the inhabitants of the town were still Yoruba even in 1953. From this judgement, it would seem that the judge was not prepared to stir the hornet's nest by calling for the establishment of a mixed court or a legislative review of the ordinance. Adetokunbo Ademola seemed to have been impressed by the argument of H.H. Marshall, Legal Secretary of Northern Region who appeared for the crown.[136] H.H. Marshall had argued that for the proper administration of the Emirate, there must be one criminal Law for all, otherwise there would be chaos.[137] The judge was prepared to disregard the principle of *audi alteram partem* in order to ease the machinery of British colonial administration in Ilorin by not sparing a group of rioters who had been sentenced to a term of twelve months imprisonment each by the lower court.

The colonial administration came under severe pressure to leave and grant Nigeria full independence. Nationalist agitations for independence received a fillip and a boost after the 1953 motion for independence moved by an Action Group Back Bencher in the Central Legislative Council, Mr. (now Chief) Anthony Enahoro.[138]

The heat was turned on with the publication and circulation of leaflets and pamphlets calling on the British Government to grant independence and put an end to colonial rule and subjugation. Such was the climate in the country especially in the Southern Regions when in 1953, One Chinaka Anozie was charged in Ibadan under Section 51 Sub Section 2 of the Criminal Code for possessing, without lawful excuse seditious publications.[139] At the trial before the Chief Magistrate Court, Ibadan, it was held that the publications were seditions but that the onus of proof of the absence of lawful excuse was on the prosecution. Since the prosecution failed to discharge it, the accused person was consequently acquitted.[140]

At the appellate level, the case was heard by Adetokunbo Ademola who realized the danger posed by the decision of the lower court presided over by Mr. (as he then was) Daddy Onyeama to colonial rule in Nigeria. Adetokunbo Ademola faulted the analogy on the proof of absence of lawful excuse and proof of absence of consent in rape cases.

> While it is peculiarly within the knowledge of the prosecutrix whether or not she gave her consent to the act in a charge of rape, in the case of possession of an unlawful article, it is only within the knowledge of the accused for what purpose he came to be in possession of the article or document and it is for him to establish that the purpose was lawful...[141]

The judge went further to offer his own interpretation of section 142 of the Evidence Ordinance, that it would not be the duty of the prosecution to prove that an excuse was unlawful. In reasoning typical of inquisitorial judicial process, Adetokunbo Ademola held:

> To say that the prosecution must prove that the appellant had no lawful excuse to be in possession of the document would be begging the question, because whether he has lawful excuse or not is a matter peculiarly within the knowledge of the respondent and the burden of proof of the fact that he had lawful excuse is upon him. He and only he knows better than any one else whether or not he had lawful excuse to be in possession of the document.[142]

The position of the judge on the issue of showing enough cause for having in possession seditious publications that could embarrass the government had started to take shape as from 1953. His performance in this case and in a similar one later in his career showed that in matters affecting the colonial set up, Adetokunbo Ademola exercised a considerable amount of self restraint which was a result of his training, the traditions of the colonial legal system and his preference to support all efforts directed at maintaining the status-quo, peace, law and order. Adetokunbo Ademola probably believed that the colonial administration did not intend to recognize the judiciary as a separate branch of government. His performance showed diffidence to the interests of the colonial administration in Nigeria which he believed could do any of the followings; unilaterally increase the number of judges, enlarge or reduce its jurisdiction as and when deemed fit, initiate the removal of judges from office, reverse specific decisions of the courts, abolish the courts or alter the role of the judiciary in government.[143]

All these possibilities necessarily imposed certain limitations on the judge in the task of judicial review of administrative activities of government. Unlike the United States Supreme Court, the Nigerian Supreme Court of the 1950's could not be described as "a stormy petrel" in the colonial administration of the country.

In the case of *Abiodun Akerele* v. *Inspector General* of police,[144] Adetokunbo Ademola believed that the word "accuses" in section 210 (b) of the criminal code bore no more than its ordinary meaning and no fanciful or legal meaning such as "makes a formal accusation by swearing to an information under oath"[145] should be attached to it. In this case, the judge refused to be a strict constructionist of the letters of the law and even rejected the incorporation of legal meaning into the interpretation of a contestable word. The history of the case, which was more partisan and political than what the judge would want us to believe, confirmed that the judge was unable to hide his prejudice against Bode Thomas, Abiodun Akerele and the Action Group.[146] It would be recalled that Abiodun Akerele was a prominent foundation member of the Action Group and he was once a partner in the law firm of Obafemi Awolowo & Co.[147] He was also prominent in the Ibadan branch of the National Emergency Committee formed by the Nigerian Youth Movement and the NCNC after the Enugu Colliery shootings in November 1949. It would be recalled that Adetokunbo Ademola was the only Nigerian member of the Fitzgerald Commission which *inter alia* seriously indicted the so called nationalists who attempted to make a political gain our of the labour crisis.[148]

The fact of the case was that Abiodun Akerele was convicted on section 210 (b) of the criminal Code in that on August 10, 1954 at Oyo, he unlawfully accused one Taiwo Amoke of being a witch. The purported accusation was to the effect that Taiwo Amoke had by her powers of witchcraft killed Chief Bode Thomas and that she was attempting to kill Akerele too.[149] By dismissing Abiodun Akerele's appeal, the judge swept a lot of background information under the carpet in order to protect the interests of government and probably those of the other political persuasion.

As early as the middle of 1953, party politics in Oyo had been established between two major camps.[150] The Alaafin, Alhaji Adeyemi II represented the illiterate and conservative group while the new class of educated men, which sought to take control of local affairs through party politics, and the new local government structure was led by Chief Bode Thomas.[151] Bode Thomas was a brilliant lawyer who could be regarded as one of the intellectual pillars of the Action Group. The growing popularity of Bode Thomas made him a marked person and even cost him the goodwill of some of his friends including the Aremo. On an occasion in April 1953, the Aremo struck Bode Thomas and for this assault, despite the indigenous political weight of his father, he was banished from Oyo by the Divisional Council. Oyo gradually split apart partly along lines of traditional rivalry. Some subordinate chiefs and the northern part of the kingdom supported the Alafin, while the majority of the Chiefs and Southern Oyo elements were in support of Bode Thomas and the Action Group.[152] It would be interesting to note that some educated elite who felt threatened by the stature of Bode Thomas formed the Egba Oyo Parapo in August 1953.[153] This group was led by P.A. Afolabi who was then the Headmaster of the Roman Catholic Mission School.[154] The Egbe, which soon aligned itself the NCNC, appointed the Alafin its patron, and the situation in Oyo made rivalry between the Action Group and the NCNC almost inevitable.

Bode Thomas, the flower of his generation in Oyo died on November 20, 1955 under mysterious circumstances. His political associates had cause to suspect witchcraft poisoning. This was what provoked the allegation of witchcraft against Taiwo Amoke by Abiodun Akerele.[155]

The performance of Adetokunbo Ademola in dismissing the appeal of Abiodun Akerele would therefore be difficult to clear as not being politically motivated. The feud in Oyo was essentially between the Action Group and the NCNC. As far back as 1947, Sir Adeyemo Alakija was a very strong member of the NCNC.[156] He was deeply interested in the Oyo matters, and arrangements had already been made by the party to support the activities of Adegoke Adelabu in consolidating the gains of the NCNC in Oyo.[157] It was therefore not a surprise when Adetokunbo Ademola held on January 7, 1955 that:

> I do not think in cases of more vulgar abuse, the words are used as an accusation; in such cases their use would not constitute an offence. it cannot be said however, that the words were vulgarly used

> in the present case. It is a clear accusation that the complainant is a witch and had used her powers of witchcraft to kill somebody[158]

The deliberate simplistic interpretation of the operative word did not take into cognizance the fact that accusation is a formal allegation of committing a particular wrong act before a constituted body who determines the case and award sanctions. The case was an instance of the inability of the judge to rise above partisan considerations in the determination of legal causes. The judgement was meant to check the activities of Abiodun Akerele and Obafemi Awolowo, who despite the death of Bode Thomas, continued to harass the Alafin who had already identified himself with the NCNC and what the party stood for. The spate of public reactions to the determination of the case confirmed the suggestion that the judge could not persuade the public that his decision was just. Arguments could not be sustained that the rules of law had been justly applied. In deed, there were shreds of evidence to buttress the contention of the appellant, that the rules of law as applied in the case, had not been fairly determined.

The judicial outlook that eventually emerged reflected the preparedness of Adetokunbo Ademola to use the agency of law in the maintenance of law and order.

Notes

1. NAI: CSO/26/2/11857 Vol. XXI Warri Province Annual Report 1946.
2. *Ibid.*
3. For details, see J.S. Coleman, *Nigeria: Background to Nationalism* (Boston: Berkeley University of California Press, 1958).
4. *Ibid.*
5. *Ibid.*
6. *Ibid.*
7. B.O. Nwabueze, *Machinery of Justice in Nigeria* .. p. 69.
8. T.O. Elias, *Groundwork of Nigerian Law* ... p. 158.
9. *Ibid.* p. 160.

10. NAI CSO/26/5/43751 Magistrates' Courts (Civil Procedure) Ordinance 1945. See the accompanying memorandum on the proposed Bill, p. 1.
11. *Ibid.*
12. *Ibid.*
13. *Ibid.*
14. NAI CSO/26/5/43751 Memorandum on A Bill for the Magistrates' Course (Civil Procedure) Ordinance, 1945 postscript p. 4.
15. NAI CSO/26/5/43751/8 His Excellency the Governor to His Honour The Chief Justice p. 9.
16. *Ibid.* Paragraph 2.
17. *Ibid.* Paragraph 2.
18. NAI CSO/26/5/43751 Memorandum on A Bill for The Magistrates' courts (Civil Procedure) Ordinance, 1945, p. 1.
19. NAI CSO/26/5/43751/8 His Excellency the Governor to His Honour the Chief Justice paragraph 3.
20. *Ibid.*
21. *Ibid.*
22. NAI CSO/26/5/43751 Attorney General to Chief Secretary, p. 1.
23. *Ibid.*
24. *Ibid.*
25. NAI CSO/26/5/43751 Memorandum on A Bill for the Magistrates' Courts (Civil Procedure) Ordinance 1945, p. 1.
26. See details below Omoniyi Adewoye, *The Judicial System in Southern* Nigeria.... p.24.
27. Omoniyi Adewoye, *The Judicial System in Southern Nigeria* ... p. 24.
28. S.A. de Smith, *Judicial Review of Administrative Action*, (London: Stevens and Sons Limited, 1973). p. 28. See also, Duncan Kennedy, *Legal Education and the Reproduction of Hierarchy* (Cambridge: Afar, 1983).
29. *Nigerian Daily Times* January 15, 1946.
30. *Isiyaku Mohammed* v. *Kano N.A.*
31. *Nigerian Daily Times, January* 15, 1946.
32. *Ibid.*
33. *Ibid.*

34. *Ibid.*
35. *Ibid.*
36. Oral interview: Justice Adenekan Ademola National Judicial Institute Lagos, February 14, 1995.
37. *Ibid.*
38. For details on the Nigerian Police Force, see.
39. Oral interview: Justice Emmanuel Fakayode 68 years, Ibadan, 1996.
40. *Ibid.*
41. NAI CSO/26/1523/51 Chief Justice to His Excellency The Governor September 19, 1947.
42. *Ibid.*
43. *Ibid.*
44. Folarin Coker, Sir Adetokunbo Ademola CJN 1958, 1972. p. 22.
45. Oral interview: Justice Adenekan Ademola NJI, Lagos February 14 1995.
46. Oral Interview: Justice E.O. Fakayode 68 year Ibadan March 10, 1996.
47. For details, See Folarin Coker, Sir Adetokunbo Ademola pp. 48-51.
48. The colonial judiciary was hedged down by law and order cases.
49. E.O. Esiemokhai: *The Colonial Legal Heritage in Nigeria* (Akure: Fagbamigbe Publishers, 1986), p. 22.
50. Folarin Coker: Sir Adetokunbo Ademola, p. 49.
51. NAI CSO/26/246650 Vol. III Supreme Court Ordinance.
52. NAI/CSO/26/11857 Vol. XVIII Report on the Warri Province for the Year Ended 31 December 1947 p. 36.
53. *Ibid.*
54. *Ibid.*
55. *Ibid.*
56. Comments of His Excellency the Chief Commissioner for Western Provinces on the 1949 Report as presented by Resident R.Wilkes. NAI/CSO/26/1857 vol. XVIII.
57. NAI/CSO/26/11857 vol. XVIII Report on the Warri Province for the Year Ended 31 December, 1`949 paragraph 102.
58. *Ibid.*

59. *Ibid.* .
60. *Ibid.*
61. Report of a sub-committee at Aba of the Association of European Civil Servants Nigeria Journal Vol. XXV, No. 4, March 1945.
62. I.F. Nicolson *The Administration of Nigeria 1900-1960: Men Methods and Myths* (Oxford: Clarendon Press, 1969), p. 250.
63. Oral interview: Justice Adenekan Ademola Nigeria Judicial Institute, Lagos 1995.
64. *Ibid.*
65. *Ibid.*
66. R.Sklar, *Nigerian Political Parties* (Princeton) New Jersey: Princeton University Press, 1963, also J.S. Coleman, *Nigeria: Background to Nationalism* (Berkeley: University of California Press, 1958).
67. T.O. Elias Nigeria: *The Development of its Laws and Constitution* (London: Stevens and Sons, 1967) p. 71.
68. *Ibid.*
69. *Ibid.*
70. *Ibid.*
71. E.A. Ayandele, *The Educated Elite in the Nigerian Society* (Ibadan: Ibadan University Press, 1974) p. 82.
72. Sir Adeyemo Alakija in 1926 with Ernest Ikoli and Richard Barrow founded the Nigeria Printing and Publishing Company publishers of the Influential *Nigeria Daily Times.*
73. For details, see T.O. Elias Nigeria: *The Development of its Laws and Constitution.*
74. *Ibid.*
75. *Ibid.*
76. A.P. Anyebe, *Ogboni: The Birth and Growth of the Reformed Ogboni Fraternity* (Lagos: Sam LAO Publishers, 1989), pp. 108-109.
77 Report of the Commission Appointed by his Excellency the Governor of Nigeria to Inquire into Report upon the Recent Disorder in Nigeria, with Special Reference to the Recent Labour Troubles at Enugu Colliery and the Events which Followed" p. 37.
78. J.S. Coleman, *Nigeria: Background to Nationalism* (California: University of California Press, 1958) p. 299.

79. *Ibid.*
80. *Ibid.* pp. 299-302.
81. Report of the Commission Appointed by His Excellency .... to Inquire .... p. 42.
82. The report stated that the tension was seized by politically minded people to further their own desires. p. 42.
83. Report of the Commission .... p. 3.
84. *Ibid.*
85. *Ibid.* p. 46.
86. *Ibid*,.
87. Report of the Commission... Paragraphs 142-153.
88. *Ibid.*
89. *Ibid.*
90. *Ibid*, p. 10.
91. *Ibid.*
92. Atanda Fatayi Williams, *Faces Cases and Places* (London: Butterworths, 1983), p. 22 .
93. Folarin Coker, *Sir Adetokunbo Ademola...* p. 11-12.
94. *Ibid*, p. 12.
95. Atanda Fatayi Williams, Faces, Cases and Places... p. 22-23.
96. *Ibid.*
97. *Ibid.*
98. *Ibid.*
99. Recovery of Premises Ordinance of 1945 was among other things an instrument for the protection of legitimate claims to land.
100. For details of Government involvement in land matters, see Crown Lands Ordinance as incorporated into the Revised Edition of the Laws of Nigeria, 1947 (No. 21 of 1947).
101. *Viatonu* v. *Odutayo and Kuyoro* (1951) 19 NLR. 119.
102. *Ibid.*
103. *Ibid.*, p. 121. The appeal to WACA was dismissed on May 19, 1952.
104. The appeal to WACA was dismissed on 19 May 1952.
105. *Ibid.*
106. *Ibid.*
107. *Ibid.*

108. *Ibid.*
109. *Ibid.*
110. *Ibid.*, p. 15.
111. *Ibid.*
112. *Ibid.*
113. This was his view in *Liversidge* v. *Henderson* (1942) A C. 206.
114. *Horvat* v. *Police* (1952) 20 NLR: 52.
115. *Ibid.*
116. *Ibid.*
117. Omoniyi Adewoye, *The Judicial System in Southern Nigeria* ... p. 198.
118. *Ibid.*
119. *Ibid.*
120. In Re Section 8 (2) of the Moneylenders Ordinance Re Marcus O. Ajaero Appellant) (1952) 20 NLR 77.
121. *Ibid.* p. 78.
122. For details of the activities of moneylenders, See Omoniyi Adewoye, The Judicial System in Southern Nigeria ... pp. 197-198.
123. *Bright* v. *E.D. Lines Ltd & General Manager, Nigerian Railway* (1952) 20 NLR. 79.
124. *Ibid.*
125. *Ibid.*
126. T.O. Elias, *Groundwork of Nigerian Law* (London: Routledge & Kegan Paul Ltd. (1954) pp. 166-169.
127. *Ibid.*
128. *Ibid.*
129. *Ibid.* The Native Courts were reorganized in line with their new judicial roles.
130. *Ibid.* p. 168.
131. *Ibid.*
132. *Regina* v. *Ilorin Native Court* (1952) 20 NLR. 144.
133. *Ibid.* p. 415.
134. *Ibid.* p. 146.
135. R.A. Adeleye, *Power and Diplomacy in Northern Nigeria: The Sokoto Caliphate and its Emi rates* (London: Longman, 1971).
136. (1952) 20 NLR 144.

137. *Ibid.* p. 145.
138. J.S. Coleman, *Nigeria: Background to Nationalism* (Berkeley: University of California Press, 1965, also Obafemi Awolowo, *Awo The Autobiography of Chief Obafemi Awolowo* (Cambridge University Press, 1960), p. 254.
139. *Inspector General of Police v. Anozie* (1954) 27 NLR. 29.
140. *Ibid.*
141. *Ibid.*, 29-30.
142. *Ibid.*
143. Interview: Justice Adenekan Ademola, Lagos February 14, 1995.
144. *Akerele* v. *Inspector General of Police* (1955) 21 NLR. 37.
145. *Ibid.*
146. Obafemi Awolowo, *The Travails of Democracy and the Rule of Law* (Ibadan: Evans Brothers Ltd. 1987), p. 130.
147. *Ibid.*
148. For details, see Report of the Commission.... to Inquire into the Recent Disorders in Nigeria with Special Reference to the Recent Labour Troubles at Enugu Colliery and the Events, which followed.
149. (1952) 21 NLR. 37.
150. Kenneth Post and Jenkins, The *Price of Liberty...*
151. *Ibid.*
152. Interview Chief Emmanuel Oriola 84 Years Retired Headmaster and Balogun Ijo Corpus Christi Catholic Church Asogo Oyo. December 19, 1995.
153. *Ibid.*
154. *Ibid.*
155. *Ibid.*
156. *Southern Nigeria Defender* October 25, 1947.
157. Kenneth Post and Jenkins *The Price of Liberty.*
158. (1952) 21 NLR at p. 38.

Chapter 4

Law, Justice and Party Politics in the Western Region 1954-1958

On 21 May 1953, the Secretary of State for the Colonies, The Right Hon. Oliver Lyttleton announced in the British House of Common that Her Majesty's Government had regrettably decided to review the Nigerian Constitution.[1] The decision was made to provide for greater regional autonomy and for the removal of powers of intervention by the centre in matters that could, without detriment to other regions, be placed entirely within regional competence.[2] Consequent on the above, at a joint meeting with the Governor of Nigeria, Sir. John Machpherson on June 19, 1953, the leaders of the Action Group, National Council of Nigeria and the Cameroon and the Northern People's Congress agreed to discuss the following terms of reference at a constitutional conference.

(a) The defects in the present constitution;
(b) The changes required to remedy these defects;
(c) What steps should be taken to put these changes into effect; and
(d) The question of self-government in 1956.[3]

To underscore the importance of judicial administration in a quasi federal set up as proposed, the conference appointed a special committee to report on the administration of justice in the country. Sir Sidney Abrahams headed the committee that was made up of the representatives of the Action Group, N.C.N.C., N.E.P.U. and N.P.C. The Colonial Office in the United Kingdom provided a legal adviser who served as secretary.[4] Among other things; the 1954 constitution marked a significant milestone in the history of judicial administration in Nigeria. In consonance with the fledgling federal system of government established on 1 October 1954,[5] each region and the federal territory of Lagos established its own separate high court. The regional high courts replaced the single Supreme Court that had been established in 1943. It will be recalled, that the Supreme Court was conferred with unlimited civil and criminal jurisdiction throughout the country, 'subject only to the jurisdiction of native courts in land tenure, family status, guardianship of children, and testamentary disposition of property under customary law.'[6] According to Aguda, [7] the jurisdiction and powers of the newly created regional high courts were similar to those of the Supreme Court that they superseded.

The regionalization of the judiciary under the 1954 Constitution was one issue on which the often mutually suspecting Nigerian political parties became strange bedfellows. The political parties showed a remarkable willingness and preparedness to regionalize the judiciary in spite of reasonable advice to the contrary. Indeed, individuals and corporate bodies had good reasons to campaign against the grand design to politicize, as it were, the judiciary believed to be the last hope of the average citizen. Regionally based Nigerian political parties sought ways to protect their bases and by an extension the use or misuse of power to frustrate the activities of rival political parties.[8] It would seem therefore, that the political parties supported the regionalization of the judiciary to remove any or all legal opposition to party supremacy in the regions.

A most articulate critic of judicial regionalization was Sir John Verity, the Chief Justice of Nigeria.[9] The Chief Justice was very constructive in his criticism of the scheme. He advocated judicial administrative system that would not be under the overwhelming influence of the political class to ensure judicial independence.[10] In a memorandum submitted to the January 1954 Constitutional Conference in Lagos, the Chief Justice argued that a developing country needed 'to maintain a single standard of learning and professional competence in the judiciary.'[11] The Nigerian Bar Association was equally opposed to regionalization of the judiciary. It was believed that the interest of ordinary people and the rule of law would be best served when the judiciary was not under the party controlled regions. The Association expressed a fear that regionalization would mean making judges what Francis Bacon called 'lions under the throne.'[12]

Adetokunbo Ademola was also opposed to the regionalization of the judiciary. He believed that a unified system of judicial administration could not be compared with the new contraption that would subsume judicial authority under the executive arm of government.[13] His assessment of the Nigerian political class, the political immaturity of its members and their limited knowledge of the requirements of a democratic system really provoked the bitter reaction of Adetokunbo Ademola.[14] He was aware of the tendency of Nigerian politicians to put the judges under the government of the day. He feared that judicial officers might lose their independence and might not be able to check or oppose the executive, if it should in any way misuse or abuse its powers.

> The day that judges have to take instructions from politicians or to acquaint them with their decisions beforehand, it will be time for us to pack up and go.[15]

Adetokunbo Ademola was perhaps not expressing these fears for his own generation, but for succeeding generations when he said:

> We feel that our present politicians will use their wisdom carefully, but what of those ten years hence? We on this side have taught [sic] that power corrupts (and absolute power corrupts absolutely). We cannot therefore but feel that in the years ahead, the appointment of judges by politicians may lead to what we call a packed bench.[16]

The introduction of a quasi-federal arrangement under the 1954 constitution therefore made it impossible to go back on the scheme of regionalizing the judiciary. By the time the constitution became effective, there was a Supreme Court for the whole country and it was headed by the Chief Justice.[17] The Governor General, acting on the instructions of the British Crown issued as letters patent by the Secretary of State for Colonies, made the appointment of the judges of the Supreme Court including the Chief Justice. Judges of the Supreme Court were therefore to hold office only when they still enjoyed the pleasure of the British Crown.[18]

Regional high courts were created to exercise such jurisdiction as might be vested in them by the regional legislatures.[19] Judges are to be appointed by the Governor of the region and the salaries and allowances of regional high court judges including the Chief Justice were to be determined by the regional legislature.[20]

Despite the advertised opposition of Adetokunbo Ademola to the regionalization of the judiciary, he was appointed the first Chief Justice of the Western Region High Court.[21] It is noteworthy that the circumstance of his appointment, the source and strength of opposition, and the unfolding political developments in the Western region, determined the relationship between the judiciary he led and the government of the region. Adetokunbo Ademola was not preferred for the appointment by politicians of the Action Group that had consistently fought for regionalization.[22] The Action Group developed a particularly ambitious programme, and realizing that 'the Yoruba were a fastidious, critical and discerning people'[23] needed a judiciary that would be highly supportive of executive programmes. To achieve this, the Action Group sent a representation to the Governor, Sir John Rankine, asking him to seriously consider the appointment of a Nigerian to the office of Chief Justice Western Region.[24] The preference of the party was obviously Mr. Justice Olumuyiwa Jibowu who was described in superlatives. According to Obafemi Awolowo:

> The preference of many people at the Bar and in the country was for Mr. Justice Jibowu. He was senior to the other two (Adetokunbo Ademola and Louis

> Mbanefo) at the Bar and on the Bench. He was second in rank to the Chief Justice of the Supreme Court of the federation of Nigeria, and had acted several times as Chief Justice in that Court. He was the first Nigerian ever to agree to sacrifice a successful and lucrative legal practice for the niggardliness of the Magisterial Bench. His probity, integrity and impartiality had never been in question.[25]

By Western Regional Notice No. 90 of 3 February 1955, Her Majesty, the Queen, approved the appointment of Adetokunbo Ademola as Chief Justice of the High Court of the Western Region as soon as the High court was created.[26] On 23 June 1955, the Governor of the Western Region, Sir John Dalzell Rankine, in accordance with sub section (1) of section 4 of the Western Region High Court Law, 1954, created the offices of the Chief Justice and other judges.[27] He thereafter, having received instructions through one of Her Majesty's principal secretaries of state, proceeded to appoint Adetokunbo Ademola Chief Justice of the Western Region with effect from 1 July 1955. He was to exercise jurisdiction accordingly and to hold office during Her Majesty's pleasure.[28]

There is no doubt that Obafemi Awolowo and the Action Group leadership were particularly embittered by the appointment of Adetokunbo Ademola who was as equally qualified as Olumuyiwa Jibowu. During a social gathering specially called to congratulate the new Chief Justice on his appointment, Chief Awolowo could not hide his disdain and even mentioned his personal disappointment that Justice Olumuyiwa Jibowu was superseded.[29] The Regional Minister in charge of Justice and who could be regarded as one of the most visible members of the Regional Executive Council was equally appalled by the appointment of Adetokunbo Ademola. Chief Rotimi Williams was both disappointed and shocked that the appointment was for Adetokunbo Ademola and not Olumuyiwa Jibowu as earlier speculated by him on very strong evidence.[30] The appointment of Adetokunbo Ademola in 1955 was a continuation of a trend that had started in 1939 when he was first appointed to the lower bench. The British colonial administrators wanted a judge who would not rock the boat and who would be highly predictable, especially during the closing years of British colonialism in Nigeria. The popularity of Olumuyiwa Jibowu among Nigerian politicians was a cause for concern, just as the overwhelming influence of Adeyemo Alakija within the circle of British colonial policy makers favoured the choice of Adetokunbo Ademola. The matter was therefore settled in favour of Adetokunbo Ademola to the chagrin of those who were uncomfortable with him..

On assumption of office, Adetokunbo Ademola was aware of the odds that were against him in the executive council of the Western Region.[31] The Action Group that had a majority in the legislative house was not impressed by the appointment and the logic of the situation suggested to Ademola, a romance with the opposition as a possible way out of the seeming impasse. The relationship that existed between the courts and the government was therefore one of suspicion and strain. What reduced the tension was however, the personality of the Regional Governor, Sir John Rankine who showed recognition of the need to protect the integrity and independence of the bench against onslaughts from politicians. Again, Adetokunbo Ademola was fully aware of the dangers of exposing the judiciary to the whims and caprices of politicians in executive council. He had distrust for overzealous politicians who believed that they alone had the panacea to all social, political and economic problems. He therefore refused to be drawn into any confrontation between his court and the executive. Indeed, the way the leadership of the Action Group conducted government in the Western Region made it virtually impossible to separate the party from the government. Perhaps this was responsible for Obafemi Awolowo's attitude to the judicial performances of Adetokunbo Ademola and some other judges in the Western Region between 1955 and 1959.

Our discussion of the tenure of Adetokunbo Ademola as Chief Justice of the Western Region, for clarity of thought and incisive analysis will focus on (i) cases involving the interests of the state and the preservation of law and order; (ii) the protection of property rights, and; (iii) the protection and promotion of interests normally associated with a particular political party in Nigeria.[32] According to the Attorney General and Minister for Local Government Western Region in 1955, the judiciary of the Western Region was the best organized, staffed and salaried in the whole federation.[33] It would seem therefore, that the administration of justice was considered a veritable tool for the establishment of peace, law and order, economic development, and harmonious social relations. In many ways, the executive of the Western Region progressively as from 1955 to 1959 was determined to promote the integrity of the judiciary and by extension the notion of the rule of law in the Western Region.[34] Western Region was painstakingly committed to the success of a regionalized judiciary, and by that token, steps were taken to considerably improve the conditions of serving judicial and legal officers.[35]

In spite of the vehement opposition of the senior cadre of the administrative services in the region, the executive displayed an 'uncompromising determination and tenacity' to push through the programmes of judicial reforms. In the words of F. R. A. Williams, the conditions of judicial service in the Western Region became a model copied eventually throughout the country.[36]

In the same vein, and pursuant to the same objective, the executive of the Western Region showed an abiding faith in the potentiality and capability of the judiciary to firmly establish the rule of law, by causing the revision and compilation of the statutory laws of Western Nigeria.[37] Added to this, was the 're-enactment with suitable modification where necessary, of all British statues, having force and effects in the Regions, which were of general application and in force in Nigeria before January 1, 1900.'[38] According to the Deputy Commissioner for Law Revision, Atanda Fatayi Williams, they intended the exercise to remove the 'annoying reference to English statues when trying to find what the law in Nigeria was in certain matters'.[39] In holistic terms, the justification for law revision and compilation might be simply the desire for 'efficiency in the administration of justice'.[40] It was to ensure that all the statute laws that had been in force in the Western Region would be on the statute books of the Region.[41] The executive in the Western Region attached the greatest importance to the revision and compilation of the laws of the Region, and had to employ the legal expertise and experience of the Chief Justice of Nigeria who had just retired.[42] Sir John Verity CJN (1946-1954) was appointed Commissioner for Law Revision while an equally hardworking and industrious legal mind (Atanda Fatayi Williams) was appointed Deputy Commissioner.[43] The crowning effort was the production of Laws of the Western Region of Nigeria in seven volumes, which introduced certainty and efficiency to the machinery of justice in the Western Region.[44]

As soon as he assumed office as Chief Justice of the Western Region on 1 July 1955, Adetokunbo Ademola showed a remarkable understanding of the zeal and enthusiasm of the party controlled executive to use the judiciary in the promotion and protection of its programmes and policies. He was equally aware of the position of the Action Group especially concerning his appointment in super succession to Olumuyiwa Jibowu. Adetokunbo Ademola therefore developed a scheme that was to ensure the independence of the judiciary without jeopardizing its interrelationship with the executive. Three interpretive approaches of adjudication could be recognized in his judicial performance as Chief Justice of the Western Region: (i) inflexibility of the conservative judicial culture inherited from colonial rule especially in respect of law and order cases; (ii) broad literal interpretation of the law especially in private law; and, (iii) abdication from adjudicating on what were perceived as political constitutional claims especially when they involved the interest of the State. Adetokunbo Ademola was however quick to distinguish between cases involving the interests of the State and cases affecting the interests of political parties. Unlike the leadership of the Action Group which believed that the executive or government of the Western Region was synonymous with the Action Group, Adetokunbo Ademola drew a line between the two, and this affected his judicial performance. The distinction necessarily brought him into some sort of no love lost relationship with the leadership of the Action Group that was at the helm of executive affairs and government in the Western Region.

Our discussion of the interrelationship of the executive and the judiciary will recognize this fact as we proceed. The greatest fear and suspicion of Adetokunbo Ademola as expressed in his view on why the judiciary should not be regionalized was the tendency of the politicians to scuttle and trample on judicial independence by using the court in the abuse and misuse of power. Therefore, as preliminary precautionary efforts, the Chief Justice attempted to play a major role in the appointment and transfer of judicial officers, in the staffing of the judicial department and in ensuring that the mediating role of the judiciary was not affected by executive action or inaction. Adetokunbo Ademola as Chief Justice of the Western Region believed that a talking Chief Justice was not a good thing for the interrelationship of the executive and the judiciary in a period of party politics. He refrained himself from making political statements that were capable of misrepresentation or misinterpretation. His court provided the only outlet and audience.

Judicial reorganization was one major area of concern for Adetokunbo Ademola when he assumed office as Chief Justice. Indeed, one of the first official duties he did was the Directions he gave under section 35 of the Western Region High Court Law. The Direction cited as the Judicial Divisions Directions that became effective on 1 July 1955 created four judicial divisions in the Western Region.[45] These included:

(i) Ibadan Judicial Division, which was made up of Ibadan and Oyo Provinces;

(ii) Abeokuta Judicial Division, made up of Abeokuta, Ijebu and Colony Provinces;

(iii) Benin Judicial Division, made up of Ondo Province and the Benin Administrative Division of the Benin Province; and

(iv) Warri Judicial Division made up of the Delta Province and the Asaba, Ishan and Kukuruku Administrative Divisions of the Benin Province.[46]

The creation of the judicial divisions was meant to ease the process of judicial administration in the Western Region by bringing the high courts nearer the people and ensuring speedy judicial intervention.[47] The magistrate courts were equally reorganized and streamlined to achieve the same purpose and objectives. Nine magisterial districts were created thus:

(i) Ibadan Magisterial District (The Ibadan Division of Ibadan Province and the Oyo Division of Oyo Province);
(ii) Ikeja Magisterial District (The Ikeja, Awori and Egun Awori Area of the Colony Province);
(iii) Abeokuta Magisterial District (The Abeokuta Province);
(iv) Ijebu Magisterial District (The Ijebu Province, the Epe and Ikorodu Administrative Divisions of the Colony Province);
(v) Ile-Ife Magisterial District (The Ile-Ife and Ilesa Administrative Divisions of the Oyo Province and the Osun Division of the Oyo Province);
(vi) Akure Magisterial District (The Ondo Province);
(vii) Benin Magisterial District (The Benin, Ishan and Kukuruku Divisions of the Benin Province);
(viii) Sapele Magisterial District (The Sapele Administrative Division of the Delta Province and the Asaba Division of Benin Province); and
(ix) Warri Magisterial District (The Delta Province excluding the Sapele Administrative Division of the Province.[48]

As envisaged by the Chief Justice, the magistrate courts in the Western Region lived up to expectations by acting as a bridge between the customary courts with their untrained illiterate personnel on the one hand and the high courts held down by elaborate procedure on the other. In 1958 alone, the magistrate courts in the Western Region in both civil and criminal jurisdictions tried a total of 32,409 cases.[49] Equally important to the reorganization of the judicial system by Adetokunbo Ademola, was the appointment of commissioners for taking affidavit and declarations, receiving and production of documents, for taking the examination of witnesses on interrogatories or otherwise, and for exercising in general the powers conferred upon Commissioner for Oaths. This became necessary and obvious in view of the creation of more judicial divisions and magisterial districts. The first set of officers appointed had earlier opportunities of judicial service, as most of them were first class clerks. The list included:

(i) Joseph Edegware Oddiri (Sapele Magisterial District)
(ii) Jonathan Olutayo Soda (Akure Magisterial District)
(iii) Anthony Emuomajewa Annubissa (Warri)
(iv) Daniel Kolawole Oshati (Ikeja)
(v) Herbert Hedwig Chuka Anene (Benin)
(vi) Clifford Ibim (Abeokuta)
(vii) Layinka Akpata (Ijebu-Ode)
(viii) Johnson Ogheneovo Odejvwedje (Warri).[50]

The only exception was Thomas Edward Nelson-Williams who was a lawyer before his appointment on 4 April 1956.[51]

By 1957, Adetokunbo Ademola was satisfied that the judiciary in the Western Region had been properly established and was therefore confident to require the high courts to play more supervisory roles over the magistrate courts. In accordance with section 42(1) of the Magistrate's Courts (Western Region) Law, 1954, the Chief Justice required that magistrates forward with the 'least possible delay,' at the expiration of every calendar month, a list of all criminal cases decided by them during that month within every judicial division of the high court in which any such cases have been so decided, to a judge sitting in such judicial division.[52] This directive took effect on 5 September 1957.

The appointment of diligent, resourceful and efficient judges by the Western Regional Judiciary gave a perfecting touch to the establishment of a sound judicial system. According to E. O. Fakayode, Adetokunbo Ademola knew how to encourage and appoint good judges.[53] His Chief Justiceship witnessed the appointments of Stephen Peter John Quao Thomas, William Henry Irwin, Charles Russell Stuart, Robert Yorke Hedges,[54] Dadi Onyeama (Acting),[55] John Idowu Conrad Taylor.[56] Richard Adeeyo Doherty

(Acting) and William Algernon Holwell Dufus, A.A. Adesigbin[57] and J.A.A. Kester[58] were both appointed chief magistrates on 1 October 1955, and the Chief Justice conferred the powers of a magistrate as set out on them.[59] The powers to adjourn proceedings and to remand in custody under sections 236 ad 238 of the criminal procedure Ordinance Cap 43 were communicated to the District Officers in Oyo, Ife and Ilesa Divisions.[60]

What could be described an infraction on the province of power of the Chief Justice by the executive was the administration of official oaths on the newly appointed magistrates and justice of the peace. With reference to the official oaths Ordinance Cap 163 of the Laws of Nigeria, the Governor appointed the Resident, Oyo Province, to administer the official oaths required by section 5 of the official oaths Ordinance Cap 163 to all magistrates and justices of the peace appointed under the Magistrate's Courts Western Region Law 1954.[61] Adetokunbo Ademola felt that it was the duty of the Chief Justice and advised the Governor accoardingly.[62]

By a special dispatch from the Governor's office on 23 November 1955, the Governor accepted the suggestion that henceforth the official oath must be administered either by His Lordship the Chief Justice or the Chief Registrar or Residents in charge of provinces.[63] The approach adopted by the Chief Justice in the matter and its acceptance by the Governor showed the willingness of both sides to differ to and accommodate each other even in the exercise of power. This attitude of the Chief Justice was typical of British trained judges who believed that court review of the administrative acts and decisions of the executive was little more than perfunctory on matters of substance.[64] Although the courts would insist on compliance with statutory requirements, it was difficult to persuade them that a member of the executive branch had acted ultra vires[65] Judicial self-restraint became more appealing than judicial activism under colonial rule. As noted earlier, Adetokunbo Ademola adopted a cautious approach to adjudication and manifested a sense of obligation toward the welfare of the state. The performance of Adetokunbo Ademola as Chief

Justice confirmed the suggestion that his judicial decisions were chiefly limited or influenced by statutory directions, traditional procedures, the demands of the judicial role of the judge and the organizational and political connections between the judicial process and the political system.[66] As an appellate judge, he realized very early in his career that, an ordinary individual through a regular law suit might raise fundamental questions of public policy.[67] Adetokunbo Ademola was convinced that the decision a litigant secures could create or confirm a rule that governs the behaviour of many persons not even contemplated. He therefore believed that the appellate court could play an important role as policy maker.[68]

One of the first cases he tried as Chief Justice of the Western Region was a civil case that bordered on the claim for declaration of title, possession and forfeiture. The Chief Justice held that since the first four defendants reached an agreement under which they surrendered their interest in consideration for at least 100 years in a representative capacity, they could not be sued for breach of covenant arising therefrom in their personal capacity.[69] In spite of the arguments of Miss Grant, (Crown Counsel) the Chief Justice averred:

> These men entered into the deed (Exhibit A) for themselves and as representing the Fedeshire family. They are sued in respect of the deed in their own personal capacity. Surely, it is clear they have not entered into any agreement in this matter with the plaintiff in their personal capacity. In my view therefore, the claim, as it is, should be dismissed, as it is not a claim against the Fedeshire family.[70]

The case is particularly relevant to the on-going discourse in that, it was transferred from the Land Court 1 (Native Court), Ibadan by the District Officer, Ibadan in exercise of powers conferred upon him by Section 28(i) of the Native Courts Ordinance Cap 142 of April 7 1954.[71] The decision of the high court in the Ibadan District Council case was an attempt to preserve the integrity of the courts in a case in which the defendants had already put to question especially when they were taken in the first instance to a court under the political and administrative control of the plaintiff. In fact, the decision was intended to protect the property right of the fifth defendant who could have been a victim in the hands of unscrupulous land speculators in Ibadan District Council.

In another case that involved the State, Adetokunbo Ademola re-affirmed the trite position of the law that irregularity in the procedure adopted by a court of justice could lead to grave injustice. The fact was that the appellant was charged with two others with stealing the sum of £325 contrary to section 390 of the Criminal Code. He was convicted and sentenced to 18 months imprisonment with hard labour (1.H.L.) The appellants' Lawyer in the course of the trial argued that the magistrate visited the *locus in quo* in the absence of the accused persons and or their counsel. Except for the reference in the judgement of the learned magistrate, there was nothing in the record of proceedings about this visit.[72]

Two major inferences could be made from the judgement. When a court visits the *locus in quo*, it forms part of the trial and it is essential that the accused should be present when the object of the visit is to see the opportunity open to the accused for committing the offence.[73] Secondly, the Chief Justice doubted the conviction of the learned magistrate on who of the three accused persons actually stole the money bag. He therefore declared:

> The court must not convict on probabilities... It must be established beyond reasonable doubt that the appellant stole the cash bag before the learned magistrate could convict.[74]

The case was similar to an earlier case, decided by Adetokunbo Ademola in 1949 at St. Anna Court, and at which the same procedural oversight was recorded. In *King v. Emmanuel Oyefolu & Others.*[75] Adetokunbo Ademola's judgment was set aside on appeal by the Supreme Court because when his court visited the *locus in quo*, the accused, Emmanuel Oyefolu was absent. On the authority of Atanda Fatayi Williams who was the first defence counsel in the Emmanuel Oyefolu case, the judgment of the Supreme Court, became the "leading case on the procedure to be adopted when a court is visiting the locus in quo.[76] By this time, it was becoming obvious that Adetokunbo Ademola had started to develop a new attitude towards the protection of individual liberty. In a number of cases, he showed a willingness to give the accused person the benefit of the doubt wherever and whenever such existed especially in circumstances where procedural errors could be established against the prosecution. A good example of the display of a new judicial attitude in criminal matters was the performance of the Chief Justice in *Regina v. Diyaolu*.[77] The accused was charged with stealing the sum of £1,815 at Ebutte Metta in the Lagos Magisterial District. He was however, apprehended at Abeokuta where he was charged before the learned magistrate in charge of Abeokuta Magisterial District who subsequently committed him for trial at the assizes holding at Abeokuta.[78]

Adetokunbo Ademola held that the learned magistrate in charge of Abeokuta Magisterial District had no jurisdiction to take the case. He conceded that the magistrate could have taken the case if he had assumed jurisdiction under section 70 of the Criminal Procedure Ordinance, (Cap 43). According to the Chief Justice,

> ...the learned magistrate, it would appear, gave no consideration to the matter, and there is no note, that he considered the matter at all. It cannot be presumed he did and if he did at all, the ground upon which he assumed jurisdiction must appear on the face of the record.[79]

He subsequently discharged the accused with an advice that fresh proceedings could be commenced against the accused if it was thought fit in a court of competent jurisdiction.

What is particularly informative in this case, was the fact that an accused who did not deny stealing the said amount was let loose by a court of appellate jurisdiction which should be concerned about the social consequences of its decisions. The

Chief Justice was interested in legal technicalities even where they seemed injurious to the establishment of a just and moral society. His dedication to the ideals of the common law tradition could be seen clearly in this case. As conceived by the declaratory theory, the common law is a fixed and immutable systems or principles; the sole function of the judge is to ascertain those principles and apply them to disputes brought before him.[80]

In another criminal case,[81] the State suffered another loss, at the high court. The accused persons were charged with the murder of one Bolaji Kasali between 14 and 15 May 1955 at Ikorodu. The prosecution relied on confessions made by the accused persons as well as on circumstantial evidence implicating the accused.[82] The Chief Justice simplified the submission of the two parties to two weighty questions i.e. what weight was to be attached to such confessions made by the accused, and whether killing was justified or not.[83] It was held that the degree of credit due to confessions must be estimated according to the particular circumstances of the case,

> in considering the whole case before the court, it is necessary to bear in mind that the statement of an accused person implicating another accused is no evidence against that other; it is only evidence against the maker.[84]

The Chief Justice averred further that the fact that an alleged confession, made in writing, had been admitted in evidence did not preclude the court from estimating what weight it would put on a document as evidence against an accused person and that the whole circumstance of the case must be taken into due consideration.[85] On the second question of justification for murder, Adetokunbo Ademola held that, unless there is evidence that a well known thief is out to commit an atrocious crime or to use lethal weapons, it would be wrong to kill him merely because he is a reputed thief.[86]

> ... to justify killing in defense of property, it must be proved that the intent to commit such forcible atrocious crime, was clearly manifested by the accused.[87]

He used the occasion of the case to warn and remind the prosecutors, that:

> ...in a criminal case, the burden of proof lies on the crown and it never shifts; and if on the whole evidence, the court is left in a state of doubt, the crown would have failed to discharge that onus of proof the law lays upon it, and the prisoner is entitled to an acquittal.[88]

The accused persons, Emmanuel Jegede, Rufai Odutola, Tukuru Shonubi, Odu Ogun, Idowu Badan and Abudu Aluko who were represented by a strong team of lawyers; T. O. S. Benson leading Akintola, Odesanya, Ogunsanya, and Awolesi, were discharged on a charge of murder but found guilty of manslaughter.[89]

The judicial attitude to give the accused the benefit of the doubt again found expression in the *Queen* v. *Joseph Kesinro*.[90] The fact of the case was that the accused was charged with the murder of a night watchman. There was no direct evidence of the murder, but the prosecution relied on an alleged confession made by the accused. Adetokunbo Ademola held that in accepting an "extra judicial" confession made by an accused person but which he denied at the trial, care must be taken that there is other evidence to support it as against the accused before the court convicts.[91] The case was essentially a bad one for the crown largely as a result of the glaring inadequacies and carelessness of the criminal investigation Department of the Police in criminal matters.[92] For example, the Chief Justice could not be convinced that the confessional statements of the accused to the police were voluntary. The accused denied the statement because from the evidence when he was taken before the officer in charge of the police, Mr. Brett, the English translation made by the police was handed over to him, while the original version in Yoruba allegedly made by the accused was read out to him. The Yoruba version was never interpreted to Mr. Brett who was therefore not in position to say that what was read out to the accused agreed with the English translation he was holding. Mr. Brett later endorsed the English translation.[93] According to Chief Justice, the whole procedure was unsatisfactory and the alleged confessional statement had lost its value, and therefore could not be relied upon as basis for conviction in a case of murder.[94]

Adetokunbo Ademola also doubted the claims of the prosecution on two further pieces of evidence and on the strength of this, the accused was granted the benefit of doubt and was accordingly discharged and acquitted. It would be seen that Adetokunbo Ademola had been extremely cautions in handling cases of murder. He believed that the prosecution must have proved its case beyond all reasonable doubts and all shadows of doubt before a court could impose the capital punishment. He however believed that it was a duty to sentence a man to death, if he felt convinced that the accused had indeed committed the offence as charged.[95] He was never against capital punishment and he was even ready to join issues with the campaigners of the abolition of capital punishment. On armed robbers and violent criminals he said:

> In a case like that, you make some people an example kill them. If a man is found guilty doing this, deal with him harshly. Then these crimes are bound to minimize and stop.[96]

In a civil suit, *Joshua Fowowe* and *H. H. Ajimoko, The Owa of Ilesha*,[97] Adetokunbo Ademola used the court to warn against extortion of money from contestants of chieftaincy titles. He showed his aversion to the politics of winner takes all.[98] In the case under reference, the defendant was the natural ruler of Ilesa, whilst the plaintiff was a contestant to the Lejoka chieftaincy title. In pursuance of this, the plaintiff paid various sums to the defendant. After the final selection, another contestant was declared the winner and yet the defendant refused to refund to the plaintiff the amount paid by him. Adetokunbo Ademola held that since the money paid to the defendant was not a bribe, but a customary guarantee that title fee would be available for distribution among the chiefs, after the selection, the plaintiff's money must be refunded to him.[99] The Chief Justice was of the opinion that, it would be morally wrong to deny a contestant both the title and the money he had paid as guarantee.[100] The judgement confirms the position of the realists school of jurisprudential thought that the moral, philosophical as well as ideological orientation and persuasions of a judge normally, either consciously or unconsciously, impinge on his judicial outlook. Oba Ajimoko Hasstrup was an influential Oba in Yorubaland, highly placed and revered by his people. In spite of his status and stature, he lost a legal battle with one of his subjects who was bold enough to bring him before a court of law. It confirms that the Chief Justice did believe that the law is no respecter of persons not even the royalty. One would have expected a crown prince of another equally important Yoruba Oba to protect the institution of Oba against the activities of daring subjects. But the provisions of the law were dearer to the heart of the Chief Justice more than mere traditional relationship with royalty.

Adetokunbo Ademola also used his court to settle chieftaincy disputes that were capable of causing disaffection and endanger public peace. Despite the provisions of the Ordinance No. 30 of 1948 (Chieftaincy Preclusion from Court etc) the Chief Justice ignored the decision of the West African Court of Appeal in *Bello Balogun & Ors.* v. *Momodu Keye of Oke Ode,* to decide the case of *Lawani Tewogbade & Others* v. *Lawani Adeyemi (Akirun of Ikirun) & Ors.*[101] The over riding concern of the Chief Justice seemed to be the maintenance of peace, law and order in the society. It was believed that, if the court had not assumed jurisdiction, there wouldn't have been any other option left for the aggrieved party other than violence.[102] The judicial resolution of the dispute reaffirmed the confidence of the parties to the dispute in the Court as an agency of conflict resolution and arbitration. The import of the Ordinance could not be readily seen as it was no more than an ill conceived means of reducing the number of chieftaincy disputes that could be brought before the High Courts.

Adetokunbo Ademola's profundity of thought could be seen in his handling of an otherwise simple, but important case.[103] The case was of particular and special interest to the executive.

Ordinarily, one would have thought that the police needed not to pursue such a minor case as traffic regulation to the High Court, but for its implications for other road users and safety on the roads. The respondent at about 8.30 p.m. parked his car on the highway in Abeokuta, put out the lights and went away for a few minutes. He was charged under Regulation 24(i) (K) of the Road Traffic Regulations for parking the car without lighted lamps. The learned Magistrate discharged him, on the ground that the car was not in use at the material time. Adetokunbo Ademola held otherwise that:

> Since it was admitted by the respondent that the car was driven to the spot where it was found and where it stopped for a few minutes, it was in use and it was immaterial whether or not its engine was running or whether it is at a standstill. To adopt the interpretation put on the word use by the learned Magistrate would reduce the law to an absurdity.[104]

By this judgment an amount of sanity seemed to have been introduced to the driving habits of Nigerians who were driving motor vehicles for the first time. The executive successfully used the agency of the court to introduce and enforce good driving habits that would show a reasonable concern for the interests and safety of other road users.

The executive arm of government in the Western Region had by June 1956 been reconstituted with the appointment of the following politicians into the executive council with specific portfolios. Obafemi AWOLOWO, Premier Dauda Soroye ADEGBENRO, Minister for Land and Labour, Adebiyi Omowonuola ADEYI, Minister for Local Government, Claudius Dosa AKRAN, Minister for Development, Gabriel AKINDEKO, Minister for Agriculture and Natural Resources, Anthony ENAHORO, Minister for Home Affairs, Alfred Olatunji OGEDENGBE, Minister for Works, Jonathan Akinremi, Olawole ODEBIYI, Minister for Education, Ayodele OKUSANYA, Minister for Health, Joseph Oduola OSUNTOKUN, Minister for Finance, Fredrick Rotimi Alade WILLIAMS,

Minister for Justice. All the appointments were made on June 7 1955 under section 109 of the Nigeria (constitution) Order in Council, 1945.[105]

What Adetokunbo Ademola had prepared the judiciary for i.e. the independence of the judiciary against the encroachment of the politicians in government, was to be tested. As discussed above, the Chief Justice had already developed a three-layer scheme that guided his judicial attitude. He was quick to determine what cases were of particular interest to the executive and therefore to proper and responsible governance. He also identified those cases that involved or touched on the interest of the Action Group, its members and leadership in and out of government.[106]

The relationship between the executive now dominated by the leadership of the Action Group and the Judiciary under the leadership of Adetokunbo Ademola suffered a set back towards the end of 1956. In spite of the moderating influence of Sir John Rankine, the Governor of the Western Region, and the Deputy Governor, Thomas Murray Shankland, a face off between a section of the executive and the judiciary became public knowledge. The era of party politics prior to, and after the attainment of self-rule status in the Western Region was characterized by mutual suspicion, hostility and distrust between the Action Group that was in power and the National Council of Nigeria and Cameroon.[107] Obafemi Awolowo as leader of the Action Group and Premier of the Western Region had cause to observe that the burden of administering the Western Region and establishing good government was then on the shoulders of the leaders of the Action Group. 'We are now free within the prescribed jurisdiction, to do just what we like, without let or hindrance from any quarter.'[108] He would therefore not consider any limiting or restraining factor in ruling the Western region, not even from the judiciary.

During the second half of 1956 and the entire 1957, there was an escalation in the strife between the Action Group and the NCNC in the Western Region. The Action Group became more entrenched in the Region especially after its electoral success. At the same time and understandably, the NCNC under the leadership of Adegoke Adelabu was bent on the removal of the Action Group from political power in the Western Region. Despite the popular showing of the Action Group, the British Governor of the Region, Sir John Rankine was still *de facto* head of the regional executive council. British Administration was still visible as the Governor took an active part in the formulation of policy and in political party affiliation. Sir John Rankine was one British Administrator in Nigeria, who believed that the sooner self rule, was granted the regions, the better. He did not therefore see any reason why he must interfere unduly with the Action Group government.[109]

While the Action Group continued to use the floor of the Western House of Assembly to attack its opposition and popularize its policies, the NCNC was equally prepared to use the British Administration in its efforts at checkmating the Action Group. On Saturday, 2 June 1956, the NCNC sent a delegation of five that included Adegoke Adelabu (Leader), J. O. Fadahunsi, P. A. Afolabi, Mojeed Agbaje and E. O. Fakayode to present a petition to the Governor.[110] The N.C.N.C. had alleged that the Action Group was involved in electoral fraud at the elections, planning to disturb the peace of the region, destroy the civil liberty of people, thinking of seceding from the federation, and hell bent in controlling the police and the judiciary. The petitioners therefore called for direct British rule, a Royal Commission of Inquiry to examine the general administration of the Action Group government during the past 4½ years among other requests.[111]

It would therefore seem that the judiciary under Adetokunbo Ademola would be called upon to intervene in the resolution of matters affecting the interests of the two parties. The judicial performance of Adetokunbo Ademola in cases involving the Action Group or its sympathizers and Adegoke Adelabu had been a subject of critical comments over the years. Obviously, Adegoke Adelabu led and personified the most critical, if not the most damaging opposition to the Action Group in Ibadan.[112] He not only described his political opponents as the peculiar messes of the Action Group; he created himself the peculiar man of the masses.[113] He therefore commanded a large following at Ibadan largely as a result of his identification with the masses, walking bare footed and eating from the same dish with the common man. He did not consider himself elite, who was once a manager at the U.A.C. or one of the detached educated politicians. He identified himself as "one of the illiterate masses" who could always refer to his father's compound among them. Adelabu believed that the Action Group that he accused of "tribalism, arrogance, technique and chicanery" must be eliminated from the seat of political power in the Western Region.[114]

In *Adegoke Adelabu & L. Ade Bello* v. *Inspector General of Police.*[115] the judgement of Adetokunbo Ademola was adjudged to be partial and partisan and against the interest of the Action Group. Obafemi Awolowo once said that he "had been under no illusion as to Sir Adetokunbo Ademola's antipathy"[116] to him and his political aspirations. The facts of the case were that Adegoke Adelabu was convicted of contempt of court, contrary to section 133(1) of the Criminal Code, while Ade Bello was convicted of common assault contrary to section 351(23) of the Criminal Code.[117] The case before the Magistrate was that during the sitting of the Oja'ba Native Court No.2 Ibadan, Adegoke Adelabu and Ade Bello with a number of rabble rousing young children and some miscreants entered the court with a view to causing the disruption of court session. Adegoke Adelabu showed disrespect to D. T. Akinbiyi, the presiding judge of the native court. Adegoke Adelabu, in fact, called Akinbiyi many unprintable names including 'a fool and a mad man'. The second appellant went to the bench and assaulted the judge by slapping him on the face. All this happened while the court that was supposed to consist of a judge and three assessors was sitting with the judge and just one assessor.

Adetokunbo Ademola rested the weight of his decision on whether the Oja'ba Native Court 2, was properly constituted at the time of the alleged contempt.[118] In spite of the submission of Noel Hay, Q. C. the Attorney General of the Western Region, that there was nothing to show on the Warrant establishing the court that the judge could not sit alone, the Chief Justice was obviously little impressed or persuaded, when he said:

> If the matter of the Assessor is as vague as the learned Attorney General puts it and there is some doubt, then it must be resolved in favour of the 1st appellant. But there appears to be no ambiguity about it. It is clear from evidence that three assessors were appointed and the three have been sitting from time to time with the Judge. Can the judge then by sitting alone or with one assessor constitute a court.[119]

The Chief Justice believed that since it was not stated in the warrant that a particular number of assessors would constitute a quorum, the only interpretation that could be put out was that the judge and all the assessors appointed or attached to the court must sit together before the court could be said to have been duly and rightly constituted. To him, the content of the warrant was grossly inadequate, but that it was not the duty of the high court to supply what it thought had been inadvertently left out.[120] It was therefore held by Adetokunbo Ademola that the Oja'ba II Native Court at the material time on the 20th day of July 1955 was not properly constituted. It therefore was unable, lawfully, to take any judicial proceedings within the meaning of judicial proceedings so called or judicial proceedings in section 133 of the Criminal Code. It follows, it was not possible at the material time for an offence under the section of the code to have been committed.[121] In consequence, and the appeal of Adegoke Adelabu, according to the Chief Justice, must succeed.

A couple of reasons could be advanced for the decision of Adetokunbo Ademola, and there are also two major perspectives on his performance. It could be said that the Chief Justice was aware of the enormous influence of Adegoke Adelabu in Ibadan and what his conviction and incarceration could lead to in Ibadan. Even in his private and extra judicial capacity, he was aware of the position of the Governor, Sir John Rankine and the attitude or disposition of his administration to Adegoke Adelabu matters.[122] Again, Adetokunbo Ademola was not oblivious of the political undertones of the case. For instance, he was aware that on the day of the incidence at the Oja'ba Native Court 2, the supporters of the Action Group and the Editor of the Nigerians Tribune witnessed the subpoena that was served on Adegoke Adelabu by the uniformed messenger of the council. Adetokunbo Ademola was equally aware of the sympathies of the native court judge, D. T. Akinbiyi for the Action Group.[123]

Perhaps this was responsible for the thinly disguised attempt of counsel to Adegoke Adelabu to score cheap political points from the case. The Chief Justice had cause to warn:

> It appears to me that the counsel for the appellants in the court below over-stepped the bounds of propriety in the conduct of the case... It should be obvious to counsel that the witness box is hardly a place to criticize judicial functions of a judge, from his own Registrar of Court at that.[124]

He went further castigating that,

> ineptitude, bad manners, irresponsibility are all hidden under the cloak of politics... the evidence shows indiscretion, abuse of power, recklessness and utter disregard of responsibility of office particularly on the part of the 1st appellant who happens to be a minister of state.[125]

What is curious in the logic and decision of Adetokunbo Ademola in this case, was his willingness to protect the integrity of the native court judge against the recklessness and 'utter irresponsibility' of politicians. This point has been succinctly made by the other viewpoint on the performance of the Chief Justice in the case. It is believed that Adetokunbo Ademola sacrificed the integrity of the judiciary to satisfy a personal wish supported by rather weak legal construct. It was proved that Adegoke Adelabu met the court in session at the time of the invasion and insult on the person of the Judge. The fact that the Judge sat with only one assessor did not detract from his status and appointment as Judge. That alone should have been enough to establish contempt since the idea was the preservation of the respect of the ordinary man for the court and its functionaries. It has also been said, that Adetokunbo Ademola was over protective of the personal and political interests of Adegoke Adelabu. For instance, on 30 March, 1953, Adetokunbo Ademola, as judge of the Supreme Court, granted an order *nisi* to an applicant which was instigated by Adegoke Adelabu and intended to sweep the Action Group sympathizers from the bench of the Ibadan native courts. These included The Chief Judge, Oba I. B. Akinyele, D. T. Akinbiyi, J. L. Ogunsola, O. H. Adetoun, Mogaji Osunware and Akinpelu Obisesan.

In spite of the earlier orientation and judicial outlook of Adetokunbo Ademola, which emphasized law and order, he found it difficult in a number of important cases involving the interest of the N.B.C.N.C. to espouse and maintain a commitment to the maintenance of public order. When he had the opportunity, he did not use the court process to check the acknowledged excesses of Adegoke Adelabu who was using his mastery of local politics and massive mass following to breach the peace not only in Ibadan but also in the Western Region. It would seem that of the two dominant parties in the Western Region between 1955 and 1958, Adetokunbo Ademola showed more sympathies for the N.C.N.C. This was not lost on Obafemi Awolowo who spoke of "an intimidated judiciary" in the Western Region during the same period.[126]

When D.T. Akinbiyi further appealed to the Supreme Court,[127] the Federal Chief Justice, Sir Foster Sutton, sitting in panel with Verity Ag. F. J. and Irwin Ag. F. J. held *inter alia*.

> We had no difficulty in reaching the conclusion that the words in question clearly mean one of the parties to the proceedings. Chief Akinbiyi clearly had no right of appeal to the high court under section 70 of the Law because he was not the prosecutor; the prosecutor being as already said, the Inspector General of Police.[128]

Furthermore the Federal Chief Justice reasoned that it

> would be odd indeed if the legislature had intended to allow a complete stranger to the proceedings in the legal sense, no right of appeal to the high court, but a right to come in at the last moment as a party to an appeal to this court. Before so holding, we should certainly require to be satisfied that the right had been conferred by language, clear, express and free from any ambiguity.[129]

In view of the fact that the learned Counsel to D. T. Akinbiyi, F. D.L. McIntyre QC with R. A. Fani-Kayode could not find any case which supported the argument put forward; an inability which did not surprise the Federal Chief Justice, it was declared that D.T. Akinbiyi had no *locus standi* to appeal in this case, and the appeal was accordingly struck out.

The position of the Federal Supreme Court in this case went a long way to support the judicial attitude of Adetokunbo Ademola in cases involving the two dominant parties in the Western Region; the Action Group and the N.C.N.C. It should however be noted that the Federal Supreme Court came to its own independent conclusion based on the basic facts presented to it and strictly in obedience to what the law said on who could bring a matter up for judicial intervention of the court. It would have been a surprise and a shock, had the Federal Supreme Court reasoned and declared otherwise. In the words of Lord Bramwell L. J., in his judgement in *Ex.parte Sidebotham*

> ...but certainly, the general rule is that an appeal must be brought by the party who has endeavoured to maintain the contrary of that which has taken place.[130]

The Federal Supreme Court referred to this position with a qualification that it meant one of the parties to the dispute, which was brought before the court for its decision.

Adetokunbo Ademola as Chief Judge was always very alert and sensitive to the judicial process at the lower courts to ensure that litigants were given adequate opportunities within the law to pursue their cases to satisfactory and logical conclusion. He showed a remarkable belief in the principle of free and unfettered access to the courts especially on the right to appeal. The Chief Justice was of the judicial opinion that appeal should not be restricted or burdened on arbitrary grounds. He was committed to the due process of law. His performance in cases on evidence confirms his belief in the relationship between a judge's understanding of the principle of evidence and top flight judicial performance. Adetokunbo Ademola believed that the Nigerian Evidence Act contains far-reaching provisions aimed at ensuring fair and just dispensation of justice.

In *A.R.Salami* v. *Joseph Nahman,*[131] the appellant (Salami) filed a motion asking for an extension of time within which to fulfill one of the conditions imposed by the court. Ayo Rosiji appearing for Joseph Nahman opposed the application on the ground that once the appeal had been entered, Rule 25 of the West African Court of Appeal Rules applied, and the high court had nothing more to do with the matter. The application according to counsel to respondent should have been made to the West African Court of Appeal.[132] After a careful consideration of the rules of the West African Court of Appeal, Adetokunbo Ademola held.

> Now Rule 16 of the West African Court of Appeal Rules permits the Registrar of the Supreme Court or High Court to settle records. Under rule 19 of the Rules, he transmits all records to West African Court of Appeal with a certificate that all conditions have been satisfied. It appears to me then that until this has been done, there is no appeal before the West African Court of Appeal. In this case, the certificate so issued by the Registrar under Rule 19 is incorrect, because all the conditions have not been fulfilled.[133]

He concluded that there was no appeal as such before the West African Court of Appeal. He therefore affirmed the competence of the high court to enlarge the time within which to perfect conditions of appeal sought by A. R. Salami.

In another case[134] where there was a visit to the locus in quo in the presence of the accused persons, but which was not recorded in the records, Adetokunbo Ademola held that,

> where the court of the first instance has visited the locus in quo in the presence of the accused persons, the absence from the records of the object of the visit, or what transpired there will not vitiate conviction, if the appellate court is satisfied that there has been no substantial miscarriage of justice occasioned thereby.

The Chief Justice drew attention to the difference between this case and two earlier cases.[135] It was of the opinion that the present case was not one of the cases where the absence of some essentials could amount to substantial miscarriage of justice. The charge was one of riot and malicious damage done to a particular house. It was most likely that the object of the visit was to see the opportunity open to the accused persons to commit the types of offences charged. Adetokunbo Ademola averred,

> I do not therefore think that a non-recording of the object of the visit or what transpired there so long the accused persons were all present create in this case a substantial miscarriage of justice.[136]

Adetokunbo Ademola's mastery of evidence and procedural law could equally be seen in his handling of the case, *Inspector General of Police (Respondent) v. Eusebius & Another* in *Re: Abudu Salami.*[137] The appellant and another person were charged with stealing and the appellant alone was charged on a second count with unlawful possession of the goods alleged to have been stolen. At the close of the case, for the prosecution, the magistrate held that there was no case for either accused to answer on the charge of stealing and discharged the other person. The prosecution then sought and obtained leave to call that person as a witness. After hearing him and the appellant, the magistrate convicted the appellant for unlawful possession.[138] The case aroused the Chief Justices's sense of justice and he believed that in such instances, the principle of natural justice must be given free reign.

> That the exercise of the discretion of the court under section 200 of the Criminal Procedure Ordinance is limited when, to exercise such discretion is unlikely to cause an injustice or tend to be against the spirit of the law.[139]

For the education of the lower courts in such matters, the Chief Justice said,

> Where reasonable suspicion of unlawful possession is based upon the alleged stealing which is not proved, a charge under section 430(i) of the Criminal Code cannot be sustained.[140]

He thereafter added that the other person in the case having been acquitted on the charge of stealing and the issue as to unlawful possession being clearly an issue between that person and the appellant, it would be difficult to see how the former could be considered an accomplice.[141]

In *Inspector General of Police v. Abu Bakare*,[142] which involved obtaining money by false pretence, it was held by Adetokunbo Ademola that the appeal court had no power to revive the charge of stealing upon which the appellant had been acquitted, and substitute a conviction thereon for the erroneous conviction on the second count. When there existed an alternative count, the Chief Justice, believed that the proper course, especially when the Magistrate was in doubt on which of the two offences and accused person had committed, was that "the court could convict on one of the counts and stay the other or make a mere order of discharge on the other charge."[143]

According to J. A. G. Griffith, judicial conception of public interest could be "reflected in cases involving the interest of the State (including its moral welfare) and the preservation of law and order."[144] The interrelationship of the executive as the guarantor of public interest and the judiciary could therefore be discussed within the context of such cases. Appellate judges are equally members of a political group who should protect the social order against threats to its stability. However, in the protection of public interest, the judge is bound to observe the due process and ensure that no injustice is done to private right of the individual.[145] Adetokunbo Ademola's judicial performance in two important cases were eloquent testimonies of the restraints the Chief Justice had to exercise in order to protect the private right of the accused persons.

In *Inspector General of Police v. Suara Sunmonu (appellant)*[146] that was determined on 27 November 1956, the appellant was convicted of indecent assault contrary to section 360 of the criminal code. He however, appealed on the grounds that, (i) the learned magistrate convicted on the uncorroborated evidence of the prosecutrix story, and (ii) the learned magistrate did not hear the evidence of a witness for the appellant on the ground that he did not understand the nature of an oath. The Chief Justice was in no difficulty before coming to his conclusion. He held that, it was "not a rule of law that in sexual offences, an accused person should not be convicted on the uncorroborated evidence of the prosecutrix."[147] The jury could convict, if satisfactory evidence of truth had been obtained. Adetokunbo Ademola further held that the evidence of a child was admissible, notwithstanding the fact that the child did not understand the nature of an oath. He believed however, that before admitting such evidence, it was the duty of the judge to satisfy himself that the child called upon to give evidence was sufficiently intelligent to appreciate what he was saying and must understand the duty of speaking the truth.[148] Having said this, he allowed, the appeal despite the fact that the charge of indecent assault was a serious sexual offence. Although it would have been impossible for the Chief Justice to be oblivious of the moral implications of the offences, he was however, of the opinion that the existence of procedural errors on the part of both the prosecution and the judicial officer of the lower court titled the balance of justice in favour of the accused. Since the principle of due process was not entirely observed, it seemed to Adetokunbo Ademola, that it would be better to hurt the morality of the society than to do injustice to an individual.

The second case was a charge of murder preferred against six accused persons.[149] The appeal was on the grounds of the existence of an alibi and the non-availability of statements made by witnesses to the police. Since murder involved capital punishment, Adetokunbo Ademola would not be satisfied until the charge had been proved beyond all shadows of doubt. It was however unfortunate for the state, that the prosecution was ill prepared to prove the charge as required by law. The Chief Justice held *inter alia*

(a) that unless there is a stronger evidence against it, the court cannot lightly disregard evidence of an alibi; and
(b) that it is the duty of the prosecution to make available during trial, statements made by witnesses who had been interviewed by the Police, especially where a witness has made different statements to the Police.[150]

On the ground that the court was of the opinion that the prosecution had not discharged the onus on it adequately and exhaustively, the appeal was allowed. In spite of his concern for the preservation of law and order typical of all colonial judges, Adetokunbo Ademola's commitment to the due process of law remained intact in his performance in this case.

By 1957, Adetokunbo Ademola was a rather confident judge. He had developed a mature attitude towards life, and his definition of society,, morality and social reality had assumed a broader sense. Having passed the 50-year mark, and having assumed positions of far more responsibility, his judicial performance showed a new presence of mind, a more determined outlook and an awareness of the relevance of the judiciary to independent Nigeria. He became confident to the extent that, he would not be disturbed or bothered about the possibility of a litigant appealing to a higher court against his judgement.

> Even when I was in a lower court and the matter goes up, it doesn't worry me at all. I know some judges who if there is an appeal on their case are shaking like leaves. That's the opinion of the higher court.

> I've given my own opinion. The higher court gives its own opinion. That's my principle it doesn't worry me.[151]

This new judicial outlook was demonstrated in two of his judgements in 1957. Although the two cases were not reported, their relevance to the book could not be over-emphasized. One of the cases really gives an insight into how extra judicial or circumstantial considerations could affect the performance of a judge. In *The Queen v. The Minister of Education (Western Region) Ex Parte Emmanuel S. Akappo (Applicant),*[152] the Chief Justice was prayed upon to make absolute an order nisi made for a writ of prohibition.

The fact of the case was that the principal and proprietor of a school known as Thomas Marshall College of Commerce, Ibadan was ordered to close down the school, following an adverse report submitted by Miss J. Miller, an Acting Senior Education Officer. The principal however objected to the minister's order on three grounds.

(i) that the report of Miss J. Miller, Acting Senior Education Officer (Technical) of February, 1956 was null and void or legally invalid;

(ii) that the purported Notice of Complaint dated 22nd February 1956 was legally invalid, null and void;

(iii) that the Minister of Education erred in law to order that Thomas Marshall College of Commerce be closed at the end of January 1957.[153]

It was argued that at the time Miss J. Miller inspected the school, she was not an Inspector as required by section 78 of the Education Law No. 6 of 1955. To that extent, Miss Miller cannot claim to be competent and entitled to perform the duty of an Inspector as specified in section 80 of the Education Act. Reacting to this, the crown counsel agreed, but that Miss Miller was entitled to report on the organization of the school that she did. She did not assume the role of an inspector.

Again, counsel for the applicant argued that notice of complaint served on him was served as a result of the report, and that for such notices to be served in accordance with section 43(1) of the Education Act, an inspection should have been made.

Section 43(1) listed eight grounds upon which Minister of Education could serve the proprietor of an institution a notice of complaint. It however starts with the operative sentence "if at any time, the minister is satisfied that an institution is objectionable upon all or any of the listed eight grounds."

Counsel to applicant contended that the minister could only be satisfied after he had ordered an inspection and that had been carried out. To him sections 77 to 84 of the Education Law dealing with Inspections were the only means whereby the Ministers could be satisfied before applying the law under section 43(1). The Chief Justice referred the court to an obvious confusion of thoughts with regard to the powers of the Minister of Education in the matter before him. He believed that the minister was not fettered in any way as to the means of his dis-satisfaction so long as he was judicious about it, and his reasons for dis-satisfaction came under one of the eight grounds in section 43(1) of the Education Law.[154] In other words, it did not matter how the Minister came to be aware of the matter complained of; It could be by a report of a visiting officer, or by a report of an inspection officer, or by an ordinary letter from an interested party calling attention to the breach or defects, or by any other means whatsoever. It would appear to Adetokunbo Ademola that the law did not even state by what means the minister should ascertain that the breach or breaches or defects had been attended to. The minister was empowered to use any means provided it was reasonable and judicious. It therefore seemed to the Chief Justice that the minister had discretion to use whatever means he considered proper. The ministerial order and administrative actions were therefore declared valid and in accordance with the law. The *Order nisi* could therefore not be made absolute as applied for by the appellant.[155]

A review of the performance of Adetokunbo Ademola in this case would confirm our earlier position that he was able to draw a line, neat and distinct between the interest of the party and the policy of the Government of the Western Region. Although it was a cardinal programme of the Action Group, the provision of free education had been accepted as a policy of the Western Region. As confirmed by Omolewa,[156] Obafemi Awolowo stood at the head of an administration that lent political weight to the programme of providing access to education for the masses. The government of the Western Region mobilized all sections of the society towards the ideal of free education. For instance, a major actor in the education sector of the Western Region, C. O. Taiwo,[157]

> The Director of Education down to clerks... chiefs, counsellors, party supporters and non party supporters, retired and serving teachers, pastors... traders, farmers, prominent citizens, missionaries both men and women became involved in the pursuit of the programme of free education.[158]

The judiciary under Adetokunbo Ademola was not left out and as it were, the courts became a strong pillar of support as could be seen in the case under review. It should be noted that, before the case was brought up for judicial intervention, several administrative attempts had been made to close down the school which was officially believed to be running contrary to the educational blue print of the government of the Western Region. The existence of the school as a post primary, commercial, and fee-paying institution was a source of concern to the government of the Western Region, especially when the middle tier school system of the Modern School was still in-choate. The continued existence of the school was considered capable of sending wrong signals to other potential proprietors of schools resulting in a proliferation of schools with doubtful academic standard. The provision of education was believed to be too sensitive to be left to individual hands especially in the era of competitive and treacherous party politics.

Adetokunbo Ademola was aware of the dilemma of the executive in closing the school. He was prepared to use the court to promote ad protect a particular public policy that was in the best interest of a greater number of the people especially the masses of the people. His judgment confirmed his preparedness to give judicial support to genuine government policy however closely tied to the fortunes of political parties. This could be corroborated by the acidic and adverse comments of Obafemi Awolowo on the judiciary in the Western Region during this period. Of the three instances of bias and impartiality Awolowo referred to, none was against the interest of the State. No attempt was made by the Western Region judiciary to thwart or frustrate the programmes and policies of the executive arm. The judiciary showed remarkable understanding of what it could do to promote good government and progressive administration.

The implication of the judgement of Adetokunbo Ademola in this case would be discussed in the next chapter with a view to confirming the suggestion that the Chief Justice was of the judicial attitude of allowing certain extra judicial consideration to influence him in matters affecting the interest of a certain political party in Nigeria as alleged by Obafemi Awolowo.

The performance of Adetokunbo Ademola in another case that was decided in 1957 would also confirm the strong suggestion that the Chief Justice had started to show obvious flashes of confidence and independence. He believed that recourse could be had to the courts of law in order to secure the annulment or variation of administrative orders or determinations or the restraining of unlawful acts by administrative bodies.[159] The courts could also be called upon to issue mandatory order for the performance of a public duty.[160] This belief could be seen in *The Queen v. The Resident Ijebu Province, Ex. Parte J. A. C. Oshinlaja*[161] which came up as an application to make absolute an order nissi granted on March 6, 1957, for a writ of mandamus to issue against the Resident, Ijebu Province, to compel him to hold an enquiry into the matter of Dagburewe chieftaincy. This was to be in compliance with an earlier order of the high court that granted a writ of certiorari for the purpose of quashing the records relating to the appointment or recognition of one Olaleye as the Dagburewe of Idowa.[162]

In order to have adequate background information necessary for a better and an enhanced appreciation of the case, as it relates to the interrelationship of the executive and the judiciary, it would be necessary to highlight the history of the matter. In 1955 J. A. C. Oshinlaja filed an application for a writ of certiorari complaining that one Olaleye was appointed and recognised as the Dagburewe of Idowa without due enquiry as required by law, despite the fact that there was a dispute about the chieftaincy. The application was filed prior in time to the promulgation of the Western Region Appointments and Recognition of Chiefs Law No. 1 of 1955 and to that extent the Chief Justice held that the Old Law i.e. the Appointment and Deposition of Chiefs Ordinance Cap 12 as amended by No. 20 of 1945 section 2 would apply and the Applicant would still be entitled to the writ of certiorari he had asked for.[163]

After hearing arguments from both parties, the court adjourned for judgement that was delivered on 16th May 1956. It is however interesting to note that before May 1956, precisely April 11, 1956 and whilst the matter still stood adjourned, the Governor in Council exercised its powers under the law to appoint and recognize Olayeye as the Dagburewe of Idowa. This was published in the Gazette of June 7, 1956. The publication of the appointment in the Gazette was after the applicant had requested the Resident or Provincial Adviser to hold the enquiry as required by law and in compliance with Section 2 of the Chieftaincy Ordinance. The reply from the executive referred the applicant to the publication and reasoned that in view of this, the enquiry would not be necessary. That was the reason for the applicant's application for a writ of mandamus to compel the Resident or provincial adviser to hold the enquiry.

After considering the role played by the Resident and the Provincial Adviser, the Chief Justice felt certain that if the Resident had put the whole position to the Governor, the matter would not have proceeded further until, the judgment of the court was known. This case afforded Adetokunbo Ademola ample opportunity to make some far-reaching judicial pronouncements that became reference materials later. For instance, he stated, "a statute or law took effect in future unless there was a specific direction in it, that it should be retrospective".[164] This position shows his distaste for and displeasure at retroactive laws that are now common feature of military decrees in contemporary Nigeria. He went further to declare, "until the executive or the legislature has passed a law to nullify a judgement of a competent court, the direction in the judgment must be carried out.[165]

According to Adetokunbo Ademola,

> ...the courts will not interfere with machinery of Government, but when the rights of a citizen is being interfered with and there is no law to justify such interference, the courts will act.[166]

He believed that the court was precluded by law from interfering in the matter of selection of a chief. They could however stand between the executive and the members of the public so far as the legislation on the point permitted. If somehow something was being done which ran contrary to natural justice or certain things required by law was not done, Adetokunbo Ademola strongly believed that the court could and should interfere.[167]

Apart from granting the prayers of the applicant, Adetokunbo concluded this judgment thus:

> One more point I would like to mention. There have been cases of this nature decided in the courts from time to time. Before 'due enquiry' is made by the Resident, the interested parties have been allowed to continue to perform the duties relating to such chieftaincies. This procedure, in my view, tends to stultify the judgement of the court. There are certain duties which cannot be left in abeyance; other duties should in such cases, in my view be suspended no matter if it causes some grave public inconvenience or hardship. It is the duty of the court to see that justice is done.

> Convenience and justice, it has been said are often not on speaking terms.[168]

The pronouncements of Adetokunbo Ademola in this case sent the necessary signals to the other arms of government as it meant a redefinition and reconceptualization of the role a fearless judiciary could play in the protection of private rights or civil liberties. Perhaps, it was also meant to warn the exponents of self-rule in the Western Region, that in a democratic set up and within the context of the rule of law, the judiciary knew the extent of its powers as the last hope of the common man against the excesses of the state and the atrocities of state officials.

As stated earlier, the independence of the judiciary was not in a straightjacket or watertight compartment in the Western Region. There were actually areas of interaction between the executive and the judiciary. In the first instance, Adetokunbo Ademola had established lasting relationship with some members of the Executive Council. For instance, Claudius Dosa Akran (later Oba C. D. AKRAN) was a former classmate at St. Gregory's Grammar School of Adetokunbo Ademola's.[169] The two lived within the same neighbourhoods as officials of state and retained their personnel friendship throughout. Again, the appointment of F. R. A. Williams as Minister of Justice and Local Government and later Minister of Justice ad Attorney General of the Western Region, paved way for the development of an inobstructive relationship between the executive and the judiciary. F. R. A. Williams was able to use the office of Attorney General as buffer between the executive and the judiciary. The judiciary had no direct constitutional access to the executive in matters pertaining to the judiciary. The overriding belief of the judiciary to come into direct contact with the executive in any matter relating to the administration of justice was to completely erode the much-needed independence of the judiciary in an era of party politics.[170]

The difference between the executive and the judiciary was at the level of personalities and they were addressed in civilized and polite manners, each using particularly important occasions to express his feelings. For example Obafemi Awolowo reviewed the performance of the judiciary in cases involving the interest of the party he led and came to a conclusion that the Chief Justice could not be absolved from partisanship. He used the floor of the legislative council to express his convictions and fear when he spoke of the "existence in the Western Region of an intimidated judiciary". Although the remarks of Obafemi Awolowo aroused "a press controversy," Adetokunbo Ademola refused to be drawn into the press war, rather, he used the occasion of the beginning of a new legal year to reply the Premier and to emphasize the point that his judicial performance and those of his learned colleagues at the various levels of adjudication in the Western Region were strictly to maintain the rule of law and ensure the liberty of the people. The judiciary in the Western Region was committed to upholding the dignity of the judiciary as an arm of government in a democratic set up.

Perhaps what was obvious in the relationship between the executive and the judiciary during this period in the Western Region was a sort of mutual suspicion of what each could do, given the prevailing situation of party politics.[171] The executive under the premiership of Obafemi Awolowo was highly suspicious of the relationship that existed between the leadership of the opposition NCNC and the judiciary in the Western Region. According to Awolowo,

> The courts of this region have several times been accused of all manner of evil things. A few days ago, however, leader of opposition paid a glowing tribute to the impartiality and incorruptibility of the judiciary in the Western Region. I do not know what the members of the bench themselves think of this piece of eulogy, coming as it did from one who has consistently conducted himself in defiance of law, order and constituted authority. Some people may regard this tribute as a compliment to the bench; but there are others who see it as a very strong evidence of a deflection from the path of rectitude and impartiality on the part of a thoroughly intimated judiciary."[172]

The performance of the judiciary in every case involving the Action Group and the NCNC was always condemned as partisan. On the other hand, the Chief Justice believed it was only a fearless, thorough and conservative judiciary that could check the perceived tendency of the Action Group and its leadership to liquidate all opposition to its administration, and rule the Region by fiat.

With the benefit of hindsight, it would seem that the judiciary in the Western Region during this period, suspected a tendency of the Action Group towards the strategy and style of Kwame Nkrumah's Convention People's Party as the party in government in Ghana. Indeed, there were a number of meeting points between the C. P. P. and the Action Group, in terms of organization, leadership style, attitude to opposition and tendency toward totalitarian rule. Adetokunbo Ademola was reared in the English tradition that allowed opposition, venerated parliamentary give and take, and which also was abhorrent of totalitarianism. The idea of left wing and militant political party that was gaining ground in Ghana, Egypt, Tanzania and Guinea, was not appealing to the Chief Justice.[173] He believed that the ideal political context or milieu must allow the existence of healthy opposition in order to allow the citizens an alternative viewpoint. The judiciary in the Western Region therefore had a different perspective to the party in government on what could lead to development and what democracy was all about.

According to Coleman,

> The dominant theory of the Action Group leaders was that under the circumstances then prevailing in Nigeria, the only certain avenue to power was a regional political party. Accordingly, one of the main themes in the group's electoral campaign was common opposition to Azikwe and to the threat of Ibo domination under a unitary scheme.[174]

As far back as 1951, the Action Group had established an electoral control over the Western Region when it succeeded in sweeping the polls by a very wide margin. The dominance was therefore seen as an opportunity to annihilate all opposition in the Region. Adetokunbo Ademola however believed that, for the democratic experiment to succeed, there must be an effective opposition, and to this extent, the Chief Justice, sought to use his court to protect the interest of the opposition against any attempt to muffle or suppress it in the Western region between 1954 and 1958. This perhaps explains the attitude of the Premier Obafemi Awolowo to and indictments of Adetokunbo Ademola as Chief Justice of the Western Region and of the Federation.

Notes

1. Report by the Conference on the Nigerian Constitution, London: July and August 1953, London, p. 3.
2. *Ibid.*
3. *Ibid.*
4. Report by the Conference on the Nigerian Constitution, London: July and August 1, 1953, London, p. 17.
5. Nigerian (Constitution) Order-in-Council, 1954.
6. B. O. Nwabueze, *Machinery of Justice in Nigeria*... p. 68.
7. Akinola Aguda, "Judicial Administration", Quarterly Journal of Administration, v (1), October, 1970, p. 79.
8. For details of the ethnic orientation of Nigerian political parties, see, J. S. Coleman *Nigeria Background to Nationalism*...O. Nnoli, *Ethnic Politics in Nigeria* (Enugu: Fourth Dimension Publishers, 1980). See also Atanda Fatayi Williams, *Faces, Cases and Places*... pp. 37-38.
9. Sir John Verity was Chief Justice of the Supreme Court of Nigeria's between 1946 and 1954.
10. Omoniyi Adewoye, *The Judicial System in Southern Nigeria* ... p. 245.
11. *Ibid.*, p. 246.
12. Quoted by Lord Denning, *What Next in the Law* (London: Butterworths, 1982), p. 235.
13. Interview: Justice Adenekan Ademola, Lagos, 1995.
14. *Ibid.*

15. Trevor Clark, *A Right Honourable Gentleman The Life and Times of Alhaji Sir Abubakar Tafawa Balewa* (Kaduna: Hadahuda Publishing Company, 1991), p. 643.
16. Trevor Clark, *A Right Honourable* ... p. 643.
17. B. O. Nwabueze, *A Constitutional History of Nigeria* (Ibadan: Longman Nigeria Limited), p. 56.
18. *Ibid.*
19. Omoniyi Adewoye, *The Judicial System* ... p. 244.
20. *Ibid.*
21. Western Regional Notice No. 90 contained in The Gazette of the Western Region No. 5, Vol. 4, 1955.
22. For details of the reactions of the Action Group and its leadership, see, Obafemi Awolowo, *My March Through Prison* (Lagos: Macmillian Nigeria Publishers Ltd., 1985), pp. 205-211.
23. Obafemi Awolowo, *Awo: The Autobiography of Chief Obafemi Awolowo* (Cambridge: Cambridge University Press), p. 261.
24. Obafemi Awolowo, *My March Through Prison*... p. 205.
25. *Ibid.* p. 206.
26. Western Region Notice No. 90 of February 3, 1955.
27. Western Region Notice No. 433 of June 23, 1955.
28. *Ibid.*
29. Obafemi Awolowo, *My March Through Prison*... p. 208.
30. Obafemi Awolowo, *My March Through Prison*... p. 208.
31. Interview Justice Adenekan Ademola, Lagos, 1995.
32. For an expansion of the theoretical framework being adapted for this discussion, see J. A. G. Griffith, *The Politics of the Judiciary* (3rd ed) (London: Fontana Press, 1985), p. 199.
33. F. R. A. Williams, "Awo's Moments in Law," The *Guardian* (Lagos), May 27, 1987.
34. Omoniyi Adewoye, "Obafemi Awolowo and the Rule of Law", Olasope Oyelaran, Toyin Falola, Mokwugo Okoye and Adewale Thompson (eds) *Obafemi Awolowo: The End of an Era?* (Ile-Ife: Ife University Press, 1989).
35. F. R. A. Williams, "Awo's Moments in Law," The *Guardian* (Lagos), May 27, 1987.
36. *Ibid.*
37. *Ibid.*

38. Atanda Fatayi-Williams, *Faces Cases and Places...* pp. 38-39.
39. Atanda Fatayi-Williams, *Faces Cases and Places...* p. 39.
40. *Ibid.*
41. House of Assembly Debates, Official Report, 4-6 February 1959, p. 1006.
42. Atanda Fatayi Williams, *Faces, Cases...* p. 38. He later became a justice of the Supreme Court of Nigeria and thereafter the Chief Justice of Nigeria.
43. *Ibid.*
44. Omoniyi Adewoye, "Obafemi Awolowo and the Rule of Law", Sope Oyelaran, etc. *Obafemi Awolowo: The End of an Era...* p. 735.
45. Western Region Notice No. 472 of 1955.
46. *Ibid.*
47. Section 3 of the Magistrate Courts (Western Region) Law, 1955.
48. Western Region Notice No. 473 of 1955: Magisterial Districts, (1955).
49. B. O. Nwabueze, *Machinery of Justice in Nigeria...* p. 146.
50. Western Region Notice No. 466.
51. Western Region Notice No. 215 of 13/4/56.
52. WRLN 231 of 1957.
53. Oral Interview, E. O. Fakayode Retired Chief Judge Oyo State, Ibadan, March 10, 1996.
54. Western Region Notice No. 481.
55. Western Region Notice No. 188 of 20/3/56.
56. Western Region Notice No. 215.
57. Western Region Notice No. 1178 of 30/11/57.
58. Mr. Justice Kester became the first indigenous Chief Judge of the Western Region Court of Appeal.
59. Western Region of Nigeria Gazette No. 45, Vol. 4 of October 6, 1955, p. 221.
60. NAI Oyo Prov. 1377, Vol. VI.
61. Western Region of Nigeria Gazette No. 45, Vol. 4, p. 223.
62. *Ibid.* p. 226.
63. Deputy Governor to Residence Oyo Province November 23, 1995.

64. S. A. de Smith *Jusicial Review of Administrative Action* (London: Steven & Sons Ltd. 1973), p. 28.
65. *Ibid.*
66. Oral Interview: Hon. Justice Adenekan Ademola, Lagos, February 14, 1995.
67. *Ibid.*
68. Oral Interview: Hon. Justice Adenekan Ademola, Lagos, February 14, 1995.
69. *Ibadan District Council v.Ishola Mosadogun & Four Others* (1955) WRNLR: 22.
70. *Ibid.,* p. 27.
71. *Ibadan District Council v Ishola Mosadogun & Four Others* (1955) WRNLR 22, p. 23.
72. *Alli Adekunle and Two Others* v. *Inspector General of Police* (1955) WRNLR: 16.
73. *Ibid.,* p. 17.
74. *Ibid.*
75. Atanda Fatayi Williams *Faces Cases and Places...* pp. 25-26.
76. *Ibid.*
77. *Regina* v. *Diyaolu*, High Court of Justice, Ibadan records Judgement delivered in 29 September 1955, also contained in (1955) WRNLR. 30.
78. *Ibid.*
79. *Ibid.,* p. 31.
80. A. E. W. Park, *The Sources of Nigerian Law* (Lagos: African Universities Press Ltd. 1963), p. 7.
81. *The Queen v. Emmanuel Jegede and Others* (1955) WRNLR. 33.
82. *Ibid.*
83. *Ibid.*
84. *Ibid.*
85. *The Queen v. Emmanuel Jegede and Others* (1955) WRNLR. 33.
86. *Ibid.*
87. *Ibid.*
88. *Ibid.*
89. *The Queen v. Emmanuel Jegede and Others* (1955) WRNLR. 33.
90. (1955) WRNLR. 56.
91. *Ibid.*

92. Oral interview of Hon. Justice Adenekan Ademola 14 February 1955. He believed that the location of the headquarters of the Criminal Investigation Department did not allow for the use of competent and qualified police officers as criminal investigators in regional courts.
93. (1955) WRNLR. 57.
94. *Ibid.*
95. *Society Magazine,* 21 June, 1990 pp. 22-25.
96. *Ibid.*
97. (1955) WRNLR. 103.
98. *Ibid.*
99. 343. (1955) WRNLR. 103.
100. *Ibid.*
101. *Lawani Tewogbade & Others v. Chief Lawani Adeyemi, Akirun of Ikirun* (unreported) High Court of Justice, Ibadan Suit No. 1/99/54.
102. *Ibid.*
103. *Inspector General of Police v. Ganiyu Oyeneye* (1955) WRNLR. 4.
104. *Ibid.*
105. NAI Px/A11 West Regional Government, 1954-63.
106. Oral Interview Justice E. O. Fakayode, Retired Chief Judge of Oyo State, Ibadan, 1996.
107. For details of the hostilities and mutual suspicion, see Kenneth and Post and George Jenkins, The *Price of Liberty: Personality and Politics in Colonial Nigeria* (Cambridge: Cambridge University Press, 1973).
108 .*Daily Times of Nigeria* 14 October 1957.
109 .Kenneth Post and George Jenkins, *The Price of Liberty... op. cit*, p. 310.
110 .Kenneth Post and George Jenkins, *The Price of Liberty... op. cit*, p. 310.
111. *Ibid.*
112. *Ibid.*
113. Anonymous "Mr. Adelabu has the Answers" West *African Pilot,* 12 March 1955, p. 221, quoted in Ibid. p. 192.
114. *Ibid.*

115. (1955) WRNLR.6.
116. Obafemi Awolowo, *My March Through Prison*... p. 210.
117. (1955) WRNLR 6.
118. *Ibid.*
119. *Ibid.*, p. 7.
120. *Ibid.*
121. *Ibid.*
122. Oral Interview, Hon. Justice E. O. Fakayode, Ibadan, 1996.
123. *Ibid.*
124. (1955) WRNLR.
125. *Ibid.*
126. Obafemi Awolowo, *My March Through Prison*, ..., p. 210.
127. Chief D. T. Akinbiyi (Appellant) in Inspector General of Police v. Adegoke Adelabu, Judgement of the Federal Supreme Court of Nigeria, Lagos delivered on 29 May 1956.
128. *Ibid.*
129. *Ibid.*
130. *Ex-parte Sidebotham* (1880) 14 ch D 458, 465.
131. (1955) WRNLR 18.
132. *Ibid.*
133. (1955) WRNLR 18.
134. *Inspector General of Police v. L. Ade Bello and Others* (Appellants) (195) WRNLR.
135. *Inspector General of Police v. Alli Adekunle in re: Stanley Bazuaye,* and *R. v. Hogan Antia and anor.*
136. *Inspector General of Police* v. *L. Ade Bello and Others.*
137. (1955) WRNLR.
138. (1955) WRNLR.
139. *Ibid.*
140. *Ibid.*
141. (1955) WRNLR.
142. *Ibid.*
143. *Ibid.*
144. J. A. G. Griffith, *The Politics of the Judiciary* 3rd Edition (London: Fontana Press, 1985), pp. 199-224.
145. J. A. G. Griffith, *The Politics*... op. cit. Pp. 223-224.

146. (1955) WRNLR.
147. *Ibid.*
148. *Ibid.*
149. *The Queen* v. *Ayodele Turner and Others*. (1955) WRNLR.
150. *Ibid.*
151. Society Magazine, June 1990.
152. Suit No. 1/20/57 of 20 March 1957 High Court of Justice Western Region Folio 377.
153. *Ibid.*
154. *Ibid.*
155. *Ibid.*
156. Michael Omolewa, "Awolowo and Seven years of Mass Education Work, 1952-1959: A Study on the Question of Number in Education" in Olasope Oyelaran et al (eds.) Obafemi Awolowo. *The End of An Era*? .. .p. 778.
157. *Ibid,* p. 789.
158. *Ibid.*
159. For expansive discussion, see de. Smith Judicial *Review of Administrative Action...*
160. *Ibid.*
161. Suit No. 1/57/55 of 14 August 1957 High Court of Justice Western Region Folio 466.
162. *Ibid.*
163. *Ibid.*
164. Suit No. 1/57/55 of 14 August 1957 High Court of Justice Western Region Folio 466.
165. *Ibid.*
166. *Ibid.*
167. *Ibid.*
168. Suit No. 1/57/55 of 14 August 1957 High Court of Justice Western Region Folio 466.
169. Oral information Hon Justice Adenekan Ademola 14 February 1995.
170. *Ibid.*
171. *Ibid.*
172. Western region Hansard 4th Session 1956 also in West African Pilot April 18, 1958.

173. According to Hon. Justice Adenekan Ademola, the forces of the left had not gained wide acceptance as at the time Adetokunbo Ademola received formal training in law.
174. J. S. Coleman, *Nigeria: Background to Nationalism...*, p. 350.

Chapter 5

Judicial Role in Parliamentary Democracy and Representative Government

> *Constitutional decisions should be 'genuinely principled' in the sense that they must rest upon reason with respect to all the issue in the case, reasons that in their generality and their neutrality transcend any immediate result that is involved... Constitutional decision should not be based on expediency, but upon reasons commanding a generality and neutrality of application.*
>
> S. Wechsler," Towards Neutral Principles in Constitutional Law" *Harvard Review*, 73 (1959), p.1

When the Federal Supreme Court was reconstituted in 1954,[1] it had an extensive original jurisdiction extending to the following matters.

(a) any matter in which a writ or order of mandamus or prohibition or an injunction is sought against an officer or authority of the federation;

(b) any matter arising under any treaty;

(c) any matter affecting consular officers or representatives of countries or of international or similar organizations outside Nigeria;

(d) admiralty matters where the court exercised the jurisdiction of a Colonial Court of Admiralty under the Colonial Court of Admiralty Act 1890;

(e) disputes between the federation and a region or between the regions *inter se*; and

(f) questions relating to the interpretation of the constitution.[2]

By the Supreme Court Act, 1960,[3] the Admiralty Jurisdiction Act, 1962,[4] the Emergency Powers (Jurisdiction) Act, 1962,[5] and the Constitutional Referendum Act, 1962,[6] the afore stated original jurisdictions were variously affected. The various Acts of parliament redefined and re-conceptualized the jurisdiction of the Federal Supreme Court to make the original jurisdiction more constitutional and the court more relevant to the federal system in Nigeria. As observed by Nwabueze, the concentration of the original jurisdiction of the courts upon an ever-increasing sphere of constitutional issues conferred greater powers on the court. These powers included the power of control over the legislative, administrative and quasi-judicial activities of government departments and parastatals. The Supreme Court was also empowered to decide the validity of laws enacted by the federal legislative houses. It became obvious that the conferment of these powers on the court, made it assume an exceptionally unique character quite uncommon in many common law countries where legislative supremacy had been accepted as a sacrosanct principle.[7]

The appellate jurisdiction of the Federal Supreme Court covered matters that were considered by the West African Court of Appeal, which ceased to be a court of appeal for Nigerian cases because of the judicial reorganization of 1954. The Federal Supreme Court became an intermediate court of appeal between the high court and the Judicial Committee of the Privy Council in London, which until 1963 was the final court of appeal.[8] Appeals lay to the Federal Supreme Court from the decisions of a high court given either at first instance or on appeal from a lower court, and from the Sharia Court of Appeal. The federal Supreme Court might also on the request of the parliament, consider and advise upon any question over which the Governor-General or the Governor of a region desired the assistance of the court for the purpose of deciding on what matters he could exercise the powers of prerogative of mercy.[9]

This chapter is therefore intended to be a discussion and an examination of the performance of the Federal Supreme Court in the discharge of these weighty responsibilities, bearing in mind the training, exposure and professional accomplishments of members of the bench during this period of experimenting in popular democracy and parliamentary system of government.

When it was obvious that Sir Stafford Foster Sutton would be retiring as Chief Justice of the Federal Supreme Court in 1958, the choice of his successor became a matter of concern and interest to the departing British Administration, the Nigerian political class and members of the legal profession. The Nigerianization policy had been well received especially at a time the political independence of the country from Britain had been assured following the successful completion of the London and Lagos constitutional conferences of 1957 and 1958 respectively.[10] A section of the political class and the press controlled by it supported and campaigned for the appointment of Olumuyiwa Jibowu.[11] As noted in chapter four, the dominant party in the Western Region believed in the judicial competence of Jibowu. He was thus preferred to succeed Sir Stafford Foster Sutton as Chief Justice.[12] On the other side of the divide was the NCNC, which was critical of the extra judicial activities of Jibowu. The Zik group of newspapers advised the colonial administration to exercise utmost restraints in the appointment of the next Chief Justice. In an editorial opinion, the West African Pilot[13] called for the appointment of a judge who "knew no tribe, colour or creed". The editorial was least impressed by the experience of Olumuyiwa Jibowu when it said;

> Experience is quite all right, but what purpose does it serve when channeled to oppress one section of the community. We would rather prefer a comparatively less experienced judge than a hate ridden, tribe conscious and party politics minded individual to sit on the highest judicial bench of the federation of Nigeria.... we want Nigerianization not at the expense of justice to all.[14]

The vehement opposition of the NCNC and its press organizations to the possible elevation of Olumuyiwa Jibowu to the office of Chief Justice, was not unconnected to the alleged hatred by Jibowu of Azikiwe's political leadership and style as contained and expressed in the so called Savage letter.[15]

The colonial administration in Nigeria had cause to institute a Commission of Inquiry to look into the allegation that Nnamdi Azikiwe was using the African Continental Bank to promote private financial interest. A chief magistrate, Mr. Savage, was a member of the commission, which was headed by Sir Foster Sutton C.J.N. Dr. Azikiwe, objected to the inclusion of Mr. Savage on the ground that Sir Olumuyiwa Jibowu had an enormous influence on Mr. Savage, which could affect his objective consideration of the case at the inquiry. It was alleged that Olumuyiwa Jibowu while serving as a judge of the Federal Supreme Court, wrote a letter to Mr. Savage in 1954 which contained critical and provocative statements against the NCNC and its leadership.[16]

It would seem that the release of the 'Savage letter' by the NCNC was detrimental to the credentials and possible appointment of Olumuyiwa Jibowu. In spite of the support of the Action Group and that of a section of the press, Olumuyiwa Jibowu was eventually by passed.

In accordance with section 139 of the Nigeria (constitution) Orders-in-Council 1954 and 1955, the Governor-General, by instrument under the Public Seal in pursuance of instructions given by Her Majesty, through the Secretary of State for the Colonies[17] appointed Adetokunbo Adeniji Adegboyega Ademola Chief Justice of the federation. The appointment was announced by Sir James Wilson Robertson, and was effective 28 April 1958 and during Her Majesty's pleasure.[18] Indeed, it would seem that the swearing in of the new Chief Justice on Monday 28 April 1958 was one of the last memorable official activities conducted by Sir James Robertson in Nigeria.[19] The ceremony was conducted privately in the council of ministers chamber at about 11.30 p.m. shortly before Sir Ralph Grey was sworn in at midnight of the same day as Officer Administering the Federal Government.[20] In the same vein, the new Chief Justice performed his first official judicial activity when he presided over the Federal Supreme Court and was received by members of the Nigerian Bar.[21] At that ceremony, Adetokunbo Ademola said he realized how difficult it was to succeed a very popular and hard working personality like Sir Stafford Foster Sutton.[22] He however, promised to do his best to maintain traditions of law and the independence of the judiciary in the country. He said that it was most unusual for pioneers to enjoy the fruits of their labour, but some how, he thought, he was fortunate to have been appointed Chief Justice.[23]

The public statements of Mr. Justice de Lestang about Adetokunbo Ademola would attest to the acceptance of the appointment by the bench. According to de Lestang,

> The new Chief Justice has the unique distinction of being the first Nigerian to be appointed to the highest judicial post in the country. During his tenure of office as Chief Justice Western Region, Sir Adetokunbo Ademola showed that he possesses those rare gems among other precious stones such as great ability, strength of character, a keen sense of justice and understanding.[24]

On behalf of the Nigerian Bar Association, Alhaji Jubril Martins described the appointment of Adetokunbo Ademola as Chief Justice as a unique opportunity and a great thing for the Bar Association.[25] The appointment was yet another confirmation, that given the opportunity, Nigerians could be entrusted with most honourable and sensitive national duties. It marked the appointment of a second Nigerian to the headship of key federal department.[26] On the day of his introduction to the Bar and exactly ten minutes after the ceremony, Adetokunbo Ademola confirmed his preparedness to maintain a tradition of promptness that was first seen at St. Anna Court in Lagos when he was magistrate. Sitting with Justices de Lestang and Dove Edwin, the new Chief Justice enrolled Christopher Okon Iyang as a solicitor & Advocate of the Supreme Court of Nigeria. Messrs Olujide Somolu and J.E.C David sponsored Iyang.[27]

Even on the eve of political independence, the departing British administration was still very conscious of the role the

Chief Justice of the Supreme Court could play in the maintenance of political stability and economic development. The provision of the 1960 constitution,[28] which made a special case for the appointment of the Chief Justice, was so constructed to achieve a particular objective. Indeed, the manner of appointment gave the Chief Justiceship a quasi-political image. According to Kasumu,[29] the holder of that office must not only know his law, but must also be acceptable politically in order to avoid a situation of setting the judiciary in direct confrontation with the executive.[30] Adetokunbo Ademola was perhaps found to be politically predictable and temperamentally suitable for the appointment as Chief Justice. This chapter is intended to highlight the competence, adequacy, creativity, and the fertile mind of Adetokunbo Ademola to sustain the argument that it was politically safe for the executive to appoint him the Chief Justice of the Supreme Court of Nigeria.

Between 1958 and 1960, the Supreme Court entertained a variety of cases that emphasized the resourcefulness and dedication of the bench. As an intermediate Court of appeal, with appeals still going to the Privy Council in London, the Federal Supreme Court lived up to the expectations of the departing colonial government. The accumulated experience of Adetokunbo Ademola on the colonial bench, his predictable judicial outlook and perhaps the extra judicial rapprochement between him and the highest echelon of the executive, all together, put him in good stead to discharge both the judicial as well as the political functions of the office of Chief Justice to the admiration and commendation of the colonial government in Lagos and London.

The first reported case of Adetokunbo Ademola, as Federal Chief Justice was *Molade & Ors.* v. *Molade & Ors.*[31] where he was empanelled with Hugh Hurley and Quashie Idun. Though a civil case, the judgment cleared some misconceptions on property law that was then a festering issue in Lagos. The substantive issue before the court was whether evidence of acts done under a deed as a guide to the intention of parties could be admitted to contradict the clear meaning of the instrument. The court held that it was permissible to give evidence of acts done under a deed as a guide to the intention of parties, but evidence of such acts could not be admitted to contradict the clear meaning of the instrument.[32]

As early as 1958, Adetokunbo Ademola was prepared to evoke the principle of natural justice to prevent a possible miscarriage of justice even when the breach was by a junior colleague on the lower bench. The Chief Justice had started the practice of using the appellate jurisdiction of the Supreme Court to educate judges below on the need to master the rules and procedure of court.

This position could be buttressed in the case of *Stephen O Adedeji* v. *Police Service Commission*[33] where Adetokunbo Ademola said;

> It is possible the appellant is corrupt and did commit the offence alleged against him. This is not what we have to consider. Was the case against him sufficiently brought home to him, that one can say that the requirements of natural justice were sufficiently observed on the facts and the circumstances.[34]

The Federal Chief Justice in *The Queen* v. *Fadina*[35] answered the questions of (i) whether a judge could give consent to file an information after discharge by a magistrate on preliminary inquiry (ii) whether sentence could be passed without a conviction grounded on a judgment not properly written before such conviction.[36] The fact of the case was that Fadina (appellant) was charged for issuing forged certificate of road worthiness for lorries. At the end of the preliminary inquiry, the magistrate discharged him. The prosecution however believed that a case had been made against him and thereafter the consent of the judge was obtained under section 340 of the Criminal Procedure Ordinance to file information. The appellant was tried by the judge who at the conclusion of the trial delivered judgment based on notes made by him during the trial, which did not form part of the record of appeal. He convicted the appellant and sentenced him to concurrent terms of nine months imprisonment with hard labour.[37]

Adetokunbo Ademola delivering the judgment of the court held that the learned trial judge rightly gave his consent. The C.J.F however believed that once a judge had pronounced judgment, it was *functus officio* and the Supreme Court cannot look at any judgment reduced into writing thereafter. He further held that the notes made by the judge during the trial were not before the court, and therefore it was impossible to compare his written judgment with them as it was not possible to say what reasons he gave for the judgment he delivered from notes. In the words of Adetokunbo Ademola;

> It seems clear from the provisions of this section, that a judge, besides pronouncing his judgment must record it in writing and must sign it at a time of pronouncing it. It follows that the judge must record his judgment before or at the time of pronouncing it; he cannot record it afterwards.[38]

He concluded that the Supreme Court could look not at the judgment on the record because it was of no effect.

In the same tradition, Adetokunbo Ademola in_*Monsour Habib* v. *Lagos Executive Development Board* answered the tricky question of whether the heading of a statute could control the plain words contained therein. He held that it was a "cardinal rule of interpretation of statute that the heading cannot control the plain words of the statute"; headings could be regarded where and only where there was ambiguity in the words of the statute.[39]

We have seen that Adetokunbo Ademola was prepared to support private or individual claims in cases where the performance of the prosecution or the judge showed obvious lapses in evidence and procedure. His English legal background and experience as magistrate and judge under British colonial rule obviously developed in him the outlook and attributes of a strict constructionist. His performances in such cases were testimonies of his good understanding of the relevance of common law to the protection of private interests, while at the same time not undermining the law and order interest of the state.

As it would be seen presently in *Obodo & Ors* v. *The Queen*, where the activities of individuals threatened the moral values of the society and the stability of the polity, Adetokunbo Ademola would not shy away from imposing or confirming the ultimate punishment. In such cases, he believed that punishments must serve as deterrents to others who might have the tendency of similar actions. In the case under reference, the Federal Supreme Court was to determine two issues (i) where persons act in concert with one another, in furtherance of an object of a society to which they belong, whether the act of one was the act of all for purposes of criminal liability, (ii) whether a single refusal to carry out an order of the head of such a society without a final repudiation of the society was sufficient to absolve from criminal liability.[40] Five persons Nwibioko Obodo, Nwegede Ogbo, Mbeke Awan, Mwugbala Nwankwo and Nwabonyi Mgbabo were convicted for the murder of one Nwangbo Igbeagu (female). The five men were members of Odozi Obodo a murder society dedicated to the killing of thieves and other parties who the society decided to get rid of.

The deceased was accused of witchcraft and found guilty by the society for the killing of her two step sons. The first man who was also the head of the society and husband of the deceased struck the woman dead with the usual instrument of murder when his four subordinates refused to carry out his instructions. They had refused to kill the wife of the head of their society.[41] After a review of the case, Adetokunbo Ademola held that when a person joined a society of which one of the objects was murder, and he was present and acquiescent when a murder was carried out in pursuance of the object of the society, it was no defense that he did not commit the murder with his own hands, or even that he refused a command to do so. For such an argument to succeed, there must be incontrovertible evidence that he not only refused the order to kill, but that he vehemently repudiated the society. The criminal culpability of the five was confirmed even when it was argued that some of them joined the society because they were threatened with death.[42]

It would seem that the existence of a murder society in 1958 on the eve of independence was considered barbaric and uncivilized by the Chief Justice. At a time when the Nigerian State was preparing for a place to stand in the comity of nations, a society was still dedicated to such criminal acts and thereby injuring the moral value of the society. The capital punishment passed by the lower court on the appellants was confirmed as their appeal to the Supreme Court failed in its totality.

In a number of cases in 1959, the contributions of Adetokunbo Ademola to the judicial process in Nigeria were brought to the fore. His performance and especially *obita dicta* refined and clarified technical procedures of adjudicating disputes between parties. As observed in chapter three, his understanding of the techniques of evidence and procedure was not in any doubt. He used his position as Chief Justice of the Federation to set the course of justice straight in the various levels of court. For instance in *Ligali & Anor.* v. *The Queen,*[43] the Chief Justice addressed the important issue of bail and made definite pronouncements on it to the effect that the Federal Court Ordinance subsequently section 35 (1) of the Federal Supreme Court ordinance (1960)[44] conferred the powers to grant bail on the Federal Supreme Court only in a number of special circumstances. The pronouncement was intended to curb the emerging tendency of the lower courts to grant bail in curious circumstances, as was the case in the case under reference. Here, after sentence had been pronounced on the two appellants, the learned trial judge granted bail to the second appellant pending the hearing of his appeal.

Again, in the case of *Guri* v. *Hadeija Native Authority,*[45] the principle of natural justice in the judicial process was better articulated. The issue that was determined was whether the Maliki law as to hiraba (highway robbery) that precluded persons accused thereof from having any opportunity to defend themselves was repugnant to natural justice, equity and good conscience. The Chief Justice believed that the principles of natural justice, equity and good conscience were not properly observed, although the strictness of the rule was to some extent relaxed. The trial did not include the identification of the accused by at least two eye-witnesses, which was an essential condition for conviction under Maliki Law.[46]

In another instance, the Islamic judicial process came under a clinical review of Adetokunbo Ademola. His attitude toward Islamic law will only confirm his conclusion that Islamic law was foreign to the Nigerian Society.[47] Although he was always suspicious of the quality of judgment obtainable under Islamic law largely as a result of the tendency of that legal system to breach the principle of natural justice, he was prepared to recognize its relative importance in certain instances A good example of the attitude to Islamic Law could be found in his judgment in *Kano Native Authority v. Obiora.*[48]

In this case, the two issues determined were;

(i) whether it was contrary to natural justice for an accused not to be given the opportunity of calling witnesses in a Moslem court.[49]

(ii) whether there was any particular method of satisfying the requirements of natural justice in a Moslem court.

In order to present a clear picture of the circumstances of the case, we state the facts of the case. The respondent was convicted by the grade A native court of the Emir of Kano for stealing. His appeal to the Moslem court of appeal in Kano failed, but his appeal to the high court was allowed. The court based its decision on the contention of the respondent that he was not given an opportunity to put forward his case and to call witnesses and that the court had a duty to ask the respondent whether he wished to call any witnesses. There was evidence on the face of the records that by the procedure of the native court which was not the same as that of the regular court that the respondent had many opportunities to put forward his case and to call any witnesses he wished to call. In simple language, the Chief Justice declared that natural justice required that an accused person must be given an opportunity to put forward his defense fully and freely, and to ask the court to hear witnesses whose evidence might help him. Quoting Lord

Justice Tucker in *Russell* v. *Duke of Norfolk & Ors*, Adetokunbo Ademola averred:

> Natural justice must depend on the circumstances of the case, the nature of the inquiry, the rules under which the tribunal is acting, the subject matter that is being dealt with and so forth"

The appeal of the Kano Native Authority against the judgment of the high court was allowed with an *obiter dictum*:

> A procedure is not contrary to natural justice merely because it is foreign to English Law so long as it is clear that substantial justice is done.[50]

Adetokunbo Ademola showed a remarkable commitment of protecting the right of the individual through the strict adherence of the courts to rules, procedure and process of court. In *Alawode & Ors*. v. *Semoh,*[51] the important question of what constituted the commencement of action was determined. Here it was held that the test of the commencement of an action according to the rule of court must be determined by whether the plaintiff had done all that was required of him by law to commence his action. As from when that condition had been met, it remained the domestic duty of the court and its staff.

According to Adetokunbo Ademola:

> In Nigeria an action is commenced by an application for a summons to the Registrar of the appropriate court for a summon and the payment of the prescribed fees. It is the date of such application and payment, and not the date on which the summons is signed by the judge or other officer empowered to sign it, which must be considered in deciding whether or not an action is within time. Once the plaintiff has done all that is by law required of him to commence an action, that action has been commenced.[52]

He further said it certainly would be a matter of grave injustice to a plaintiff who had delivered his application for a writ and had paid the prescribed fees if he was deemed not to have commenced an action, merely because for one reason or the other, the court could not sign the writ for some time.[53] The decision of the federal Supreme Court in this case has been a reference point to the courts and a lot of frustrations were removed from the process of gaining access to the courts. It also curbed the atrocious and sinister activities of some interested parties that might want to frustrate their opponents through the back door.

Although the position of Adetokunbo Ademola on visits by the court to the locus in quo had been discussed earlier, reference to this particular case is intended to examine and discuss the importance attached to a visit to the locus in quo by any court of law thereby emphasizing its relevance to the judicial process in Nigeria. In *Arutu* v. *Queen,*[54] four substantive questions were raised for the Federal Supreme Court to answer.

i Whether a decision based on an irregularly conducted inspection of the locus in quo for a crime could stand",

ii At what time of a trial could an inspection of the locus be made?

iii what irregularities in the inspection of a locus could amount to substantial miscarriage of justice?'

iv. whether a judge's notes of evidence of inspection thus irregularly conducted could be admissible as evidence as the basis of a criminal conviction?[55]

After a careful review of the facts of the case and with due regard to the obita dictum of Lord Denning in *Tameshaw* v. *The Queen*, where it was submitted that,

> Slow as their Lordships are to interfere, yet, if it is shown that something has taken place which tends to divert the due and orderly administration of the law into a new course which may be drawn into an evil precedent in the future, then their Lordships may well think it necessary to advise Her Majesty to allow an appeal.[56]

The Federal Supreme Court answered the four questions of law to guide the lower courts. It was held that

i. where an inspection of a locus in quo takes place, the rules and procedure applicable must be carefully observed, and a decision based on an irregularly conducted inspection cannot stand;
ii. that although an inspection of the locus in quo can be made at any time in the trial; before or after judgment has been reserved in a case, however, where the inspection raises matters which are prejudicial to an accused person, he or his counsel has every right to put questions to witnesses who made statements and demonstrated to the judge at the scene of the crime,
iii. an irregularity which amounted to a denial to an accused of the right to cross examine a witness for the prosecution was grave enough to have amounted to a substantial miscarriage of justice; and
iv. in an irregularly conducted inspection of the locus, the judges' notes of it should not have been regarded as an admissible evidence, much less as basis for the decision.[57]

The position of the Federal Supreme Court in this case easily provoked bitter reactions from the political class especially the sympathizers and leadership of the Action Group who believed that Adetokunbo Ademola was too protective of the interests of Adegoke Adelabu, his motley crowd of followers and the NCNC. It was submitted that the principle of *venire de novo* should have been considered and a fresh trial ordered in view of the severity of the crime.[58]

Alonge v. *Inspector General of Police*[59] provided an opportunity for the Supreme Court under Adetokunbo Ademola to make definite pronouncement on the trite position of the law on who should discharge the onus of proof in a criminal procedure. The central issue raised for determination was whether it was necessary for the prosecution in order to discharge the onus of proof, it needed to call every available piece of evidence. It was also asked whether a magistrate could convict on what was called oath against oath. The fact of the case was that the appellant was convicted on the evidence of one witness supported by certain corroborative facts. An expert witness who had examined the forged document was not called to give evidence. Adetokunbo Ademola held that it was not necessary for the prosecution, in order to discharge the onus of proof lying upon it to call every available evidence. According to him, the commission of a crime by a party must be proved beyond reasonable doubt. "The burden of proving that any person is guilty of a crime rests on the person who asserts it". The Chief Justice declared;

> the burden of proof lies on the prosecution and it never shifts; and if on the whole evidence, the court is left in a state of doubt, the prosecution would have failed to discharge the onus of proof which the law lays on it, and the prisoner is entitled to an acquittal.[60]

This declaration was however qualified when the Chief Justice added that it was not wholly compulsory for the prosecution to call every available piece of evidence to prove its case. It would be enough, if sufficient evidence was called to discharge the onus that the law placed on the prosecution. In conclusion, Adetokunbo Ademola said a Magistrate could convict on oath against oath provided he had sufficient reason to prefer the evidence of the prosecution witness to that of the accused.[61]

The judicial process as hinted earlier consists in the hearing by impartial persons of a complaint by one party to a dispute and of a defense by the other party. This would be followed by a decision that one or the other has the superior claim. In 1959, the Federal Supreme Court was called upon to give a proper and correct direction to the judicial process in Nigeria. The case *Igwe and Ors.* v. *The Queen*[62] showed the level of performance of judges in Nigeria and the parlous understanding of the judicial process by some of the judges of the lower bench. In deed, the period before independence was characterized by procedural mistakes on the part of some Nigerian judges. The Supreme Court had to make definite pronouncements on a number of procedural issues that had the possibility of affecting the quality of justice obtainable at the Nigerian courts. In the case under discussion, the trial judge, owning to the absence of counsel for the prosecution, personally conducted the examination -in- chief of the principal witness for the crown. The Federal Supreme Court was required to determine whether a trial judge could in the absence of the counsel for the prosecution conduct the examination-in-chief of the principal witness for the crown.[63] Adetokunbo Ademola did not believe that such a course of action could vitiate a trial before a Magistrate who could make summary conviction. He however contrasted this to a situation in which case it could not be said that the accused persons were tried in the atmosphere in which it was possible for them to feel that they were tried by a judge whose mind was unbiased by his having assumed the role of prosecutor during the trial.[64]

In another case, the Federal Supreme Court determined whether in a trial, where the charge was amended, the accused should be called upon to elect to be tried summarily on the amended charge.[65] Adetokunbo Ademola, for the education of the lower bench on procedure held that, the accused must be asked, if not the whole proceeding would be a nullity. Similarly in *Queen* v. *Aderogba,*[66] the central issue was whether it was proper for a judge to call as a witness for the crown, a person who was charged along with an accused and discharged after the close of the prosecution's case. Perhaps it is necessary to state the facts of the case in view of its import on our assessment of the judicial performance of Adetokunbo Ademola in the treasonable felony trial. The appellant was on trial with another person who in the course of prosecuting the case was discharged. When the case for the prosecution was closed, the trial judge thought in view of the appellant's statements that, it was necessary to call the person discharged as a witness, and in spite of the objection of the defense had him examined by the counsel for the crown, and cross examined by counsel for the defense and later himself put questions to the witness.[67]

Adetokunbo Ademola was apparently disappointed by the unnecessary efforts of the trial judge to help the prosecution. It was held that the trial judge erred in calling a witness to help the crown and in treating him as a witness for the crown. It was however submitted that there was no substantial miscarriage of justice because the defense counsel was allowed to cross-examine the witness and on the facts of the case, the judge could have arrived at the guilt of the appellant without the evidence of that witness.[68]

As direction to judges in similar situations in the future, Adetokunbo Ademola, averred:

> Where the presiding judge calls a witness, neither the prosecution, nor the defense is entitled to cross-examine him without the leave of the judge which leave should be granted to any side to which the evidence is adverse.[69]

It would seem that the chief Justice was particularly interested in taking advantage of the appellate jurisdiction of the Federal Supreme Court to prepare the judiciary for a more effective role and relevance in independent Nigeria. The Supreme Court became the clearinghouse for the correct directions to the bench. This was made possible by the absence of a federal institution for the retraining of judges. Many of the judges still had to learn the rules of court and master procedures, the violation of which could affect the quality of justice obtainable at the courts.

On the eve of independence, the Federal Supreme Court was given an opportunity to pronounce on an administrative action. In *Irem* v. *Obubra District Council*,[70] the Supreme Court was required to determine whether a council could terminate the appointment of an employee, where there was no power of termination vested in the council by its enabling statute. The facts of the case were that, the plaintiff sued the council for wrongful termination of his appointment because he was retrenched as super-numerary and given notice of termination without the consent and approval of the Minister. His appointment was terminated with the same benefits as on retirement. The Minister later approved the termination. The Law on the matter provided *inter alia*, for retirement at a certain age but a council without the Minister's approval shall dismiss no employee.[71]

Adetokunbo Ademola delivering the opinion of the Court held that the power to enter into a contract of employment implied the power to terminate the appointment and the Council could therefore terminate the plaintiff's employment without having the Minister's approval, there being no regulations on the subject made in pursuance of the law. The Chief Justice however differentiated termination from dismissal. According to him, a dismissal from the service carried such infamy that a termination did not suggest in the least. A terminated officer could still enjoy certain benefits like gratuity.[72]

The eve of political independence was particularly conducive to the strengthening of relationship between the executive and the judiciary. As long as the judiciary saw herself as an inobstructive junior partner in the discharge of government responsibilities to the people, the executive was determined to use the agency of law and the courts to ensure its continued relevance. A major step in this regard was taken in October 1959 when the Federal Government accepted the report of the Committee on the future of the Nigerian Legal Profession headed by Mr. Unsworth. The Committee recommended *inter alia*:

(a) that Nigeria should establish its own system of legal education;
(b) that a faculty of law should be established first at the University College Ibadan and subsequently at any other University to be established in future;
(c) that a law school to be known as the Nigerian Law School should be established at Lagos for practical training and examinations in certain subjects; and
(d) that a council of Legal Education be established.[73]

Pursuant to this acceptance, the Federal Government proceeded to implement some of the recommendations immediately. The Prime Minister, Alhaji Abubakar Tafawa Balewa directed the Federal Chief Justice, Adetokunbo Ademola and the Attorney General of the Federation, T.O. Elias to set up a board to arrange for the establishment of a Law School. The board which was made up of the Chief Justice of Nigeria, the Attorneys - General of the Federation and Regions, Chairman of the Nigerian Bar association met in December 1962 and recommended the setting up of the Nigerian Law School.[74] Statutory effect was given to this recommendation by the enactment of the Legal Education Act, 1962.[75]

The Legal Education Act, 1962 was a testimony of the relationship subsisting between the executive and the judiciary during this period. Despite the fact that the Bill was introduced as an executive Bill, the Prime-Minister showed a remarkable recognition of the primacy of the judiciary in legal education matters by making the Chief Justice Chairman of the Council.[76] Section 1 (2) provides that the Council shall consist of the Chief Justice of the Federation who shall be chairman of the Council. Further more, the composition of the council was essentially made up of legal minds except under subsection 2(1) where the Prime Minister could appoint two persons to the membership of the Council[77] The hold of the Chief Justice on the Council was further strengthened when he was allowed to appoint two persons who had held high judicial office.[78]

The Legal Practitioners Act, 1962 was also passed by parliament to confer on the Supreme Court disciplinary jurisdiction.[79] Enrolment of legal Practitioners in Nigeria was based on three conditions, viz;

(a) he is a citizen of Nigeria;
(b) he produces a qualifying certificate to the registrar; and
(c) he satisfies the Chief Justice that he is of good character.[80]

It would seem that the Chief Justice by virtue of section 3(c)[81] had the right to accept or reject any application for enrolment to practice law in Nigeria. The legislation could not have given the Chief Justice the ultimate power of acceptance or rejection if the relationship between the judiciary and the executive had not been cordial.

The 1960 independence constitution provided for a parliamentary system of government. It emphasized the rule of the legislative houses through a committee of its own members. The executive derived from and was responsible to the legislature. According to Nwabueze,[82] what justified the appellation parliamentary government was the fact that the right to govern flowed through the legislature to the executive. The 1959 General Election was the only popular election that produced members of the parliament as no separate election was conducted for the executive. The only popular mandate for the government was the one conferred by the votes that elected the members of the legislature. Thus, the authority to govern belonged to parliament. For the purpose of convenience, the parliament delegated its authority to some of its members. The 1960 parliamentary system was characterized by four main features, viz; the nominal position of the Governor-General who represented the British Crown and his separation from the leader of government business who was the effective head of government, plurality of the effective executive which was made up of cabinet of ministers headed by the Prime-Minister; the parliamentary character of the executive; and the responsibility of the ministers individually and collectively to the legislature.[83] This arrangement necessarily imparted on the relationship between the executive so composed and constituted on the one hand and the judiciary on the other. To the extent that the 1960 constitution did not expressly provide for the exercise of judicial power by the Nigerian courts, the supremacy of the parliament was ensured.

Essentially, the interrelationship of the executive and the judiciary under the 1960 constitution was guarded and with a lot of caution. The parliamentary system fused governmental power and the constitution failed to separate judicial power from legislative and executive powers. The Chief Justice was also to be appointed by the Governor-General on the advice of the Prime Minister.[84]

The judicial performance of Adetokunbo Ademola in the major cases that came up before him between 1960 and 1963 reflected a judicial behaviour guided by temperament, experience, and association. Trevor Clark strongly believed that Adetokunbo Ademola was wholly suited to become one of the most trusted friends of the Prime Minister. The Chief Justice subsequently became a friend and a confidant of the Prime Minister.[85] It would seem that both the Prime Minister and the Chief Justice had a concurrence of opinions on the nature of Nigeria's peculiar federal structure. Unlike the exponents of legalistic and formalistic federalism of the Whearean School, Adetokunbo Ademola believed that unitary and federal systems were not mutually exclusive.[86] The peculiar origin of the Nigerian federal system from the centre to the federating units made the experiment difficult to understand and operate in reality. It would be remembered that the 1954 constitution, which introduced federalism, took a reverse process. This was noted and recognized by the Committee, which drafted the 1951 constitution. According to the report of the Committee.

> The Federal Governments of the United States of America, Canada and Australia, for instance were built based on separate states surrendering to a federal government some of their powers for the benefit of all. The reverse process on which we are engaged - that of the creation of a federal government by devolution - is a political experiment for which ... there is no precedent to guide us and we are very conscious of the dangers inherent in such an experiment.[87]

Adetokunbo Ademola had consistently argued against regionalization especially of the judiciary, which he feared could be turned into an instrument of mass oppression by the political class. The Chief Justice believed that the period 1960-63 provided opportunity for the re-establishment of strong central power, capable of checking possible abuse of power by the regions. His long career as colonial magistrate and judge, the experience he garnered from the Chief Justiceship of the Western Region where he became a sympathizer of the opposition and most importantly the preference of the central government were enough to compel a maturation of the principle of Federal supremacy in Adetokunbo Ademola. The Federal Supreme Court was established by the constitution order, 1960 and while it existed, occupied a special position in the judicial arrangement under the federal constitution. The Federal Supreme Court was vested with jurisdiction nation wide and it was an institution of the central government. The 1960 constitution provided not only for the appointment of the Chief Justice of the Federation by the Federal Government, but also that the Federal Government would fix and pay the salaries of the court's personnel.[88] The original jurisdiction, powers and procedure of the court were matters exclusively for the central government.

The interrelationship of the executive and the judiciary in establishing the principle of federal supremacy over the federating units became real when parliament passed series of laws known as Emergency Powers Act,[89] 1961 that were passed based on Section 64 (i) of the 1960 constitution. The section gave the Federal parliament the power to make laws

(a) for the peace, order and good government of Nigerian (other than the Federal Territory) or any part there of with respect to any matter included in the legislative lists..."[90]

Specially and for the purposes of precluding regional courts from intervening in actions related to and carried out under the Emergency Powers Act, 1961, the parliament under the authority of section 65 passed the Emergency Powers (Jurisdiction) Act, 1961 which stated *inter alia.*

> The Federal Supreme Court, to the exclusion of any other court in Nigeria, shall during any period of emergency within the meaning of section sixty five of the constitution of the Federation have original jurisdiction with respect to any question as to the validity of the Emergency Powers Act, 1961, of any regulation, order or other instrument having effect,

> or purporting to have effect by virtue of that Act, and of anything done or omitted, or purporting or proposed to be done, or omitted, in pursuance of that Act or any such instrument.[91]

The emergency powers had been described the most potent power possessed by the central legislature that could be used by the Federal Government and to the disadvantage of the federating units. According to Nwabueze, the power vested in the federal government by the Emergency Powers Act of 1961, was wider than its power to preserve the federal character of the constitution.[92] The power to deal with emergency situations and crisis was enough to destroy the basis of federation. The legal aftermath of the 1962 Western Region crisis provided judicial opportunity for the Chief Justice to confirm his preference for a strong central government having leverage over and the right of intervention in the affairs of the regions. The Prime Minister, in exercise of his power under the Emergency powers Act, 1961, appointed Dr. M.A. Majekodunmi as Administrator of the Western Region.[93] This appointment was made after the Prime Minister had declined a suggestion to appoint Adetokunbo Ademola as Administrator.[94] According to Trevor Clark, the Prime Minister declined because he felt that the appointment would compromise the judicial position of Adetokunbo Ademola.[95] The Administrator of the Western Region served a number of restriction orders, including one on Chief Rotimi Williams, which restricted his movements to a distance of three miles from an address in Abeokuta.[96]

The appellant admitted to being a member of the national executive council of the Action Group as well as its Legal Adviser, but he had tried to no avail to arbitrate between the two factions of the party. He further disclosed that he was not at the meeting, which deposed S.L.A. Akintola from his position as leader.[97] Consequently Rotimi Williams commenced an action at the Federal Supreme Court against the Administrator. He sought declarations to the effect that the 1961 Act or at least section 3(1) of that Act which authorized the administrator to restrict him, and the restriction order itself were *ultra vires*, unconstitutional and void. He sought an injunction restraining the Administrator from restricting his movement.[98]

While ruling on the *ex-parte* application for an interim injunction restraining the Administrator from giving effect to the order of restriction pending the determination of the substantive suit by the court, the Federal Supreme Court held that parliament had declared a state of emergency and that, at that stage at any rate, there was nothing to show that the law under which the restriction order was made was invalid or irregular. It stated further that section 26 of the 1960 constitution permitted restraint on movement in the interest of public order provided it was reasonably justifiable in a democratic society.[99] At the substantive suit, the plaintiff argued that such an extensive delegation of power to the Governor-General-in Council under the 1961 Act and by the Governor-General in Council under the various regulations was unconstitutional. It was further submitted that the Nigerian Constitution carefully balanced the powers of the central government and the regions while at the same time preserving individual rights from encroachment by government. The delegation of power under the Act was enough to destroy the whole purpose of the constitution. With respect to the relevant sections of the constitution, which conferred authority on parliament to make laws during emergency, the plaintiff believed that the authority conferred by section 65 was limited by the authority conferred by section 64.[100] The plaintiff concluded his argument by saying that the mere fact that he was Legal Adviser to the Action Group was not enough reason to restrict him and the restriction could not be reasonably justifiable in a democratic society.

The Federal Supreme Court held per Bairamian F.J.

> If parliament can make a law to restrict movement which has effect at all times, it can make one which restricts movement only during periods of emergency for the greater includes the less. The Emergency Powers Act, 1961 was enacted with a view to use in such periods only; parts of it may be valid

> under section 64 and parts of it may be valid under section 65; the grand question is that the part which is relevant to a case in hand should be valid; and it is immaterial under which section of the constitution it is valid.[101]

Ruling on the justifiableness of the restriction, the court said; Apparently the learned Attorney-General left it to be inferred that the mere fact of being legal adviser made it reasonably justifiable to restrict the plaintiff's freedom of movement. Merely from that fact, such an inference could not legitimately be done.[102] The court then declared that the restriction order be set aside, but that the existence or non existence of a state of public emergency was a "matter apparently within the bounds of parliament, and not for this court to decide.[103] This was perhaps seen as another opportunity to re-emphasize the powers of the centre to interfere with the regions through the Emergency Powers Act of 1961.

In *Akintola* v. *Governor of Western Nigeria and Adegbenro,*[104] the Federal Supreme Court showed a thinly disguised preference for the establishment of federal government hold over the affairs of one of the constituent units of the federation, the Western Region. It was obvious even to the casual observer of Nigerian government and politics during this time that the Federal government was particularly interested in the unfolding events in the region especially with the hurried passage of the Emergency Power Act, 1961 by parliament.[105] The case was of constitutional law on the removal of premier from office by the Governor under section 33 (10) of the Constitution of Western Nigeria. The salient issue for determination by the lower court was whether such removal was valid without prior resolution or decision of the House of Assembly to the effect that the Premier no longer enjoyed the support and confidence of the majority. The lower court was also seized with the question of whether the Governor could rely on extraneous materials or information in the exercise of his power to remove the Premier. When the matter came up at the High Court Ibadan on 5th June 1962 and after preliminary arguments from counsel for both sides, the Chief Justice of the region referred two questions for the determination of the Federal Supreme Court under section 108 (2) of the Constitution of the federation. The High Court, Ibadan, believed that the two questions involved substantial question of law. Precisely, the Federal Supreme Court was asked to determine, whether the Governor could validly exercise power to remove the Premier from office without prior decision or resolution on the floor of the House of Assembly showing that the Premier no longer commanded the support of a majority of the House and secondly, whether the Governor could rely on materials or information extraneous to the proceeding of the House in exercising such powers.[106]

By the time the case came up for determination by the court, the Action Group crisis had divided the party into two ideological camps. While the Awolowo faction advocated democratic socialism and strong regional government, the Akintola group that later metamorphosed into the Nigerian National Democratic Party believed that the survival of the Western Region depended on its relationship with the central government.[107] Akintola therefore represented a movement for more cooperative relationship with the central government. The performance of Adetokunbo Ademola in this particular case could therefore be better understood as another attempt to enhance the position of the central government over the Western Region.

The Supreme Court per Ademola CJF, held:

> that section 33(10) of the Constitution of the Western Region was an attempt to write down the constitutional convention of the English constitution, and that in fact, and examination of sections 31-39 of that constitution reveals that they were based on constitutional conventions of the English system of cabinet government whereby the Prime Minister of England depends upon the support of the majority of the House and which conventions provide the example of a Government defeated in the House of Commons on the budget in 1841, but yet the Queen did not remove the Prime Minister when he refused to leave office.[108]

The Chief Justice believed that the constitution of the Western Region contemplated proceedings in the House as being the touchstone whether the Premier commanded the support of a majority of the members or no longer commanded such support.[109] In an apparent answer to the question of law raised, Adetokunbo Ademola said:

> I think that the House of Assembly cannot be relieved of its responsibilities and duties as the House by a letter to the Governor signed by members of the House. It will be an unduly narrow and restrictive interpretation of the powers of the House, and a correspondingly unduly wide interpretation of the powers of the Governor, if in the circumstances, section 33(10) is interpreted in any other way except in a way which make it clear that the evidence emanates from proceedings of the House.[110]

Consequently, the Supreme Court answered the first question in the negative when the Chief Justice averred that the Governor could not validly exercise power to remove the Premier from office under section 33(10) of the constitution of the Western Region except in consequence of proceedings on the floor of the House whether in the shape of a vote of no confidence or a defeat on a major measure or of a series of defeats on measures of some importance showing that the Premier no longer commanded the support of a majority of the members of the House of Assembly.[111]

In the address of the Prime Minister to the Federal Parliament, while seeking the approval of the House to declare a state of emergency in the Western Region, it was obvious that the federal government believed that the purported removal of the Premier by the Governor was unconstitutional and regarded government as having broken down in the region from that time.[112] It would seem that the fiasco in the Western House of Assembly on 25 May 1962 was only the apparent and not the real cause of the federal government's rapid reaction to events in the Western Region. What was probably upper most in the thinking of the central government was how to contain the Action Group dominated

Western Region and establish a strong federal presence. This was not lost on the Federal Supreme Court that became over protective of the interest of the Federal Government.

The dissenting opinion of Lionel Brett F.J. and the decision of the Privy Council on the appeal filed by Alhaji D.S. Adegbenro confirmed that the constitution of the Western Region did not restrict the Governor's power to remove the Premier.[113] The hidden intention of the Federal Government found expression in its attitude to the decision of the Privy Council. Immediately the decision was known, efforts were made to amend the Western Nigeria Constitution. On 3 June 1963, the Prime Minister in the House of Representatives supported an amendment to the Western Nigeria Constitution that forbade the removal of the of the Premier from office by the Governor until the House of Assembly had been afforded an opportunity to express its wishes.[114] This amendment was enacted retroactively to 2 October 1960 to render the purported removal of S.L. Akintola as Premier by the Governor null and void.[115]

The period 1960-62 was auspiciously used by the Federal Government to consolidate the base of its authority and strengthen its hold on power. In spite of vehement and articulate opposition led by the Action Group in the federal parliament, the executive had its way largely as a result of the marriage of political convenience between the NPC and the N C N C; the two parties had entered into an understanding to form the federal executive council on the basis of senior and junior partnership. The sheer majority of the coalition in parliament paved the way for the enactment of a number of enabling legislation, which significantly affected the relationship of the central government with the other centres of powers.

In July 1961, the federal parliament passed the Commissions and Tribunals of Enquiry Act, 1962 which empowered the Prime Minister to use his discretion to issue a commission appointing commissioners to hold a commission of inquiry into any matter or thing within or affecting the welfare of the federal territory.[116] The commission could also inquire into any matter within the legislative competence of the federal government any where within the federation.[117]

It would seem that parliament intended the Commissions of Enquiry Act, 1961 to provide statutory strength to federal government interference in regional affairs. Section 3 (4) of the Act specifically attempted to oust the jurisdiction of the courts in the exercise of the Prime Minister power when it provided inter alia.

> The fact that a commission is issued under this section shall be sufficient proof of the proper exercise by the Prime Minister of his authority to do so; and neither the commission itself nor any action of the Prime Minister in relation thereto shall be enquired into in any court of law.[118]

The Federal Supreme Court had an opportunity to express an opinion on the Commissions and Tribunals of Enquiry Act, 1961 when the High Court of Lagos referred three questions of constitutional interpretation to it viz;[119]

1. Whether or not the Commissions and Tribunals Act, 1961 is within the competence of the legislative powers of the Federal Parliament in so far as the said Act purports to have effect in relation to matters and things within federal competence anywhere within the federation;
2. Whether or not section 3(4) of the said Act is constitutional and valid or contravenes sections 21, 31 and 108 of the constitution of the federation of Nigeria; and
3. Whether or not sections 8 (c), 8(d) 15(a) and 18 1) (b) of the Commissions and Tribunals of Enquiry Act, 1961 (or any of them) are constitutional and valid or contravene section 20 or 21 of the Constitution of the Federation of Nigeria.

Adetokunbo Ademola delivering the opinion of the court stated that, in so far as it applied to the whole federation, it exceeded the power of parliament under the constitution. The Act was declared invalid on the ground that particular provisions exceeded the power of parliament and that these invalid provisions could not be "severed" from the valid provisions or "read down" so as to comply with constitutional requirements.

Section 3(4) of the Act, which ousted the jurisdiction of courts, was also declared void when the chief Justice said;

> We do not think that the wording of the sub section is capable of the construction that it applies only to the discretion of the Prime Minister, and we consider that the subsection is clearly contrary to the provisions of Sections 21, 31 and 108 of the constitution.[120]

Answering the last question, the Federal Supreme Court per Ademola CJF maintained the validity of section 8(c) that conferred on the commission the power to summon any person in Nigeria to attend any meeting of the commissioners to give evidence or produce any document or other thing in his possession. It also provided that the commissioners could examine any person as a witness or require him to produce any document or other thing in his possession, subject to all just exceptions.[121] Contrary wise, sections 8(d), 15(a) and 18 (1) (b) were declared void to the extent that they empowered the commissioners to impose a sentence of fine or imprisonment.[122]

Adetokunbo Ademola's performance in this particular case on the surface might reflect an attempt to protect the regions from the interference of the federal government. More fundamental however, was the need to protect the sanctity of the constitution and to establish the principle of constitutional supremacy over the Acts of parliament. The constitution was accepted as the fundamental law (grundnorm) under which every power (executive, legislative or judicial) was subsumed and against which all inconsistent enactments were void.[123]

The decision of the Federal Supreme Court in this case obviously embarrassed and considerably irked the Prime Minister who had wanted to use the National Bank inquiry to expose the fraud and scandal of the bank and thereby justify some actions he intended to take against the authorities of the Western Region and the Action Group dominated cabinet.[124]

The Prime Minister called a press conference at which he dispassionately absolved the judiciary of any blame because he believed the justices did their duty in the best tradition of the law. He however expressed the regret that the Nigerian constitution was too rigid and therefore not flexible enough to accommodate a resolution of emerging moral issues. The Prime Minister believed that an erratic or ineffective constitution could be amended but meanwhile it must be obeyed. According to Trevor Clark, the Prime Minister had the greatest respect for the person and office of the Chief Justice. Even in his embarrassment, he told Adetokunbo Ademola about his personal feelings when he said;

> Chief Justice, I am glad you gave that judgment, because I want you to feel free. If I commit a crime or do wrong in your opinion say so... If I am brought before you, send me to jail. This is the way I want the judiciary to perform; you will never waver from the truth.[125]

The Federal Supreme Court presided over by Adetokunbo Ademola in *Akwule & Ors* v. *The Queen*[126] would not allow the use of its own judicial opinions as expressed in *Senator Chief T.A. Doherty v Sir. A.T. Balewa* by the appellants to escape from severe punishment.[127] Section 311 of the penal code (Northern Region law) provided for the offence of criminal breach of trust, while section 312 provided a general punishment of seven years and/or fine. Section 315 further provided a term of fourteen years in the case of a banker and some others in far more responsible positions of trust. The appellant was convicted of criminal breach of trust in his capacity as a banker. The sum involved was £100,089.85s 5d. He was also convicted of an offence under section 371 of the Penal Code of falsifying a clearing account relating to other banks in what was known as the impersonal ledger.[128] Akwule also forged a current account ledger. In spite of its belief that ancillary legislation must come either within well-established rules relating to matters incidental to the subject matter of legislation or be incidental to the execution of a specific existing power,[129] the Supreme Court could not over look the moral implications of the case. It was held that since the legislature of Northern Nigeria had power to make laws for the peace, order and good government of the region, there was no suggestion that, in including bankers in section 315 of the penal code, the legislature was using its powers on an offence such as criminal breach of trust as a cloak for encroaching on a matter on the exclusive legislative list. The chief Justice further said:

> We are of the opinion that section 315 of the Penal Code is constitutionally valid in so far as it includes bankers in the category of persons liable to heavier punishments for criminal breach of trust. We are of the view that this is not legislation in respect of banks and banking but merely an incidental provision in penal legislation enacted, for the peace and good government of Northern Nigeria.[130]

The federal executive sponsored the Defamation Bill that was eventually passed by parliament as Defamation Act, 1961 to impose certain qualified restrictions on the individual's freedom of expression in the interest of public safety, defense, health, moral judicial authority and independence.[131] The Supreme Court had an opportunity to give its considered opinion on freedom of expression as a basic human right in the case of *Director of Public Prosecution* v. *Chike Obi.*[132] It would be recalled that the Henry Willinks Commission of 1958 recommended the entrenchment of a Bill of Rights in the independence constitution because,

> their presence defined beliefs widespread among democratic countries and provides a standard to which appeal may be made by those whose rights are infringed... a government determined to abandon democratic courses will find ways of violating them, but they are of great value in preventing a steady deterioration of standards of freedom and the unobtrusive encroachment of a Government on individual rights.[133]

As rightly observed by Akande, the rights guaranteed by the independence constitution could be categorized into personal, political and moral, proprietary, procedural and equality rights.[134] The constitution however, provided for occasions when some of these rights could be derogated in the interest of public order, public safety, national defense, public morality, public health or for the purpose of protecting the rights and interests of other persons. The experiences of other common law countries have shown that the survival and the realization of individual rights ultimately depend on judicial performance.[135] This makes the issue of court jurisdiction very important and crucial in constitutional cases. The Federal Supreme Court under Adetokunbo Ademola behaved as part of the institutional structure of the federal government to the extent that the Chief Justice was even accused of deep involvement in partisan politics.[136] It could not be denied that Adetokunbo Ademola was both a judge and a statesman during this period. His judicial attitude especially on constitutional cases smacked of what Martin Shapiro called political jurisprudence.[137] The Federal Supreme Court probably became an active participant in government and its decisions in some notable instances were based on premises, which were reflective of the social results of such opinions. This judicial attitude of the Federal Supreme Court could be best seen in the "illiberal and restrictive" interpretation of human rights provisions as demonstrated in the *Chike Obi case.*[138]

In *DPP* v. *Chike Obi*, the Supreme Court was called upon to consider whether the provisions of sections 1 and 24 of the Independence Constitution, 1960, regarding the supremacy of the constitution and freedom of expression respectively had invalidated sections 50 and 51 of the Criminal code that were in regard of seditious publication. Chike Obi, a Professor of Mathematics and leader of a political party who under normal circumstances, had good information about government activities, was prosecuted on the charge that in August 1960 he distributed a pamphlet called "The People: Facts that you must know.[139] It was alleged that the publication was seditious because it contained the following:

> Down with the enemies of the people, the exploiters of the weak and oppressors of the poor... The day of those who have enriched themselves at the expense of the poor are numbered. The common man in Nigeria can today no longer be fooled by sweet talk at election time only to be exploited and treated like dirt after the booty of office has been shared among the politicians.

The prosecution submitted that the words used violated sections 50 and 51 of the criminal code which provided punishment for any person who published any material which could subject or which attempted to subject the government to hatred, contempt or disaffection or which could excite the subjects to procure changes otherwise than by lawful means. Defense counsel led by F.R.A. Williams submitted that the law of sedition could not be said to be reasonably justifiable in a democratic society because it contravened section 24 of the 1960 constitution, which provided guarantee for freedom of speech. It was further argued that the two sections could severely restrict the freedom of political expression that was considered vital in any democratic set up.[140]

Adetokunbo Ademola found it hard to agree with the defense and went great length to establish a link between the publication and the probable excitement of the public to violence against government. His expositions on the dictionary and contextual meanings of government, hatred and contempt were such as to create an impression that the words contained in the pamphlets were in fact weightier than what they said.

The Chief Justice admitted that a person had a right to discuss any grievance or criticize, canvass and censure the acts of government and its public policy as long as he kept within the limits of fair criticism. He however left the determination of fair criticism in the hands of his court without making the features of fair criticism unambiguous. This obvious loophole was exploited when he said:

> It is clearly legitimate and constitutional by means of fair argument to criticize the government of the

> day. What is not permitted is to criticize the government in a malignant manner as described above, for such attacks; by their nature tend to affect the public peace.[141]

Adetokunbo Ademola held that where the seditious intention was clear and patent, truth could not be a defense.[142] He believed that sedition was clear and patent in the Obi pamphlet and to that extent its truth could not be considered as defense. Accordingly, it was held that sections 50 and 51 of the criminal code in the Chike Obi case did not invalidate the provision of the constitution relating to fundamental human rights because it was the duty of the "court to decide the real intention of persons charged on the facts of each particular case".[143]

The performance of the Federal Supreme Court in this case was a demonstration of undisguised preparedness to safeguard the interest of the federal government against acidic criticisms of the critical public, the press and articulate opposition. The determination of the "real intentions of persons charged" by the court left ample room for expedientiary considerations without uniformity and generality. This attitude and judicial orientation could be seen in the determination of other constitutional cases since the decision of the Supreme Court were meant to achieve the objectives of enhancing the position of the central government and protecting its total control of power within the Nigerian federation. Constitutional decisions were reduced to preferred moral choices unrelated to and irreconcilable with one another and lacking an underlying and controlling principles. Perhaps this was why Ezejiofor said that the ultimate collapse of the first Republic could be blamed on the "failure of the courts to interpret the constitution fearlessly, impartially and liberally".[144] The grounds and principles of adjudication continued to shift, as cases were determined on the basis of expediency in respect of particular cases.

As in the *Chike Obi* case, the Supreme Court in *The Queen* v. *The Amalgamated Press of (Nigeria) Ltd.& Fatogun*[145] held that sections 1 and 24 of the constitution did not abrogate the law of sedition as contained in sections 50 and 51 of the criminal code. The Chief Justice in a most restrictive interpretation of section 24 said that fundamental human rights provisions "guaranteed nothing but ordered freedom".[146]

As rightly observed by Ezejiofor,[147] the paucity of constitutional cases could be explained largely by the restrictive interpretations of the constitution by the courts. Ogan who believed that the performance of the Supreme Court did not justify the confidence reposed in it as a court of justice made this same point.[148] It would seem that the congruence of outlook between the Prime Minister and Adetokunbo Ademola on the position of the Federal centre *vis a vis* the regions was responsible for the over supportive performance of the Supreme Court in constitutional matters. It may be difficult to agree entirely with the suggestion that judges probably feared that an "active interventionist policy" of interpreting the constitution might provoke a clash between the judiciary and the politicians with the possibility of weakening judicial authority. It could be safely said that the educational background of the majority of Nigeria judges including Adetokunbo Ademola was deficient in constitutional adjudication. As rightly analyzed by Fakayode, the lack lustre performance of judges in constitutional cases was a result of their limited understanding of the principles of constitutional law.[149] The British model of legal education did not contain instructions and training in constitutional law. Many of the first generation Nigerian judges approached constitutional cases with trepidation and generally on the basis of trial and error.[150] The performance of counsel was equally not helpful as many of them received training from the United Kingdom. Those who became involved in constitutional cases had to do a lot of self-training, personal development, and improvement.[151]

More importantly, constitutional cases were scarce during the period under review largely because the constitution did not make certain socio-welfare matters justiciable. Apart from outright political cases, which were brought as violation of fundamental human rights guaranteed by the constitution, litigations could not be entertained on what eventually became known as fundamental objectives and directive principles of state policy under the 1979 constitution. It was indeed the preferred position of the federal government that there would be very few constitutional cases.[152] For instance when the Prime Minister was opening the seminar on the constitutional problems of federalism in Nigeria on August 15 1960, he said *inter alia*:

> The Federal Supreme Court has not yet been called upon to decide any constitutional issues, and this I count another advantage. Nevertheless, during these early years of the federation the Supreme Court has been able to build up a reputation for itself and to get that reputation firmly entrenched. All constitutional arguments tend to become charged with emotions and prejudice especially if they are between two governments, and so the longer they can be avoided the more likely are we, in my opinion, to accept the verdict without question.[153]

The above explains the abhorrence of the Prime Minister for constitutional cases and the need to ensure the continued support of the central government by Federal Supreme Court. The Prime Minister would seem to have preferred a compliant and conservative statesman as Chief Justice of the Federation who would be sympathetic to and supportive of government policy. The rapport between Adetokunbo Ademola and the Prime Minister was such that it would not be too far fetched to believe that the two would be discussing state policies at private and inter personal levels. In the words of Trevor Clark, Adetokunbo was both a trusted friend of the Prime Minister and a confidant.[154] Adetokunbo Ademola obviously gave in to the Prime Minister's overtures of genuine friendship perhaps to spite the leadership of the Action Group. Having secured the understanding of the Chief Justice, the federal executive in parliament successfully passed a number of legislations, which were meant to strengthen and enlarge the jurisdiction of the Federal Supreme Court.[155]

It is important to note that the central government in spite of the appointment of T.O. Elias as Attorney General, paid lip service to the sanctity of the judiciary during this period. Elias was in fact criticizing the decision of the courts on the floor of the House of Representatives when he said;

> But on the issue of consent, we and I think I can speak for the majority of the people in this country, do not accept that the ruling on consent is consistent with established principles of law/[156]

The central government was also in the habit of intimidating the judiciary by amending the law when the court had given judgments against it. For instance, after the judgment in the *Doherty case*, the executive rushed through parliament the National Bank of Nigeria Ltd. (Commissions of Enquiry Recall) Act, 1961[157] in order to save itself more embarrassment. A.M.A Akinloye adequately captured this situation while contributing to debate on Federal Supreme Court. (Habeas Corpus) Bill when he said,

> It does not give anybody credit that it is only when our Government is pulled up by the Court that we run to the House and amend the law... It is unfortunate, if it is only at the last moment when the Minister finds himself in a fix then he will run to this House asking for amendment.[158]

Adetokunbo Ademola was also disturbed by the penchant of the executive to nullify court decisions through the amendment of laws.

> Well, personally I don't like any decision of the court being nullified by the executive. Any judgment of the court must be adhered to, more so when a superior Court overruled the judgment of an inferior court.[159]

By the Nigeria Constitution Second Amendment Act of 1962, the federal executive confirmed its preparedness to use the judicial process in protecting its interest and that of the political party in power. The Act modified the position of the Director of Public Prosecutions by putting him under the administrative control of the Attorney General who was a political appointee of the Prime Minister. The powers conferred on the Director of Public Prosecutions by section ninety-seven of the constitution of the federation was hence forward exercised in accordance with any general or special directions given by the Attorney General of the federation acting in his discretion.

The Act equally restrained the courts from questioning the new powers of the Attorney General when it stated

> But except at the instance of the Attorney General the question whether any such directions have been given, or what the directions were shall not be enquired into by any court.[160]

Between 1 October 1960 and 30 September 1963, the Federal Supreme Court under Adetokunbo Ademola had to tackle constitutional cases with what was believed to be unjustifiable equanimity. The Supreme Court did not recognize a cardinal principle of constitutional adjudication that under unwritten law like the English law, parliament is supreme, but where there is a written constitution like Nigeria, the constitution is supreme. The first generation of Nigerian judges did not readily appreciate this principle mainly because of their background and training in British institutions that were ill equipped to teach constitutional law of written constitutions. The Federal Government became strengthened in its position and was thus prepared to use parliament in its grand design to redefine the nature and scope of the federal structure. The Federal Supreme Court while giving a broadening construction of existing powers attempted to assign to the central government powers explicitly granted to the regions. The court became politically involved when it attempted to restructure the federation through the process of interpretation it adopted in some important constitutional cases.[161]

Notes

1. Nigeria (Constitution) Order-in-Council, 1954. The Federal Supreme Court did not however begin to function until early 1956.
2. B.O. Nwabueze, *The Machinery of Justice in Nigeria p.*180.
3. Laws of the Federation of Nigeria, 1960 .
4. Laws of the Federation of Nigeria, 1962.
5. Emergency Powers (Jurisdiction) Act, 1962, Supplement to Official Gazette Extraordinary No 38 vol. 49 of 29 May 1962 p. A 47.
6. B.O. Nwabueze, *The Machinery of Justice in Nigeria...* p. 181.
7. *Ibid.*
8. Akinola Aguda, "Judicial Administration" *The Quarterly Journal of Administration,* Vol. 5 No. 1 October 1970, p.79.
9. Sections 94, 95 and 96 of the Constitution of the Federation, 1960.
10. Nigeria Constitutional Conference, London and Lagos, 1957 - 1958. Report by the resumed Nigeria Constitutional Conference held in London in September and October 1958 (Cmnd. 569).
11. Obafemi Awolowo, *My March Through Prison...* p. 205.
12. Ibid.
13. *West African Pilot*, "The Judge we want" February 24, 1958.
14. *Ibid.*
15. *Daily Times August* 11, 1956.
16. For details, see J.D. Ojo "The Independence of the Judiciary in Nigeria" Lecture Series Department of Constitutional and Public International Law, University of South Africa, Pretoria South Africa 1995.
17. N.A.I. CSO / 26.
18. *Ibid.*
19. *West African Pilot* "Swearing in of the Chief Justice" April 25, 1958.
20. *West African Pilot* April 25, 1958.
21. West African Pilot May 3 1958.
22. Ibid.
23. Ibid.
24. Ibid.

25. Ibid.
26. Sir Samuel Manuwa was the first indigenous Medical Adviser of the Federation.
27. West African Pilot May 3, 1958.
28. Section 105(1) The Nigeria (Constitution) Order-in-Council, 1960. Supplement to Official Gazette extraordinary No. v. 47 no 61, September 1960 Part B LN. 159 OF 1960.
29. A. B Kasumu, *The Supreme Court of Nigeria...* p.12.
30. Ibid.
31. Molade & Ors v. Molade & Ors. (1958) NSSC.
32. Ibid.
33. *Stephen O Adedeji* v. *Police Service Commission* [1958] NSCC.
34. *Ibid.*
35. The Queen v. *Fadina* (1958) NSCC.
36. Ibid.
37. Ibid.
38. Ibid.
39. Monsour Habib v. *Lagos Executive Development Board Suit* No. FSC/29/1958.
40. Obodo Ors. v. *The Queen* Suit No FSC/93/1958.
41. Ibid.
42. Obodo & Ors. v. *The Queen* (1958) NSCC.
43. Ligali E Anor. v. *The Queen Suit* no FSC 168/1958.
44. Federal Supreme Court Ordinance (1960).
45. Guri v. *Hadeija Native Authority* FSC 158/1958.
46. Ibid.
47. For an elaboration of this view, see *Society Magazine* August 1990 Edition, p. 56.
48. *Kano N.A.* v. *Obiora* Suit No FSC 360/1959.
49. *Ibid.*
50. *Ibid.*
51. Alawode & Ors. v. *Semoh* FSC 177/1958.
52. Ibid.
53. Ibid.
54. Arutu v. *The Queen FSC* 192/1958.
55. Ibid.

56. Quoted by Adetokunbo Ademola while delivering judgment .
57. Arutu v. *The Queen* (1958) NSCC.
58. Obafemi Awolowo, *My March through Prison*...p.209.
59. *Alonge* v. *Inspector General of Police* suit No F.S.C. 222/1959.
60. *Ibid.*
61. *Ibid.*
62. *Igwe &, Ors.* v. *The Queen* Suit No FSC 174/1959.
63. *Ibid.*
64. *Ibid.*
65. *Jones Robert Adeniyi* v. *Inspector General of Police* (1959) NSCC.
66. *Queen* v. *Aderogba* F.S.C. 133/1960.
67. *Ibid.*
68. *Ibid.*
69. *Ibid.*
70. *Irem* v. *Obubra District Council* FSC 239/1959.
71. *Ibid.*
72. *Ibid.*
73. Nigeria Federation Report of the Committee on the Future of the Nigerian Legal Profession (Lagos. Federal Government Printer, 1959), p.11.
74 E. Nwogugu. *A Quarter Century of Legal Education in Nigeria: An Appraisal* (Lagos: Nigeria Institute of Advanced Legal Studies 1985).
75 Legal Education Act, 1962 Supplement to Official Gazette Extraordinary No 12 of vol. 39 December 1962 Part A P. A41.
76. Section 1 (2).
77. Section 1 (2)(c).
78. Section 1 (2)(g).
79. Legal Practitioners Act, 1962 Supplement to Official Gazette Extraordinary No 106, Vol. 49 of 31 December 1962 Part A Section 8.
80. *Ibid.* Section 3.
81. *Ibid* Section 3(c).
82. B.O. Nwabueze, *A Constitutional History of Nigeria* (London: Longman Group Ltd; 1982), p.96.
83. *Ibid.* P.97.
84. 1960 Federal Constitution S.105 (1).

85. Trevor Clark, *A Right Honourable Gentleman: The Life and Times of Alhaji Sir Abubakar Tafawa Balewa* (Zaria: Hudahuda Publishing Company, 1991). p. 363.
86. Adetokunbo Ademola described the 1960 Constitution as a piece of African art characterized by its simplicity and great detail see F.O. Awogu, *Proceedings by and Against the State in Nigeria* (Onitsha: Pacific College Press, 1981), and p.v.
87. Colonial Office, Review of the Constitution of Nigeria dispatch from the Secretary of State for the Colonies, July 1950. Also Nigeria Legislative Council Sessional Paper No. 20 of 1950.
88. The Nigeria (Constitution) Order in Council 1960 Supplement to Official Gazette Extraordinary Nov. September 1960 Part B LN 159 of 1960.
89. Laws of the Federation of Nigeria 1961, Emergency Powers Act, 1961 No.1 Supplement to Official Gazette Extraordinary No 38, vol. 49 LN 54 of 1962.
90. Section 64 Nigeria (constitution) order in Council 1960.
91. Emergency Powers (Jurisdiction) Act, 1962 No 14 Supplement to official Gazette Extraordinary Part A p.47.
92. B.O. Nwabueze, *A Constitutional History*... p. 144.
93. Trevor Clark, *A Right Honourable Gentleman*... p. 550.
94. M.A. Majekodunmi was a non-partisan personal physician and trusted friend of the Prime minister.
95. Trevor Clark, *A Right Honourable Gentleman*...p. 551.
96. *Ibid.* pp. 552-553.
97. *Ibid.*
98. *Williams* v. *Majekodunmi* (1962) All N.L.R. 324.
99. Adetokunbo Ademola C.J.F. concurred to decision of the Federal Supreme Court.
100. (1962) All N.L.R. 413.
101. *Ibid.*
102. *Ibid.*
103. *Ibid.* Per Adetokunbo Ademola C.J.F in *Williams* v. *Majekodunmi* (1962) All N.L.R. 413.
104. *Akintola* v. *Aderemi and Adegbenro* (1962) 1 All N.L.R 442, 452, 457.

105. For details of the situation and circumstances of the case as they existed in the Western Region, Se D.O. Aihe and P.A. Oluyede, *Cases and Materials on Constitutional Law*... pp 2-9 also see, K.W.J Post, and M. Vickers, *Structure and Conflict in Nigeria* (London: Heinemann Books Ltd., 1973).
106. (1962) 1 All N.L.R. 442.
107. B.J. Dudley, "Federalism and Balance, of Political Power in Nigeria", *Journal of Commonwealth Political Studies* v. 1966, pp. 16-29.
108. (1962) 1 All N.L.R 442.
109. *Hon S.L. Akintola* v. *His Excellency, Sir Adesoji Aderemi and Alhaji D.S. Adegbenro* NMLR (1962) 185.
110. (1962) N.M.L.R. P.192.
111. *Ibid.*
112. *Sam Ekpelle, Nigeria Speaks* (Lagos: Longman of Nigeria, 1964), pp. 129-133.
113. *Alhaji D.S. Adegbenro* v. *Chief S.L. Akintola and Sir Adesoji Aderemi [*1963) 3 WLR 63.
114. Sam Ekpelle, *Nigeria Speaks*...pp.165-169.
115. S.G. Davies, Nigeria: 'Some Recent Decisions on the Constitution' *International Law and Comparative Law Quarterly* vol.11 October 1962], pp.919-936 .
116. Laws of the Federation of Nigeria 962 Commissions and Tribunals of Enquiry Act, 1961 No 26 p. A 251 Section 3(1-4).
117. Section 3(1).
118. Section 3(4).
119. *Senator Chief J.A. Doherty* v. *Sir A.T. Balewa* (1961) All N.L.R. 604.
120. *Ibid.*
121. *Ibid.*
122. *Ibid.*
123. For a discussion of the grundnorm from divergent interpretive perspectives see J.M. Elegido, *Jurisprudence* (Ibadan: Spectrum Law Publishing, 1994), pp. 85-94.
124. Trevor Clark, *A Right Honourable Gentleman*...p.941.
125. *Ibid.*
126. (1963) 1 All N.L.R. 194.

127. *Ibid.*
128. *Ibid.*
129. For a critique of the performance of the Federal Supreme Court in this case especially its inconsistency, see Abiola Ojo, "The Role of the Supreme Court in the Resolution of Power Conflict Between the Federal and Regional Governments under the Constitution of the First Republic" *Nigerian Law Journal* vol 5. No. 8 (1974).
130. *Akwule & Ors.* v. *The Queen* (1963) N.N.L.R. 105 per Ademola C.J.F.
131. Laws of the Federation of Nigeria 1962, Defamation Act, 1961 no. 66 p. A425.
132. *Director of Public Prosecution* v. *Chike Obi* (1961) 1 All N.L.R. 188.
133. Report of the Commission to Enquire into the Fears of Minorities and Means of Allaying them (Cmnd. 505 1 HMS.O. 1958).
134. J.O. Akande "Securing Individual Rights and Federalism" in Constitutions and Federalism: Proceedings of the Conference on Constitution and federalism. Held at the University of Lagos, Nigeria 23-25 April 1996 under the auspices of Fredrick Ebert Foundation, Lagos. pp. 89-90.
135. *Ibid.*
136. Obafemi Awolowo, *My March through Prison*...p. 226.
137. K.A. Kasumu, *The Supreme Court of Nigeria*...p. 15.
138. *Ibid.* p. 80.
139. (1961) 1 All N.L.R. 188.
140. *Ibid.*
141. *Ibid.*
142. For details and critical discussion, see D.L. Grove "Sentinels of Justice" .
143. (1961) 1 All N.L.R. 188.
144. G. Ezejiofor, "A Judicial Interpretation of Constitution: The Nigerian Experience during the First Republic in K.A. Kasumu, *The Supreme Court of Nigeria*...p. 67.
145. (1961) 1 All N.L.R. 199.
146. *Ibid.*
147. *Ibid.*
148. G. Ezejiofor,: A Judicial Interpretation ..." p. 80.

149. S.S. Ogan The Supreme Court of Nigeria Ph.D. Dissertation University of Ibadan 1995).
150. Akinola Aguda, *The Challenge of the Nigerian Nation 1960-1985* (Lagos N.I.A. L. S. 1985 p. 37.
151. *Ibid.*
152. Sam Ekpelle, *Nigeria Speaks...* p. 54.
153. *Ibid.*
154. Trevor Clark, *A Right Honourable Gentleman...* p.363.
155. The Legislations included,
    1. Federal Supreme Court (Miscellaneous Provisions) Act, 1961 No 47 .
    2. Administation of Justice (Habeas Corpus) 1961 No 49.
    3. Emergency Powers (Jurisdiction) Act, 1962 No. 14.
    4. The Nigerian Constitution Second Amendment Act, 1962 No.21.
156. Debates of the House of Representatives 20 July 1961.
157. Laws of the Federation of Nigeria National Bank of Nigeria Limited (Commissions of Enquiry Recall) Act, 1961 No. 25.
158. Federal Parliamentary Debates July 20, 1961.
159. Interview with Sir Adetokunbo Ademola 7 October 1986 in Ogan the Supreme Court of Nigeria. pp. 374-379.
160. The Nigeria Constitution Second Amendment Act, 1982 Section 1(1).
161. For details, see Abiola Ojo, The Role of the Supreme Court, *Nigerian Law Journal* vol. 5 No.8 (1974) pp. 77-70.

Chapter 6

The Republican Constitution of 1963 and Judicial Independence

Individual judgment and feeling cannot be wholly shut out of the judicial process. But if they dominate, the judicial process becomes a dangerous sham.

Per Baron Parke in *Egerton* v. *Brownlow* 1853, 4 H.L.C.1

This chapter specifically examines the constitutional changes of 1963 as the most important single factor responsible for the definition and re-conceptualization of the interrelationship of the executive and the judiciary during the era of representative government and parliamentary democracy.

A careful review of the Nigerian political environment especially the zero-sum-game of the First Republic will confirm that the Republican Constitution of 1963 was introduced among other things, to allay the fears of insecurity by the Prime-Minister, bolster the powers of the executive, regulate cabinet/legislature relationship and enhance the leverage of the executive over the judiciary through subtle intimidation. The Prime Minister believed that Nigeria should review her relationship with Britain to reflect the fact of her sovereignty and independence.[1]

This belief could not however be divorced from the decision of the Privy Council in *Adegbenro v. Akintola*[2] and of course the highly controversial build-ups to the case.[3] It would seem that the Prime Minister felt insecure in office based on the provisions of the 1960 Constitution that gave the Governor-General wide discretionary powers to remove the Prime Minister, as it was the case in the Western Region between the Governor and the

Premier.[4] The Government Sessional Paper of 1963 that stated government proposals on the constitutional amendment contained a sentence that reflected the apprehension of the Prime Minister:

> The Prime Minister himself will not be removable from office by the President unless he no longer commands the support of most of the members of the House of Representatives as a result of a vote of no confidence in the government, secured on the floor of the House of Representatives.[5]

The recent experience of the Prime Minister of the courts in the Doherty case[6] and his personal distaste for adversarial arguments based on precedents and procedure aroused in him a need to revise the administration of justice.[7] He believed in and felt safe with a practice that would allow the choice of a wise man of honour rather than a learned man who had impeccable credentials among his professional colleagues.[8] This formed the touchstone of the abolition of the Judicial Service Commission as a body responsible for the appointment and removal of judicial officers.[9] Beyond the argument that the proposed changes were on the grounds of "bringing the Nigerian practice in line with what obtains in the United Kingdom," it could be seen that the appointment of the Chief Justice by the President on the advice of the Prime Minister was meant to be a clear warning to the judiciary to defer to the position of the executive always. Adetokunbo Ademola was right when he said that the abolition of the Judicial Service Commission was enough to encourage judges dance to the tune of any government.[10]

Pursuant to the same objective of enhancing the leverage of the executive over the other arms of government, the abolition of all appeals to the Privy Council and the elevation of the Supreme Court to the Final Court of Appeal on all Nigerian cases[11] within a context of constitutional inferiority smacked of executive tyranny.[12] Section 120 of the constitution provided that "no appeal shall lie to any other body or person from any determination of the Supreme Court." The Supreme Court was also allowed to retain its original jurisdiction in any dispute between the federation and a region and between regions."[13]

Kasumu[14] seems to miss the point when he supports the abolition of the Judicial Service Commission by arguing that the attainment of judicial independence should in the final analysis depend on the quality, courage and integrity of the individual judges regardless of who appoints them. The fact however is that, the abolition of the Judicial Service Commission[15] would preclude the appointment of judges who could be of high intellectual quality, courage and integrity. These qualities, according to Adetokunbo Ademola, could be better discovered and appreciated in any judge by the Judicial Service Commission. Nwabueze was equally right when he described the Commission as an "insurance against the injection of political and tribal considerations into judicial appointments in a pluralized society.[16] The analogy drawn by the executive with the English practice to justify the abolition of the Judicial Service Commission was incorrect since the decisive voice in all English judicial appointments was that of the Lord Chancellor's Department who, according to English traditions, was far removed from partisan politics.[17] This effort will proceed on the premise that the constitutional changes in respect of judicial administration within the context of enhanced executive powers of a more confident Prime Minister affected the institutional safeguards of judicial independence during the period 1963-1966.

The abolition of the Judicial Service Commission according to Adetokunbo Ademola was ill advised and in the words of W.O. Briggs, "the twin brother or preventive detention Act."[18] Adetokunbo Ademola believed that although the machinery of justice worked with many wheels, the judge was the central figure in the scheme of things and it was around him the whole machinery of justice revolved.[19] The judge occupied a unique position as the arbiter of rights and duties not only between citizen and citizen but also between the state and the citizen and in a federal constitution, between the constituent regions.[20] The Chief Justice further contended that however good and however democratic the constitution might appear to be, it had in the last resort, to depend and be greatly influenced by the quality of its judges who would interpret the constitution.[21] "The more detached or impersonal the judge, the more likely will the intention of the framers of the constitution be realized."[22] It was therefore submitted by the Chief Justice that the recruitment of judges should be left in the hands of a non-partisan and professional body that would be able to assess and appreciate the basic qualities of a good judge.[23]

Adetokunbo Ademola gave the followings as the basic qualities of a good judge:

(a) Sound knowledge of the law. The judge must possess a sound logical mind, which would help the assimilation and application of knowledge of the law.
(b) A good judge should be objective in assessing facts. A judge should never allow his own personal feelings or his own preconceived notions to displace facts, which had been proved before him.
(c) Sound common sense. A judge must also be good on facts and his assessment of facts, that is, evaluation of the evidence before him and deductions from facts. Common sense was considered an indispensable factor in the attributes of a good judge.
(d) A judge should be humane. This attribute played an important role in the relation between the judiciary and the public. The human element in the administration of justice had always strengthened the position of the judiciary.
(e) Freedom from fear, prejudice or corruption.[24]

The Chief Justice submitted that modern constitutions provided for the appointment, renewal of appointment, dismissal, general welfare and promotion of judges.[25] In order to ascertain all these attributes, the Judicial Service Commission was the best suited. The abolition of the Commission was therefore seen as an attempt to expose the independence of the judiciary to gross abuse by the political class. As noted by Clark, the Chief Justice could not be convinced why the politicians abolished the Judicial

Service Commission and he continued to plead with the Prime Minister and Premiers to reconsider the decision and reconstitute the Judicial Service Commission.[26] He believed that the Nigerian politicians were never in sympathy generally with any system which excluded their right to determine important state appointments." We cannot therefore but feel that in the years ahead, the appointment of judges by politicians may lead to what we call a packed bench".[27] Time and the political turbulence of the period 1963-1966 did not however allow for the fulfillment of this prophecy.

By September 1964, it was obvious that the executive was not prepared to reconsider its stand on the abolition of the Judicial Service Commission in spite of the general and overwhelming conclusion that it was both deplorable and premature considering the character and features of the Nigerian Federal System. The Supreme Court and its Chief Justice had to readjust to the new reality and this regulated or moderated the relationship with the executive. It is however feared that considering the depth of the inter personal relationship between the Prime Minister and the Chief Justice,[28] the public condemnation of the abolition of the Judicial Service Commission by Adetokunbo Ademola was only a professional duty. It would seem that the Prime Minister would never contemplate any judicial appointment without an input of his friend, the Chief Justice. In view of his recent experience of the role of the courts, the Prime Minister would prefer to deal with the Chief Justice in his private capacity with regard to judicial appointments. The Judicial Service Commission seemed too formal, independent and difficult to manipulate in carrying out the dictates and preferences of the Prime Minister.

One recurrent and perhaps serious defect of both the 1960 and 1963 constitutions was the attempt to practise a West Minster cabinet system in a supposedly federal framework plagued by ethnic, religious, educational and economic disparities.[29] Intra-class conflicts assumed dangerous dimensions when such conflicts were presented and fought deceitfully as inter regional hostilities and rivalries. The actual manifestations of these rivalries undermined the objective base of the artificial federal system because the apparatus of the Nigerian State became structurally suspect. The political class as composed in the major parties and in shifting combinations and alliances could not resolve and arbitrate the differences among them and this led to an escalation of political disturbances in many parts of the country.[30] These were clear indications of the existence of a deep resentment against government.[31]

A major cause of concern for some politicians during the first republic especially the opposition was the existence of an arrangement that gave a particular section of the country the opportunity to dominate Nigerian politics and central government.[32] The Northern Region was much bigger in total land area and in population strength than all other regions including the federal territory of Lagos put together. In the allocation of seats in the House of Representatives, the Northern Region was allocated 174 seats out of the 312 seats. The Eastern Region had 73 while the Western Region and Lagos had 63 and 3 respectively.[33] This imperfection in a federal system that was created through the peculiar process of devolution negated one of the conditions necessary for the practice of a truly federal government.[34] In the words of John Stuart Mills:

> There should not be any one state so much powerful than the rest as to be capable of vying in strength with many of them combined. If there be such a one, and only one, it will insist on being master of the … deliberations; if there be two, they will be irresistible when they agree and whenever they differ, every thing will be decided by a struggle for ascendancy between the rivals.[35]

The fact that the ruling elite in the North was consciously using the North's political weight to decide major issues and to promote private, political as well as economic interests at the expense of their disparate southern counterparts led to mistrust and suspicion.[36] The Prime Minister was more determined in using the central might at his disposal to redefine and rearrange the basis of the federal system; an attempt that was seen as a clever design to entrench the domination of the Northern oligarchy over the federation. It would appear that it was the extent to which the judiciary headed by Adetokunbo Ademola became involved in this design that provoked Ezejiofor's conclusion that the crises which ultimately led to the collapse of the First Republic was the failure of the courts to "interpret the constitution fearlessly, impartially and liberally."[37] The Supreme Court and its leadership became involved in the national question; an involvement which affected public perception of its role as the final arbiter in constitutional matters. As the Chief Justice of Nigeria, a statesman and confidant of the Prime Minister, Adetokunbo Ademola could not but participate in the effort to arrest the drift of the State, as it were, to anarchy.[38]

The 1962 census controversy erupted in the course of the treasonable felony trial of Obafemi Awolowo and others that most people in the Western Region felt was a political vendetta in an attempt to liquidate the Action Group. The initial and unconfirmed figures had shown that the South had more population than the North; a claim the N.P.C. rejected immediately. The Prime Minister cancelled the 1962 exercise because virtually everyone became a "willing liar of the first magnitude."[39] A new board headed by Sir Kofo Abayomi was set up to produce a more credible figure. The 1963 head count preserved the numerical supremacy of the North over the southern regions. The Southern politicians however had a free day contesting the figures and after serious negotiations, the Economic Council adopted the figures in May 1964.[40]

The appeal of Obafemi Awolowo and 17 others came before the Supreme Court with Adetokunbo Ademola presiding and empanelled with Lionel Brett, J.I.C. Taylor, Vahe Bairamian and Louis Mbanefo.[41] The accused persons were charged with three counts of offence, viz: treasonable felony contrary to section 41(b) of the Criminal Code; conspiracy to commit a felony contrary to section 516 of the Criminal Code and conspiracy to effect an unlawful purpose contrary to section 518(6) of the Criminal

Code.[42] There is evidence to believe that Adetokunbo Ademola had a prior knowledge of the case against Obafemi Awolowo and his associates since he had the benefit of a privileged discussion of this with the Prime Minister.[43] According to Trevor Clark, the Prime Minister had shown some of the impounded firearms to Adetokunbo Ademola to convince him that the leadership of the Action Group had indeed, master minded a plan to overthrow the central government through non-constitutional means.[44]

When the appeal in the case eventually came up before the Supreme Court, it was wholly dismissed in respect of Michael Omisade, Gabby Sasore, Samuel Akanbi Onitiri, Sebastian James Umoren, Sunday Ebietoma, Lateef Jakande, Uzodinna Iroegbu Nwaobiala, Samuel Adesanya Otubanju and Chief Obafemi Awolowo.[45] The performance of Adetokunbo Ademola in the treasonable felony trial on appeal at the Supreme Court was not a surprise to Obafemi Awolowo who believed that the Chief Justice was decidedly against him and his party, the Action Group.[46] Awolowo believed that the Chief Justice as far back as October 31, 1962 confided in Adewale Thompson that Awolowo would be arrested on 2 November 1962, charged with treasonable felony, convicted and sentenced.[47] This confirms Trevor Clark's claim that the Chief Justice had discussed the matter with the Prime Minister and that the latter had a strong case against the leadership of the Action Group.[48] It further confirms our submission that Adetokunbo Ademola seemed to have been convinced by the evidence of the Prime Minister and that he was prepared to allow the Supreme Court protect the person and office of the Prime Minister.

Michael Omisade[49] believed that the treasonable felony charges, trial and the dismissal of the appeal wholly by the Supreme Court were a part of a grand design to eliminate any opposition to government in the Federal Parliament. The Action Group provided a robust opposition to the government side in the legislature. Obafemi Awolowo also referred to an instance when Adetokunbo Ademola equated him to a man in a village who thought it was his duty to oppose everything done in the village.[50] Awolowo seemed to believe that the Chief Justice and the Prime Minister were too simple minded to know that in a dynamic society and in politics, there was always something for thinking people to oppose. He accordingly said:

> However, the business of the opposition in a democracy was something totally beyond the ken and comprehension of our Chief Justice. Otherwise, he would not have spoken the way he did. It were better if in future he kept his wits within the confines of the Bench so as to avoid behaving like a fish out of water.[51]

From the foregoing, it could be inferred that the executive and the judiciary believed that the opposition was detrimental to the unity and stability of the Nigerian State and to orderly conduct of government business. The Prime Minister was an apostle of peaceful negotiation. According to his friend Adetokunbo Ademola:

> Sir Abubakar was a peace loving man and he accepted the Prime Ministership of Nigeria with a view of establishing peace, unity and love among the several tribes and peoples of Nigeria.[52]

The Federal Election of 1964, which was characterized by the alliance of strange bedfellows, mutual distrust and boycott created "a lot of tension and upheaval". The President, Dr. Nnamdi Azikiwe was obviously disturbed about the state of the nation in 1964 when he confided in an interviewer on his 60th birthday that "what is happening in Nigeria today does not inspire me to be optimistic that we shall survive as a nation."[53] The Northern Peoples' Congress and the Nigerian National Democratic Party formed the Nigerian National Alliance. The National Council of Nigerian Citizens and the Action Group became the United Peoples Grand Alliance. UPGA lost faith in the ability of the electoral body to organize a free and fair election devoid of persecution and intimidation of political opponents especially in the Northern Region.[54] It therefore decided to boycott the elections. The NNA was sure of electoral victory and therefore went ahead to hold the elections as scheduled. The boycott was effective and total in the Eastern Region and some parts of the Western Region. The Mid Western Region belatedly participated when the Premier, Sir Dennis Osadebay realized that the boycott would improve the chances of the NNA candidates at the polls.[55] The haphazard conduct and participation of the elections raised the question of credibility especially when the Chairman of the Electoral Body had cause to resign his appointment.[56]

On December 30, 1964, elections were held in the Northern Region, in many parts of the West and in some parts of the Mid West. They were completely boycotted in the East.[57] The results that were eventually released showed that the NNA had won 190 seats and the UPGA only 40 seats.[58] Many people called for the cancellation of the elections and urged the President Nnamdi Azikiwe to assume executive powers, nominate a caretaker government under a Prime Minister of his choice and later hold a new and more credible election.[59] Tafawa Balewa, on the other hand, strongly believed that the results of the elections were truly reflective of the political preference of the majority of Nigerians. On 1 January 1965, the President informed the Prime Minister that the elections were "unsatisfactory in view of the violations of freedom of recent weeks."[60] The President believed that the results of the elections could not be relied upon in calling up a new parliament and that he had no intention of appointing Tafawa Balewa or any person to form a government.[61] Azikiwe further said he preferred to resign as President of the Federal Republic of Nigeria than accepting the results of the elections.[62] The Prime Minister responded that he was still the Prime Minister until a new one was appointed within the provisions of the constitution.[63] He believed that the clear majority votes of the NNA gave the President no alternative than to reappoint him. He concluded that, if the President was not prepared to carry out the duty of this office, he should resign.[64]

It was in the thick of this national crisis that Adetokunbo Ademola became involved in finding a workable solution to the impasse. The Prime Minister confided in Adetokunbo Ademola his intention to appoint Sir Kofo Abayomi to succeed Azikiwe as President.[65] Adetokunbo Ademola however disabused his mind and assured him that Nnamdi Azikiwe would not resign.[66] The President had wanted to call in the Armed Forces and the Police in strengthening his bargaining position *vis a vis* the Prime Minister's.[67]

At a joint meeting with Major-General Welby-Everard, Commodore J.R.A. Wey and Mr. Orok Edet, the Inspector General of Police, the President sought to secure the allegiance and loyalty of the forces.[68] It was however at this stage that he called for legal advice as to which office the forces should pledge their loyalty. It would seem that the constitutional interpretation that was provided by Mr. Justice Lionel Brett of the Supreme Court was with the foreknowledge and concurrence of Adetokunbo Ademola.[69] It was submitted that the constitution gave the Federal Parliament sole powers to legislate for the forces. The army and Navy Acts laid down general control to be wielded by the Army Council and the Navy Board. They were both responsible to the Minister of Defence. The operational control of the forces was said to be by the commanders who were under the policy direction of the cabinet. With respect to the maintenance of public safety and order, the directive must come from the Prime Minister.[70]

This legal position emphasized the figurehead position of the President who had no operational control or command over the forces. The position of the law on the matter was conveyed to the President on Sunday 3 January 1965 by Adetokunbo Ademola and Louis Mbanefo and with a six-point proposal on how best to resolve the crisis. The six points as proposed were:

(i) reaffirmation of the federal unity of Nigeria, with equal opportunities and no oppression;

(ii) strict observance of the constitution till it is properly amended;

(iii) a broad-based national government formed on the declared election results to avoid chaos;

(iv) detailed legality of the election to be determined by the courts and the constituency results upheld, except where the small turn-out had made an obvious mockery and common sense required a re-run;

(v) a one-year eleven man commission to be set up within six months, to review the constitution and electoral machinery with a view to a constituent assembly (the President to nominate a member and the Prim Minister and Premiers two each); and

(vi) the Western government to be dissolved to allow a free expression of regional electoral will.[71]

In spite of the uncompromising position of the activists who surrounded him, the President Nnamdi Azikiwe on Monday, 4 January called on Tafawa Balewa to form a government on the basis of the 1964 election results.[72] In his acceptance speech, the Prime Minister said *inter alia*:

> ...The President and I have once again showed [sic] that the things that bind us together are much stronger than those that sometimes divide us... it is my intention to try and form a broadly based (sic) government that will cater for all our peoples.[73]

Between 1963 and 1966, the fragility of the Nigerian federation was quite apparent.[74] The Chief Justice became involved in the resolution of the national crisis. His performance as head of the judiciary could therefore be understood in view of his avowal to use the agency of the courts especially the Supreme Court to ensure the survival of the federation. The political situation and circumstances of the period called for enlightened self-restraint and not judicial activism. As noted by Cardozo, the judge could not help being uninfluenced by prevailing values[75] and in the words of Wright; value choice is the most important function of the Supreme Court, because of constitutional causes.[76] This would be better determined when judges prefer a process of selecting values to one of constructing and articulating principles.[77] Adetokunbo Ademola believed that the problem of the country was how to weld the diverse ethnic groups together and bring about a balance between national unity and regional autonomy.[78] The constitution, which he described as a piece of African art in its detailed simplicity[79] would only succeed if the politicians approached it with care and tolerance and the judges with prudence and restraints. The Bench in Nigeria must always take cognizance of the 'peculiar Nigerian circumstance and situations while considering constitutional issues and allowance must be made for spatial and historical differences.' According to Adetokunbo Ademola while commenting on the Nigerian situation during the first republic:

> Much had been said about the liberal method of interpretation, but one must remember that conditions are different from country to country and whilst therefore judicial interpretations in Nigeria may not necessarily follow those of other countries, it was to be hoped that courts would evolve their own distinct jurisprudence.[80]

The case *Attorney-General Western Nigeria* v. *African Press Limited and Ayo Ojewunmi* provided an opportunity for the Supreme Court presided over by Adetokunbo Ademola to make more definitive pronouncements on sedition. The facts of the case were that the Director of Public Prosecutions, Western Region, initiated in the name of the Attorney General of the Western Region, criminal proceedings against African Press Limited and Ayo Ojewunmi by means of information that he signed personally. The charges that were preferred against them were:[81]

(i) Publishing seditious publication contrary to Section (C) 47(1) of the Criminal Code, Cap 28, Laws of the Western Region of Nigeria, 1959.

(ii) Publication of false news with intent to cause fear and alarm or to disturb public peace contrary to Section 54(1) of the Criminal Code, Cap 28, Laws of the Western Region of Nigeria, 1959.

(iii) Publication of defamatory matters contrary to Section 316 of the Criminal Code, Cap 28, Laws of Western Region of Nigeria, 1959.[82]

Relying on the Republican Constitution of 1963 that placed the Director of Public Prosecutions under the Attorney General, the respondents at the lower court submitted that the crown could not prove that the Attorney General's written consent that was a prerequisite had been obtained before the prosecution was initiated.[83] The lower court thereafter, despite reference to Western Nigeria Legal Notice 293 of 1963 which gave a general consent of the Attorney-General to the Director of Public Prosecutions, the Deputy Director of Public Prosecutions and all grades of State Counsel in the Department of Public Prosecutions to exercise on his behalf and acting under and in accordance with such general and special directions, the powers of the Attorney General[84] acquitted the respondents. At the Supreme Court, Adetokunbo Ademola was concerned with the policy implications of the case and perhaps more importantly by the political climate of the Western Region in particular and the country in general. Relying on the 1962 Second Amendment of the Constitution Act as contained in Section 47(1), (2), (3) and (6) of the Constitution of Western Nigeria,[85] the Chief Justice held that the submission of the respondents that the power to institute proceedings differed from the duty of giving consent and that the latter could only be personal and could not be delegated was a misunderstanding of the constitution.[86] Accordingly, the Chief Justice said:

> The Attorney-General may exercise the power to institute criminal proceedings which the constitution of the Region gives him in any case in which he considers it desirable to do so, and in exercising it, he is not subject to the control of any other person or authority.[87]

With reference to the clause ousting the intervention of any court of law in the proper exercise of the powers of the Attorney General to delegate powers, Adetokunbo Ademola acquiesced that:

> The question whether in instituting these proceedings, the Director of Public Prosecutions was acting

> in accordance with any instructions he may have received from the Attorney General has no bearing on the question whether the proceedings were validly instituted and is not one into which the court can inquire.[88]

It was therefore declared that:

> Generally, there is no need for a Judge to know what instructions the Attorney-General has given to the Director of Public Prosecutions in regard to the conduct of a case and the courts must normally take it for granted that if the Director of Public Prosecutions begins a prosecution under Section 47 of the Criminal Code, he has done so in accordance with instructions given him by the Attorney General..."[89]

Commenting on the case under review, Ijalaye contends that the Supreme Court sat on the fence when it had the opportunity to review the rules of evidence relating to the exclusion of evidence on the ground of state privilege.[90] It would however seem that the Chief Justice was more concerned about the stability of the country at the material time more than any other consideration. Sedition was considered seriously as disruptive of all efforts at healing the wounds of the country. Indeed, the African Press Limited case was the only criminal case that called for a decision of the court on privilege claims of the state under Section 219 of the Evidence Act.[91]

The restrictive interpretation of the constitution by the Supreme Court and the fear that it had compromised its separateness and independence as an arm of government affected the confidence of the people in the court as protector of individual liberty, rights and privileges.[92] As noted by S.S. Ogan, the number of constitutional cases that came up for determination by the Supreme Court reduced in number progressively from 1963 to 1965. He believes that the reduction in number was a clear indication that the public had lot confidence in the ability of the courts to settle constitutional disputes impartially.[93] It could however be argued that the reduction in the number of constitutional cases was the result of a combination of factors. In the first instance, the federal government by 1963 had succeeded in assuming a position of leverage over the regions and had penetrated the Western Region, the hotbed of opposition to its rule.[94] The leader of opposition and his lieutenants in the Regional and Federal Houses of Assembly had been silenced.

The Supreme Court under Adetokunbo Ademola became characterized by being over-protective of the interest of the federal government. His extra judicial activities during this period confirmed that he was very close to the Prime Minister and would not mind using his position as Chief Justice of Nigeria to protect the interest of the government led by his soul mate. The personnel of the court became involved in hotly partisan matters giving political advice to political actors.[95] The political climate was not conducive to constitutional litigations as the business of government was conducted on the basis of political bargaining, compromise, mutual and ethnic mistrust and suspicion.[96] The preferred position of the Prime Minister was to have a little recourse to the courts as possible and this appeared to have been appreciated by Adetokunbo Ademola.[97]

The Western Regional election of October 11, 1965 was a landmark in the history of federalism and political party activities in Nigeria.[98] The various political parties were all interested in the outcome of the elections just as the political stakes were high. The political calculations were that, if the NNDP won, the AG would probably collapse and the NCNC would then be isolated in a federation completely dominated by the Northern Region and its leadership. If the AG defeated the NNDP, all three Southern Regions (East, Midwest and West) would then be under parties opposed to the NPC. By acting together, they might be able to cause sufficient political upheavals to force the federal government conduct a new round of general elections that they might possibly win.[99]

Adetokunbo Ademola's support for the NNDP through the *Egbe Omo Olofin* was well known.[100] The election was characterized by electoral fraud of frightening proportions in order to secure victory for the Nigerian National Democratic Party.[101] Some electoral officers disappeared or refused to accept nomination papers of opposition candidates, thereby declaring NNDP candidates unopposed. Ballot papers were widely found on unauthorized persons on election day and some returning officers refused to declare the result of the polls after their count to enable false returns to be made from the regional capital.[102] The Chairman of the Electoral Commission resigned in protest and declared that he had no confidence in the conduct of the elections.[103]

The Federal Government, for inordinate political interest, became most insensitive to the situation in the Western Region. In spite of public outcry, the NNDP went on air through the federal government-owned radio network to declare its victory in 73 out of the 94 seats.[104] These returns were transmitted to the Governor of the West, Sir Odeleye Fadahunsi who immediately called on S.L. Akintola to form a new government in the Western Region.[105] The rump of the Action Group, led by Alhaji Dauda Adegbenro were arrested and charged for illegal assumption of office.[106] The supporters of the AG felt that the injustice was unbearable and this led to a complete break down of law and order in the region.[107] Many farmers saw the cut in guaranteed price of cocoa from £120 to £65 as an attempt by the Premier S.L. Akintola and the Northern dominated Federal Government to repress them politically and economically.[108]

The Federal Government watched the mounting tension and remained generally indecisive. Some observers however believe that the Federal Government was waiting for the escalation of the crisis to a point that would justify the use of the armed forces as army of occupation in the Western Region.[109] The 15 January 1966 coup pre-empted the execution of an alleged plan by the Federal Government to use the army to pacify the Western Region.[110] In fact, it is believed that 15 January 1966 became the D-Day because Major K.C. Nzeogwu and his collaborators were aware of the intention of the central government to use the army to settle a sectional and political cause in the Western Region.[111]

From an analytical class perspective, the January coup that ended the life of the First Republic was as a result of the zero-sum-game politics, which was compounded by a winner-take-all strategy.[112] The Nigerian political class competed amongst themselves for access to the corridors of power and by extension the acquisition of substantial wealth.[113] The federal state structure was not founded on any enduring principle and so the institutions of state, including the judiciary, were not prepared or equipped to resolve deeply rooted structural conflicts and contradictions.[114]

Adetokunbo Ademola thought that the judiciary under him in its relationship with the executive was independent to the extent that it could not be said that the Supreme Court was under the control of the executive. It is however obvious that the Chief Justice failed or pretended not to see the thinly disguised maneuvers of the Prime Minister to build up the powers of the central government at the expense of the regions and to ensure the protection of the political interest of the NPC by all the institutions of state including the judiciary.

Notes

1. Legislative Council Debates, House of Representatives Debates, 1963.
2. *Alhaji D S Adegbenro v. Chief SL Akintola and Sir Adesoji Aderemi* (1963) 3 WNLR 12, 63.
3. For details of the political undertone of this case, see B J Dudley, '*Instability and Political Order: Politics and Crisis in Nigeria*, (Ibadan: Ibadan University Press, 1973), pp. 1- 86.
4. Constitution of the Western Region of Nigeria, 1960 Section 33 (10) Proviso A.
5. Government Sessional Paper No. 3 of 1963 which contained proposals for the new constitution adopted by the all party constitutional conference held in Lagos, July 1963.
6. *Doherty v. Balewa* (1963) 1 All N.L.R. 604.
7. Trevor Clark, *A Right Honourable Gentleman: The Life and Times of Alhaji Sir Abubakar Tafawa Balewa*. (Zaria: Hadahuda Publishing Company, 1991), p. 595.

8. *Ibid.*
9. Constitution of the Federal Republic of Nigeria, 1963 Section 112 (1) related to judges of the Supreme Court of Nigeria. See also Abiola Ojo, "Constitution and Constitutional Changes since Independence" in J.A. Atanda and A Y Aliyu (eds.), *Proceedings of the National Conference on Nigeria since Independence. Vol.1, Political Development.* (Zaria: The Panel on Nigeria since Independence Project, 1985), pp.348 – 349.
10. *Daily Times* 19 January 1972.
11. Constitution of the Federal Republic of Nigeria, 1963 Section 120.
12. The 1963 Constitution did not provide for judicial review of executive action because judicial power was not expressly granted to the courts. This inadequacy was corrected in the 1979 Constitution.
13. 1963 Federal Constitution, section 120.
14. A.B Kasumu (ed.), *The Supreme Court of Nigeria 1956 – 1979* (Ibadan: Heinemann Educational Books (Nigeria) Ltd.), p.10.
15. Oral Interview: Hon. Justice Adenekan Ademola, Lagos, 14 February 1995.
16. B.O. Nwabueze, *Nigerian Constitutional Law* (London: Butterworths, 1966), p. 290.
17. A.E.W Park, "The Constitutional Changes of 1st October 1963" *Nigeria Law Journal (1964),* p. 97 .
18. W.O Briggs was an Action Group politician representing Degema at the House of Representatives. See House of Representatives Parliamentary Debates Vol. 13, 1963, p. 2953. . Also Trevor Clark, *The Right Honourable Gentleman*...p. 601.
19. Adetokunbo Ademola, "Personnel Problems in the Administration of Justice in Nigeria" *Law and Contemporary Problems. Vol. 5 No.27 Autumn, 1962), pp. 576 – 577.*
20. *Ibid.*
21. *Ibid.*, p. 577.
22. *Ibid.*
23. *Ibid.*
24. *Ibid.*, p. 578.
25. *Ibid.*
26. Trevor Clark, *A Right Honourable Gentleman*..., p. 600.

27. *Ibid.*, p. 643.
28. For details of this relationship, see, Trevor Clark, *A Right Honourable Gentleman....*
29. A Alao, "The Military and National Integration in Nigeria, 1966 – 1979" (M.A. (History Thesis), Obafemi Awolowo University, Ile-Ife, 1987. Chapter 2.
30. B.J. Dudley, *Instability and Political Order...*, p. 78.
31. *Ibid.*
32. *Ibid.*
33. Oyeleye Oyediran, *Nigerian Government and Politics under Military Rule, 1966 – 1979* (London: Macmillan Publishers, 1979).
34. For theoretical expositions on the evolution, nature and character of the federal system in Nigeria, see Adele Jinadu, "Federalism, the Constitutional State and Ethnic Conflict in Nigeria" in Publius*: The Journal of Federation*, vol. 15 Spring 1985, R.A. Olaniyan (ed.) *Federalism in a Changing* World. (Lagos: Office of the Minister of Special Duties, 1988).
35. John Stuart Mills, *Representative Government*. (New York: Everyman Doubleday, 1948), pp. 367 – 368.
36. See Oyeleye Oyediran, *Nigerian Government and Politics....*
37. G. Ejiofor "A Judicial Interpretation of the Constitution: The Nigerian Experience during the First Republic" in A.B. Kasumu (ed.). *The Supreme Court of Nigeria...*p. 67.
38. Oral Interview: Hon. Justice E.O Fakayode, Ibadan 11 March 1996.
39. I.K. Jakande, *The Trial of Obafemi Awolowo*. (London: Secker Warburg, 1966), also R.L. Carter (ed.) *Politics in Africa – 7 Cases*. (Harcourt: Brace and World Inc., 1966.
40. The figures were, North: 29,177,986, East: 12, 288, 646, West: 10,278,o50, Mid west: 2,533,337, and Lagos: 675,352.
41. *The Queen v. Omisade & 17 Ors*. (1964) NMLR. 67.
42. *Ibid.*
43. Trevor Clark, *A Right Honourable Gentleman*...p. 555.
44. *Ibid.*
45. *The Queen v. Omisade & Ors*. (1964), NMLR. 67.
46. Obafemi Awolowo, *Adventure in Power: My march through Prison*. (Ibadan: Macmillan Nigeria Publishers Ltd., 1985), pp. 203-236.

47. Ibid., p. 204.
48. Trevor Clark, *A Right Honourable Gentleman*...p. 555.
49. Oral Interview: Chief Michael Omisade, Lagos 4 August 1994.
50. Obafemi Awolowo, *My March Through Prison*...p. 211.
51. *Ibid.*
52. Trevor Clark, *A Right Honourable Gentleman*...p. viii.
53. *Ibid.*, p. 683.
54. For details, see Olav Stokke, *Integration and Disintegration: The Case of the Nigerian Federation up to June 1967.* (Upsalla: Scandinavian Institute of African Studies, 1970), p. 24.
55. J.D. Ojo, " Constitutional Breakdown in Nigeria" Lecture delivered at the University of South Africa, September 1995.
56. Sir Kofo Abayomi resigned his appointment as the Chief Electoral Commissioner and his membership of the commission.
57. For details, see Olav Stokke, *Integration and Disintegration....*
58. *Ibid.*
59. Trevor Clark, *A Right Honourable Gentleman*...p. 698.
60. *Ibid.*
61. *Ibid.*
62. *Ibid.*
63. *Ibid.*, p. 698.
64. *Ibid.*
65. *Ibid.*
66. *Ibid.*
67. *Ibid.*, p. 699.
68. *Ibid.*, p. 700.
69. *Ibid.*
70. *Ibid.*
71. *Ibid.*, p. 701.
72. *Ibid.*, p. 703.
73. *Ibid.*
74. Oyeleye Oyediran believed that all that happened between 1962 and 1966 were signposts to disaster.
75. Benjamin Cardozo, *The Nature of the Judicial Process* (New Haven: Yale University Press, 1967).

76. Robert H. Borke ' Neutral Principles and some First Amendment Problems" *Indiana Law Journal.* Vol. 47 No I p. 5 (Fall 1971).
77. *Ibid.*
78. Lionel Brett (ed.), Constitutional Problems of Federation in Nigeria. Proceedings of a seminar held at Kings College Lagos 8 – 15 August 1960, p. 134.
79. *Ibid.*, p.v.
80. *Ibid.*
81. *Attorney general Western Nigeria v. African Press Limited and Ayo Ojewumi* (1965) N. M. L. R 159.
82. *Ibid.*
83. *Ibid.*
84. *Ibid.*
85. 1963 Constitution of the western Region, Nigeria section 47, sub-sections 1, 2, 3, and 6.
86. *Ibid.*
87. *Ibid.*
88. *Ibid.*
89. *Ibid.*
90. D.A. Ijalaye " The Impact of the Supreme Court Decisions in the Administration of Criminal Justice " in A.B. Kasumu, *The Supreme Court of Nigeria*...,p. 183.
91. *Ibid.*
92. S.S. Ogan, History of the Supreme Court of Nigeria. Ph.D. (History) University of Ibadan 1989, p. 268.
93. *Ibid.*
94. The NPC in collaboration with the NNDP established a visible presence in the electoral and political fortunes of the Western region during this period. Many politicians found it convenient to cross the carpet over to the party in government. For details, see Douglass A. Anglin, "Brinkmanship in Nigeria: The Federal Election of 1964 – 1965" *International Journal.* Spring 1965.
95. Trevor Clark, *A Right Honourable Gentleman*...pp. 700 – 702.
96. *Ibid.*, pp. 674 – 712.
97. Sam Ekpelle, *Nigeria Speaks* (Lagos: Federal Government Printer, 1966), pp. 54 – 55.
98. Douglas A. Anglin , "Brinkmanship in Nigeria...".

99. Trevor Clark, *A Right Honourable Gentleman....*
100. Obafemi Awolowo, *My March Through Prison*...p. 219.
101. John P. Mackintosh (ed.), *Nigerian Government and Politics* (London: Allen & Unwin, 1966).
102. *Ibid.*
103. Trevor Clark, *A Right Honourable Gentleman*...p.656.
104. Toyin Falola, A. Ajayi, A. Alao and B. Babawale, *The Military Factor in Nigeria, 1966 – 1985* (Lewiston: Edwin Mellen Press, 1994), p. 67.
105. *Ibid.*
106. *Ibid.*
107. Adewale Ademoyega, *Why We Struck* (Lagos: Evans Brothers Nigeria Publishers Ltd., 1981), p. 67.
108. Olutayo Adesina, " A Historical Evaluation of Western Nigerian Government Agricultural Policy 1951 – 1966" M.A. Thesis History Department Obafemi Awolowo University, Ile-Ife, 1989.
109. One of the principal planners of the mutiny, as it turned out to be, believed strongly that the plan to put an end to the disquiet in the Western Region was foremost in the plan of the NPC led central government.
110. For details, see Adewale Ademoyega, *Why We Struck* especially the introduction.
111. *Ibid.*
112. Toyin Falola et al, *The Military Factor*...p. 68.
113. Toyin Falola and Julius Ihonvbere, *The Rise and Fall of Nigeria's Second Republic, 1979-84* (London: Zed Books Ltd., 1987), p. 254.
114. Ibid.

Chapter 7

Limits of Judicial Review of Executive Action under Military Rule

> *The Judiciary owes its present existence to the military regime, which has the power to abolish if it had so wished, the whole constitution and rule the country by Decree.*
>
> Law Notes and Review (1970) No. 6, pp. 30-31.

The military putsch of January 15, 1966[1] led by some ideologically committed middle rank officers of the Nigerian Army[2] was hijacked by the upper echelon of the military on the night of January 17, 1966.[3] By January 18, it was obvious that the rump of the executive was not in any way in control of the affairs of state.[4] The inability of the federal executive council to decide on a successor played into the hands of the Army when Aguiyi Ironsi straightforwardly told Nwafor Orizu that, since the cabinet could not appoint a successor immediately, he. Aguiyi Ironsi, must assume supreme command of the administration of the country[5]. After taking some legal advice from the Attorney- General of the Federation, Dr. T.O. Elias, the Acting Council of Ministers under the leadership of Alhaji Zanna Bukar Dipcharima announced that the rump of the cabinet had come to a "unanimous decision voluntarily to hand over the administration of the country to the Armed Forces and Police of the Republic in view of the present situation in the country[6]. In a swift follow up, the new Supreme Commander of the Federal Military Government made a public pronouncement to accept the invitation and he later decreed the suspension of the offices of President, Prime Minister, Governors and Premiers. The National Parliament and the Regional Houses of Assembly were also dissolved. Each Region would have a Military Governor and regional military governments would be responsible to the Federal Military Government, Regional Governors, Premiers and executive councils were equally suspended. The Chief Justice and all judges would continue to function normally as would all civil servants, the Nigeria Police Force and special constabulary; but all native authority and local government police would be under the control of the Inspector General of Police.[7] The Supreme Commander suspended the constitution of 1963 until another was drawn in accordance with the wishes of the people.[8]

The decision to preserve the judiciary and especially its personnel in view of the rapprochement between the Prime Minister and the Chief Justice could have been as a result of the covert British influence on the new Military Commander. It would be recalled that during this brief period of constitutional, administrative and security uncertainty, Messrs Marsden, George Duckett and Stacey Barham, three high ranking police officers played important roles as a advisers and legal draughts men.[9]

In spite of the preservation of the judiciary, the military administration for all practical purposes did not consider the judiciary as an arm of government, separate from and coordinate with the executive arm. According to Nwabueze, the most significant characteristic of the military government of Nigeria was the "absolute power of the Federal Military Government and the supremacy which that implied".[10] The military government was not created by any constitution and therefore could not be restrained or fettered by any constitution. The nature and circumstance of military rule made the grundnorm of military legal order the Federal Military government itself.[11] Indeed, the continued existence and operation of some sections of the 1963 constitution were as a result of the permission and reluctant allowance of the Federal Military Government. The absence of a constitution establishing the military government and defining its powers in the words of Nwabueze "meant that its powers to make law were not limited by a constitutionally prescribed form of law making".[12]

The Supreme Court had to function within this new dispensation and context. This chapter examines of how the court, a creation of the constitution, managed its relationship with a sovereign body existing beyond and unrestrained by the constitution. By virtue of section 3 (1), (2), (3) of Constitution (Suspension and Modification) Decree No. 1 of 1966, the Federal Military Government could make laws on any subject whatsoever and no court of law had the power to entertain any question as to the validity of a Decree. The saved provisions of the 1963 Constitution were also put in inferior relationship with a decree or an edict when the Federal Military Government said:

> This constitution shall have the force of law throughout Nigeria and if any other law (including the constitution, of a region is in consistent with this constitution, this constitution shall prevail and the other law shall, to the extent of the inconsistency be void. Provided that this constitution shall not prevail over a decree and nothing in this constitution shall render any provision of a decree void to any extent whatsoever.[13]

Apart from the above restrictions on the judicial function of the courts, the Federal Military Government also reviewed the procedure for the appointment of judges to the higher bench.[14] Judicial appointments to the Supreme Court, the Western State Court of Appeal, the Northern States Sharia Court of Appeal and the Court of Resolution and all High Courts in the Federation were to be made by the Supreme Military Council, after Consultation with the Advisory Judicial Committee.[15] Adetokunbo Ademola leading the Supreme Court had the opportunities of three important cases coming before him to react to the status of the judiciary *vis a vis* the superior legislative position of the Supreme Military Council. In all the three cases Adetokunbo Ademola delivered the opinions of the court and not a single dissent was recorded. The unanimity of the decisions was an eloquent testimony of the shared predilections of the Supreme Court Justices including the Chief Justice to military rule, law, order, individual rights, and personal freedoms.

Isaac J.A. Boro and Ors. V. The Republic,[16] a case which was decided on December 5, 1966 gave the Supreme Court the opportunity to describe its understanding of what happened mid- January 1966 as simply, a hand over of power to the military authorities by the former civilian government of Nigeria. The facts of the case were that Isaac Boro in collaboration with others; Samuel Owonaru and Nottingham Dick, between February 20 and March 7, 1966 at Yenagoa in the Port Harcourt Judicial Division and in diverse other places levied war against the State in order to intimidate or overawe the Head of the Federal Military Government. The three young men who were members of the Delta Volunteer Service were convicted of treason on June 21, 1966 in the High Court of Port Harcourt and sentenced to death.[17] On appeal to the Supreme Court, Adetokunbo Ademola showed his abhorrence of violence and unconstitutional means of effecting power change. It would seem that the brutal assassination of his friend, the Prime Minister by the coup plotters of January 15, 1966 was too fresh in his memory to have allowed yet another set of impatient young stars to live after planning and partially executing high treason against the State.[18] Counsel to appellants submitted that references in section 37 of the Criminal Code to the Head of State must be taken to mean reference to the person of the Head of the Federal Military Government and that to prove an offence under the section, it must be established that, the Head of the Federal Military Government was personally intimidated or overawed in the sense that he must be afraid of injury to his person. "Unless the acts complained of are directed against the head of the Federal Military Government personally no offence could be said to have been committed".[19] Replying Adetokunbo Ademola held:

> We do not agree with the submission by counsel for the appellants that there is a difference between intimidating and overawing the state and intimidat-

> ing and overawing the Head of State. We consider the Head of State is the embodiment of the State and in our view; to intimidate the Head of State is the same as intimidating the State.[20]

The unpreparedness of the Supreme Court and Adetokunbo Ademola to take violence, attempted secession, disruption of public order, and youthful irresponsibility lightly, in view of recent developments in Nigeria, could be seen in the concluding statement of the Chief Justice when he said;

> Mr. Amachree has urged upon us the fact that the appellants are very young men whose excesses in this matter were merely due to youthful exuberance and we should give due consideration to the effect of the verdict against them. Much as we agree with counsel about the impetuosities of these young men, we trust that this aspect of the matter will receive due consideration in the proper quarters[21]

The appeal was dismissed, the conviction upheld and the sentence of death was eventually carried out. The decision tacitly accepted the fact of the military as *de facto* government when it said that the events of January 1966 were a straightforward hand over of the reins of government by the civilians to the military.[22] The Supreme Court pretended not to be aware of the July 29 Coup that overthrew the government headed by Major General Aguiyi Ironsi who became Supreme Commander as a result, of the mid January events. The July 29 coup was not a spontaneous reaction by some misguided soldiers, rather it was planned and executed as a grand design to fore-stall Igbo domination of the country.[23]

The extent of constitutional changes and the predisposition of the Head of State should not have been lost by the Supreme Court as to be under the delusion that the administration headed by General Yakubu Gowon was a continuation of the Ironsi regime, and that the former derived its legitimacy from the latter.

The Supreme Court had the next opportunity to review executive actions performed under the cover of a military edict, In *N.K. Adamolekun v. The Council of the University of Ibadan*[24] the Supreme Court capitalized on the conflict between an edict and section 117 of the 1963 Nigeria constitution to review the legislative action of the Military Governor of the Western Region. At the High Court of Justice, Ibadan, Kester, Acting Chief Justice (as he then was) gave judgement against the Council of the University of Ibadan on November 1, 1966. Not satisfied that the case had been justiciably considered, the Council filed a notice of appeal to the Supreme Court against the decision. On 19 May 1967, the Military Governor of Western Nigeria made the Court of Appeal (Commencement of Provisions) Notice 1967 which brought into operation with retroactive effect from April 1, 1967, the provisions of sections 52 and 53 of the Constitution of Western Nigeria, which related to a Court of Appeal within the region. On the same day, 19 May 1967, the Military Governor also made the court of Appeal Edict, 1967, No. 15 of 1967 which by virtue of Section 1 thereof came into force retroactively on 1 April 1967. The Edict contained provisions that spelt out the powers of the new Court of Appeal and Section 35 specifically made transitional provisions in relation to pending appeals from the High Court of the Region to the Supreme Court. Sub section (2) provided *inter alia* that "any notice of appeal given before April 1. 1967 with respect to any proposed appeal (not being a pending appeal) to the Supreme Court from any decision of the High Court shall be deemed for all purposes to have been given with respect to a proposed appeal... to the Court of Appeal". Subsection 4 defined a pending appeal as an appeal which had been entered in the Supreme Court, and so however that "an appeal shall be regarded as having been entered as afore said only where the records there-of have been received" in the Supreme Court and entered on the cause list in accordance with the rules of that court.[25]

Section 117 of the 1963 Nigerian Constitution however provided that such appeals from the High Courts shall lie direct to the Supreme Court. To emphasize the supremacy of the

Federal Military Government over the Regional Governments especially, with regard to Decrees and Edicts, Section 3 (4) of Constitutional (Suspension and Modification) Decree No. 1 of 1966 provided that:

> If any law enacted before 16 January 1966 by the Legislature of a Region of having effect as if so enacted or made after that date by the Military Governor of a region, is inconsistent with any law (i) validly made by Parliament before that date or having effect as if so made, or (ii) made by the Federal Military Government on or after that date, the law made as mentioned in (i) or (ii) above shall prevail and the Regional Law shall to the extent of the inconsistency void.[26]

Section 6 of the Decree ousted judicial intervention when it provided that no question as to the validity of this and of any other Decree or any Edict shall be entertained by any court of law in Nigeria". This Section gave the Federal Government strong leverage over the regions.

After reviewing the submissions of both sides and considering the privileged contributions of Dr. T.O. Elias to the effect that an Edict could not amend the Constitution which section 35 of the Edict contemplated, Adetokunbo Ademola held that it was clear that the legislative powers of the Military Governor of a Region were limited by virtue of Section 3 of Decree No. 1 of 1966. The Supreme Court held that; "If the Military Governor of a Region when making an Edict exceeds those powers, it is void to the extent of the inconsistency"[27]

On using the ouster clause as defense by the learned Attorney General of the Western Region the Chief Justice averred:

> "We feel unable to accept this submission. This submission creates the situation that the Supreme Court cannot decide on the application before it whether an appeal lies to the Court or not and whether or not the Court can entertain the application before it. In effect, the Court is reduced to the position that if an Edict is itself inconsistent with a Decree or with

> the Decree no. 1 of 1966; the court cannot make a pronouncement. This, in our view, will not be giving effect to Section 3 (4) of Decree No. 1 of 1966 and it becomes a dead letter.[28]

It was held that section 6 of Decree No. 1 did not disallow the courts of law in Nigeria from enquiring into the question whether an Edict was void to any extent under section 3(4) of the Decree. The Decree and appropriate section only barred the courts from questioning the validity of the authority of the Head of State and the Military Governors to legislate by Decree or Edict respectively.[29]

As observed by Abiola Ojo, the Supreme Court did not discuss the nature of military regime, as the language of the court was unequivocal and rather simplistic.[30] The choice of words by Adetokunbo Ademola would however seem deliberate in order to avoid making provocative statements on the nature and character of military rule in Nigeria. As a major participant in the events leading to 1966 coup d'etat, Adetokunbo Ademola was disturbed by the circumstances of the coups, the high death toll and the disability introduced into the Nigerian state system. The impact of what he described as the military take over of government was not immediately appreciated in its totality. Adetokunbo Ademola still believed that in a sense, Decree No. 1 of 1966 kept alive the 1963 Nigerian Republican Constitution.[31] One major fall out of the judgement was the admission of the limitless legislative competence of the new military administration. Instructively, the Chief Justice said;

> Reading the Decree as a whole, we are not in doubt that section 6 does not preclude the courts from enquiring into any inconsistency that may *arise, but merely bars the Courts from questioning the validity of the making of a Decree or an Edict on the ground that there is no valid legislative authority to make one*[32] (Emphasis mine)

The Supreme Court then declared its jurisdictional competence to entertain the application before it and directed that the appeal in question should come to the Supreme Court directly, by-passing the newly created Western Region Court of Appeal. The decision of the Chief Justice in this particular case could best be explained and understood as an attempt to protect the private right of the applicant to keep his job and have unfettered access to the courts, against the thinly disguised intention of the government of the Western Region. The creation of the Western Region Court of Appeal by The Court of Appeal (Commencement of Provisions) Notice, 1967 and the Court of Appeal Edict 1967, No. 15 released on May 19, 1967 back dated to take effect from April 1, 1967 was for all practical purposes directed at certain cases including the one under review. Adetokunbo Ademola had a strong aversion to retrospective laws especially when he suspected that they were directed at certain individuals. His beliefs in the generality and neutrality of law were strongly established to the extent that he was prepared to defend individual right against public policy in situations that such actions would not jeopardize public peace and order.

Adetokunbo Ademola believed that by hearing the appeal, the Supreme Court would do justice and better still, would remove the impression from the mind of the appellant, that the government of the Western Region created the Court of Appeal Western Region in order to use the court in frustrating his effort at obtaining justice.[33]

Arguably, the most celebrated case on the inter relationship of the executive and the judiciary in recent times was the *Lakanmi case*.[34] The political situation of the country, the attitude of the court to individual freedom and ownership of property, the puritanistic and messsianistic pretenses of the military regime all played their parts in the case. In order to underscore the role of Adetokunbo Ademola in this case, it would be necessary to give the antecedents that would probably present the background for a better appreciation of the context of unfolding events leading to the case at the Supreme Court.

By Edict No. 5 of 1967 titled The Public Officers and other Persons (Investigation of Assets) Edict 1967, the Military Governor of Western State Brigadier Adeyinka Adebayo ordered an inquiry into the assets of public officers who held public office between October 1, 1960 and January 17, 1966. According to the Governor, this was done as part of the task to clean the public life of the Western State of all forms of corruption before the return of the state to civilian administration.[35]

The five-man Tribunal headed by Justice Olujide Somolu was to inquire whether or not any of the public officers covered by the inquiry or any other persons connected with them corruptly or improperly enriched themselves or any person by virtue of their offices or by any means abused their offices or otherwise in the discharge of their public functions. Other members of the Tribunal were Olatunde Ayoola, a Chartered Accountant, Professor E.A. Tugbiyele, a Political Scientist, S. Ade Masominu, an Estate Manager and Lt. Col T. Oyedele, a Senior Army Officer. The Secretary of the Tribunal was O. Ogunowo, a Senior Assistant Secretary while the Leading Counsel was Adegboyega Odunsi, a Principal State Counsel.[36]

The total number of Officers involved in the exercise was seven hundred and twenty five (725), Seventy five (75) of whom were Ministers; one hundred and eighty six (186) Corporation Chairmen and Directors; Fifty-one (51) members of House of Assembly; One hundred and twenty (120) members of House of Chiefs; two hundred ad forty six (246) Senior Civil Servants, thirty-five (35) Corporation Senior Officials and twelve (12) Customary Courts Legally Qualified Presidents. The Tribunal began public sitting on July 18, 1967 and by the end of the year, investigation into the assets of thirty three (33) public officers had been concluded and recommendation made to the Governor.[37]

Following the recommendation of the Tribunal, the Military Governor, Western State, on December 1, 1967, ordered the confiscation of the properties of five former public officers after it was established that the officers had unjustly enriched themselves during the period they served in the Western State. The affected public Officers were;

(i) Oba, C.D. Akran, former Minister of Finance who improperly enriched himself to the tune of £924,000:
(ii) Emmanuel Lakanmi, former Chairman of the Western Nigeria Housing Corporation who unjustly acquired the sum of £64,000;
(iii) Chief A.B. Bello, former Minister of Trade and Industry who corruptly acquired a total sum of over £20,000
(iv) Chief S.A. Tinubu, a former Minister of State who enriched himself improperly to the tune of over £12,000; and
(v) S.L.A. Fajimi, a former Minister of Home Affairs who enriched himself improperly to the tune of over £4,000.[38]

The seizure of these assets was a fulfillment of the Governor's promise to spend the ill gotten gains recovered from any public officer under probe for the general good of the people. In 1968, the following officers were asked to pay reparations to the state or forfeit their properties.

These included:

(i) Chief J.O. Adigun	£120,368	15s	7d
(ii) Dr. S.D. Onabamiro	£113,743	12s	8d
(iii) Chief A.O. Adeyi	£257,795	1s	9d
(iv) Prince Ademiluyi	£130,329	18s	5d[39]

By December 1968, the Tribunal had 196 days of public sittings during which 481 people testified and 2,230 exhibits were tendered.

Specifically, the following assets of E.O. Lakanmi were seized:

(i) Land and House at NW 5/540 Salvation Army Road, Ibadan;
(ii) Plot 15 Block 7, I.C..C. Mokola Layout registered as No. 57 at page 57 in volume 821 in the Land Registry in Ibadan in the name of Mojoyinola Oke;
(iii) Plot 12 Block 7, I.C.C. Mokola Layout registered as No. 56 in volume 821 in the Land Registry in Ibadan;

(iv) Plot No. 20 Low Density Area, Wura Esan Street, Ikeja, Lagos;
(v) Land and House at Aromire Avenue, Ikeja, Lagos.
(vi) Land and House at 10 Queen Elizabeth Road, Ibadan;
(vii) Land and House at NW 5/255, Ekotedo, Ibadan;
(viii) Land and House at 1 Lakanmi Close, Ibadan;
(ix) Land and House at 2 Lakanmi Close, Ibadan
(x) Land at Osoba Road, Oke Bola, Ibadan, registered as No. 42 at page 42 in volume 356 in the Land Registry in Ibadan;
(xi) Land at Idi-Ape, Ibadan registered as No. 5 at page 5 in volume 683 in the Land Registry in Ibadan.
(xii) The sum of £3,174 12s 6d being balance in bank accounts kept at Barclays Bank, Band Road, Ibadan[40]

E.O. Lakanmi believed that great substantial injustice had been committed against him and therefore applied to the High court for an *Order* of *Certiorari* to remove an order dated August 31, 1967 made by Mr. Justice Somolu in his capacity as the Chairman of the Tribunal of Inquiry into court, for the purpose of being quashed.[41] The order forbade E.O. Lakanmi to dispose of the said property and with his daughter Kikelomo Ola operate their bank accounts. It was further ordered that all rents due on the properties should be paid by the tenants into the Western State sub Treasury at Ikeja or the Treasury at Ibadan. On December 21, 1967, the High Court dismissed the application for an order of *Certiorari* sought by E.O. Lakanmi when it was held that the order was not *ultra vires* and that Edict No. 5 of 1967 was validly made in spite of The Public Officers (Investigation of Assets) Decree, 1966 (No. 51). While the appeal against this judgement was still pending at the Western State Court of Appeal, the Federal Military government promulgated three new decrees [42]

Armed by the new Decrees, the Acting Principal State Counsel filed in the Western State Court of Appeal a notice of preliminary objection to the effect that the court had no jurisdiction to entertain the appeal on the following grounds;

(i) That the proceedings in this appeal relate to a challenge of the validity of an order which had been validated for all purposes under the provisions of Section 1 (2) of the Forfeiture of Assets, etc. (Validation) Decree no. 15 of 1968;

(ii) That the said proceedings have abated as from 28 August 1968 by virtue of section 2 (2) of the aforesaid Decree.[43]

The Western State Court of Appeal ruled on October 22, 1968 that Decree No. 45 of 1968 was valid and that (i) the order, which was the subject matter of the action had been validated by Decree No. 45 of 1968; and (ii) that the Decree had also ousted the jurisdiction of the Court. The substance of the appeal that came before the Supreme Court was therefore whether the Validation of Decree No. 45 of 1968 by the Western State Court of Appeal was correct.[44] The Chief Justice delivered the opinion of the Supreme Court that Decree No. 45 of 1968 was nothing short of legislative judgement, an exercise of judicial power, hence "It is in our view *ultra vires* and invalid". In a bold attempt to declare and assert the independence of the judiciary, the Chief Justice said:

> We are in no doubt that the object of the Federal Military Government when it engaged in this exercise, is to clean up a section of the society, which had engaged itself in corrupt practices- those vampires in the society whose occupation was to enrich themselves at the expense of the country. But if, in this pursuit, the Government, however well meaning, fell into the error of passing legislation which specifically in effect passed judgement and inflicted punishment or in other words eroded the jurisdiction of the courts in a manner that the dignity and freedom of the individual once assured are taken away, the courts must intervene...[45]

Adetokunbo Ademola delivered the judgment of the Court and for reasons we shall examine later, held that the order dated 31 August 1967 made by the Assets Tribunal and which was admitted in evidence as Exhibit 'B' in the proceedings at the High Court, Ibadan must be quashed and so it was. The appeal of E.O. Lakanmi and that of his daughter Kikelomo Ola was allowed and both Edict No. 5 of 1867 and Decree No. 45 of 1968 were declared *ultra vires*, null and void.[46]

The decision of the Supreme Court on this case has continued to generate heated debates amongst jurists, scholars and political commentators. There is however a consensus of opinion that the decision of the Supreme Court, as bold and far reaching as it seemed, was grounded on weak and unconvincing legal premise. According to Aihe, if the doctrine of necessity as propounded by the Supreme Court was anything to go by, nothing stopped the court to uphold the validity of Decree No. 45 of 1968 "as a measure of necessity in a state of emergency.[47] Aihe further contended that the Supreme Court as it did in *Chief S.L. Akintola v. Sir Adesoji Aderemi & Ors.*[48] imported extraneous matters into its consideration.

In a detailed analysis of the Lakanmi case, Popoola believed that the decision of the Supreme Court in the case was both "curious and startling" He said that:

> The Lakanmi case inevitably raised the following questions: (1) does the 1963 constitution contemplate a transfer of government power in the manner suggested by the court? The answer is certainly No; as there was no constitutional provision for such; (b) is the so called transfer of power not in actual fact an inevitable abdication of power by what remained of the Council of Ministers in the circumstances of the so called transfer? The answer in our view is a clear, unhesitating Yes; (c) at the time of the so-called transfer of power was there a validly constituted council of Ministers (in the absence of the Prime Minister) as assumed by the Court? Again the answer is No; (d) is a complete abrogation of the existing constitution

> a prerequisite of a group as suggested by the court? It is certainly not as the new government can permit whatever it so wishes to remain, (e) finally what, if any, is the import of the second coup of 29 July 1966 on the contentions in the judgement of the court? In our view, it had overtaken these contentions, as this second coup cannot be regarded by any stretch of the imagination also as a "transfer of power" [49]

Popoola therefore concluded by saying that not withstanding the so called transfer of power by the Acting President and the so called acceptance by Major General J. T. Aguiyi Ironsi, what happened was a revolution which subverted the grundnorm of the old system in the 1963 Nigerian Constitution and established in its place a new fundamental legal order which by the time of the Lakanmi Case resided in the Federal Military Government.[50]

As rightly submitted by Abiola Ojo, the Supreme Court in that case was too daring laying down sweeping rules and caring less for the probable variations in the circumstances to which they will be applied. The Court seemed to have misconstrued its role under the Constitution that gave it the power of being the apex court in the land. He submitted that any search for a "*grundnorm* in Nigeria away from Decree No. 1 of 1966 is a futile judicial and academic exercise"[51]

In our own consideration, the Lakanmi case marked a departure in the judicial attitude of Adetokunbo Ademola in his relationship with the executive. Despite the fact that the Chief Justice realized the intention of government to sanitize the society and deal harshly with those he described as 'vampires', Adetokunbo Ademola as Chief Justice of the Federation, did not consider it necessary to use the law in this particular case as an agency of social control even in the era of gross abuse of office by the political class and their collaborates in the public service. Perhaps, this was why the *New Nigerian* newspaper said;

> In declaring null and void the Federal Decrees No. 45 of 1968 and the Western State Edict No. 5 1967, the Supreme Court took its stand on a banana skin....

> by nullifying the forfeiture of stolen public money, the court did give the impression that fraud is being encouraged by legal technicalities... The Supreme Court chose a singularly inappropriate and unpopular measure on which to challenge the authority of government. *It* cannot expect sympathy from any quarter on this particular issue. The decision of the Supreme Court in declaring decrees and edicts null and void was one that threatened to undermine the stability of the country.[52]

The only aspect of the decision of the Supreme Court that fits into the attitude of Adetokunbo Ademola, to which reference was made in the Adamolekun case, was the distaste for laws specifically promulgated by the military regime to deal with specified individuals. In considering sections 1 (1-3) and 2(1-2) of Decree No. 45 of 1968, Adetokunbo Ademola believed that they were meant to shut out the Western State Court of Appeal from hearing the appeal of the appellants. According to him,

> "not only are the provisions of the Decree No. 45 of 1968 designed to oust the jurisdiction of the courts generally, but there was a schedule tied to sub sections 1 (1) and 1(2) of the Decree... Part A of the Schedule sets out *inter alia* the names of particular officers whose forfeiture orders however made are validated. The name of the 1st appellant is shown as item No. 4 (a) Part B of the schedule contains the names of officers and other persons affected by the Decree and the names of the appellants appear as item No. 5. It is therefore clear what the Decree (No. 45 of 1968) set out to do and that the object of the legislature was directed to the appellants and their pending appeal.[53]

The decision of the Supreme Court in the *Lakanmi case* has also brought up two important issues. One, the attitude of Adetokunbo Ademola to official corruption and fraud. Secondly the case was yet another instance of possible partisan consideration in judicial decisions. In a number of cases, Adetokunbo

Ademola's interpretation of the letters of the law could not be said to agree with the spirit of the law. In almost all the cases considered, Adetokunbo Ademola allowed certain individuals to escape the long arms of the law by sporting minor technical flaws in the judicial performance of judges who heard such cases at first instance. A good example was the case *Odofin Bello* v. *The State*[54] in which Adetokunbo Ademola's interpretation of the law conflicted with and inflicted wounds on the moral conscience of the society. At the material time, Odofin Bello was the Commissioner of Police and indeed the most Senior Police Officer in Western Nigeria. He was charged with the offence of corruptly enriching himself by receiving the sum of Two Thousand Five Hundred Pounds (£2,500) from Oba C.D. Akran, a patron of the Nigerian National Democratic Party of S.L. Akintola. The payment was intended to be part of a fee for the protection of any offender or intending offender belonging to or supporting the N.N.D.P. from police detection or punishment.[55]In spite of the evidence produced by Chief Adeyi[56] and his remorse, Adetokunbo Ademola preferred to believe that Chief Adeyi was either motivated by "ill will or serving some unworthy purpose of his own". The Chief Justice therefore allowed the appeal on the grounds that it would be wrong for any trial judge to rely on the evidence of a corrupt person to convict someone who was presumed to be innocent.[57]This according to him would amount to doing "something admittedly dangerous" A Senior Police Officer who must not only be clean but be seen to be clean was let off the hook through a restrictive interpretation of the letters of the law. By being a strict constructionist, Adetokunbo Ademola was probably of the persuasion that individual right was more sacred and sancrosant than societal morality.

In the *Lakanmi case*, the fact that as Chairman, Western State Housing Corporation, E.O. Lakanmi corruptly enriched himself and some other persons was not in dispute.[58] What Adetokunbo Ademola was saying in allowing the appeal and quashing the confiscation order was that, the law under which the order was given was wrongly made. The prevailing climate of opinion in the country was in support of accountability on the part of public officers. The judgement was therefore against public opinion and this was perhaps responsible for the little sympathy the Supreme Court had from the public when the Federal Military Government overruled the court.[59]

It would appear that the decision of the Supreme Court in the Lakanmi Case defied theoretical legal postulations, as it was indeed a clear departure from the attitude of the Court to the power and prestige interests of the executive arm of government. This clearly introduces a temptation to discuss the case in relation to the historical and political context of Western Nigeria and even the Nigerian State during this period. The temptation is difficult to ignore in view of the insinuation of partisanship and extra-judicial considerations made against Adetokunbo Ademola. Sociological jurisprudence has shown that the judge is not completely insulated against political happenings in the society and in one way or the other gives vent to these predilections in his judicial performance.

As rightly observed by Cardozo,[60] judges cannot help but be influenced by the traditions and values of the society in which they have been reared. In deciding individual cases, judges chose between different public policies that may flow from a decision and to that extent a choice between specific values becomes inevitable.[61] Experienced judges especially at the appellate level would have formed strong convictions about what specific values are necessary for the development of the society.[62] In practical terms, the statutes, ordinances, decrees and constitutional provisions that judges apply are not always unambiguous as not to be amenable to two or more reasonable, logical and convincing interpretations especially in the hard cases.[63] This line of thought must have prompted Justice Oliver Wendell Holmes submission that; "the felt necessities of the time, the prevalent moral and political theories, intuitions of public policy and even the prejudices"[64]and idiosyncrasies which judges share with their folks, have had a good deal more to do than logical deductions in the determination of the rules by which the society should be governed. The judge's perception of alternatives as well as his selection of such alternatives will be influenced by his values. Judicial decisions especially on matters of high constitutional importance often involve a choice between moral values[65]

After the January and July 1966 *coups d'etat*, the military organization in Nigeria assumed a puritanical attitude and set for itself the task of cleaning the mess created in the first Republic. It was, in pursuit of this, that Edict No. 5 of 1967 titled "The Public Officers and Other Persons (Investigation of Assets) Edict 1967" was promulgated by Brigadier Adeyinka Adebayo as the Military Governor of the Western State.[66] The tribunal of enquiry was appointed as discussed earlier, to inquire into the assets of public officers who held public office between October 1, 1960 and January 17, 1966.

The executive council of the Western State was made up of sympathizers of the Action Group and politically neutral professionals. The Governor himself had thinly disguised loyalty to Chief Obafemi Awolowo leader of the Action Group who was recently released from prison and who not only became the Federal Minister for Finance but also the Deputy Chairman of the Federal Executive Council.[67] Those who were indicted by the Tribunal and whose properties were ordered confiscated were Oba C.D. Akran, E.O. Lakanmi, S.A. Tinubu and S.L.A Fajimi who were all Ministers and Chairman of a Public Corporation under the Premiership of Chief S.L. Akintola in the Western Region between 1962 and January 1966. They were also notable anchormen for the nascent central cultural body for the Yoruba that was master minded and put together by Adetokunbo Ademola. The new body was intended, according to Chief Awolowo, to usurp the role of Egbe Omo-Oduduwa in Yoruba land and in the national politics.[68] Indeed, Adetokunbo Ademola's role in the new organization attracted both positive and negative comments depending on the political leanings of the commentator. While Awolowo described the body as a new political party in disguise, T.O.S. Benson and R.A. Fani-Kayode defended Adetokunbo Ademola's involvement saying;

> .... leading Yoruba citizens like Sir Adetokunbo Ademola are bound to play a noble role in the establishment of a central cultural body for the Yorubas. And we consider it devilish for anybody to misconstrue the role of the Chief Justice"[69]

It would seem that while the Action Group sympathizers in the Western State Government in collaboration with the Federal Military Government which promulgated Decree No. 45 (while the appeal was still pending), were dismantling and destroying the legacy of the NNDP government and leadership in the Western State, the Supreme Court under Adetokunbo Ademola was waiting for the opportunity to protect private interests of the political orphans of S.L. Akintola. The Lakanmi case for what it was should be regarded as a singularly inappropriate instance of protecting private property rights because the decision of the Supreme Court was as controversial as it was unpopular.[70]

The decision of the Supreme Court in the Lakanmi case brought sharp reaction from government. It promulgated the Federal Military Government (Supremacy and Enforcement of Powers) Decree No. 28 of 1970. The singular implication of the Decree was that it almost abrogated judicial review of executive and legislative actions of the military government. It stated that the coups of January and July 1966 were revolutions and that both revolutions abrogated the entirety of the existing legal order in Nigeria except what Decree No. 1 of 1966 saved of the 1963 Nigerian constitution. The Federal Military Government permitted certain provisions of the 1963 Nigeria Republican Constitution to remain in operation as supplementary to Decree No. 1 of 1966. Decree No. 28 of 1970 restated section 6 of Decree No. 1 of 1966 that prohibited the courts from entertaining any question as to the validity of any Decree or any Edict.[71] Decree No. 28 of 1970 further provided:

> With a view of assuring the effective maintenance of the territorial integrity of Nigeria and the peace, order and good government of the Federation, any decision, whether made before or after the com-

> mencement of this decree, by any court of law in the exercise or purported exercise of any powers under the constitution or any enactment or law of the Federation or of any state which has purported to declare or shall here after purport to declare the invalidity of any Decree or of any Edict (in so far as the provisions of the Edict are not inconsistent with the provisions of a Decree) or the incompetence of any of the governments in the Federation to the make same is or shall be null and void and of no effect whatsoever as from the date of the making thereof.[72]

The kernel of this provision was that the Federal Military Government not only barred the courts from determining the validity of a Decree or Edict but also of any instrument made under them. Kayode Eso captured the essence of the Supreme Court decision in the Lakanmi case when he said:

> The Judgment in Lakanmi's case must have been the grandest day for the judiciary to whom by that judgement, even the guns were sublimated to the interpretive jurisdiction of the court....[73]

He however quickly assessed the implications of the promulgation of the Decree No. 28 of 1970 and commented;

> The position had been reversed; and the reverse was made absolute. The Grundnorm, if any, would not be shared by the Executive with or abdicated to the judiciary. The Military Government would have none of this... It was a Military devastated blow to the judiciary from the jurisprudential point of view. The courts reverted to their literal and sometimes dull interpretive role.[74]

Adetokunbo Ademola and the other Supreme Court justices felt irked and provoked by what they preferred to consider as ill advised over reaction of the military Government to a court decision. In all stable societies, a judicial decision normally disposed of the dispute between the parties. A renunciation by the Executive, of a particular decision outside the judicial system is often considered a violation of the doctrine of separation of powers.

In spite of a threat to resign from the apex bench in the country, the Chief Justice and some other justices continued to hold office, but with a lot of circumspection and caution. The decision of Adetokunbo Ademola to continue in office was not unrelated to the fact that by 1970, he was on the eve of retirement from the bench having served the country for an unbroken period of thirty-one years. He was due to retire in 1971 when he would have attained the age of sixty-five years.

The implications of the Lakanmi case for judicial administration in Nigeria could be seen in the reversion of the Supreme Court to judicial self-restraint. Adetokunbo Ademola realized that under a military dispensation, judicial review as a method of resolving disputes over constitutional boundaries had only moral appeal. In the period immediately after the civil war; the era of post war conciliation, rehabilitation and reconstruction, the nature, character, command, and authority structure of the military could not tolerate detraction from its power and authority through any legal niceties like judicial review of executive actions. The state officials of the law treated the courts not as a separate and coordinate arm of government, but as a traditional and conservative agency for social control. Perhaps this was responsible for the elaborate use of tribunals of enquiry, probe panels and other extra judicial *ad hoc* bodies during military regimes.

Probably the realization by the Chief Justice that the military was using the extra judicial bodies to side track the regular courts led to his new attitude of emphasizing the principle of natural justice while reviewing the conduct of these tribunals and Commissions. For instance in the case of *Dr. Denloye*, v. *Medical and Dental Practitioners Disciplinary Tribunal,*[75] Adetokunbo Ademola, delivering the judgement of the Supreme Court, said that, it was a fundamental rule of natural justice that a man charged before any tribunal should know the nature and full details of allegations and charges preferred against him prior to the trial. He should be allowed to have adequate knowledge of the case before hand having been supplied with the facts and evidence available to the panel and tribunal.[76] The Chief Justice submitted that it would amount to a breach of the rules of natural justice to deny him all the necessary facts and evidence. Dr. Denloye was alleged to be issuing sick certificates on various dates to three different persons after they had paid him and without carrying out any medical investigation on them. He was not allowed to give evidence before the panel that took evidence from Tai Solarin and others. It was only at the tribunal that the accused person and his counsel became aware of the nature of evidence against him. In spite of the plea of his counsel, the Tribunal refused the production of evidence given before the panel because the evidence was said to be confidential. Witnesses were not recalled for cross-examination.

The gross inadequacies of the procedures adopted by the panel as well as the tribunal forced Adetokunbo Ademola to aver;

> While it is not in dispute that any tribunal of this nature is entitled to decide its own procedure and lay down its own rules for the conduct of the inquiries regarding disciplines, it is of utmost importance that the enquiry be conducted in accordance with the principles of natural justice.[77]

The appeal was allowed; the decision of the Tribunal to strike out the name of the appellant from the Medical Register was quashed and set aside. For Adetokunbo Ademola, the limit of judicial review was reached in the Adejumo case[78] when the Chief Justice impliedly admitted that the decision of the Supreme Court in the Lakanmi case was wrong. The appellant, Chief Adebiyi Adejumo, by an *order of Certiorari,* challenged the competence of an order made by the Military Governor of Lagos State for the forfeiture of the assets of his son, Adenrele Adejumo. He also wanted to obtain a declaration of the court that the Order was invalid. Relying on Section 1 (2) (b) of Decree 28 of 1979, the State argued that the court had no jurisdiction to entertain the case. In spite of the argument of counsel to appellant that the particular order of the Military Governor could not be sustained Adetokunbo Ademola held;

> The first part of the Decree no. 28 of 1970 established and otherwise confirms the already existing ouster of the jurisdiction of courts of law in respect of a Decree.[79]

As succinctly explained by Ojo, the admission by the Supreme Court that there was in existence an ouster of jurisdiction of the court before the promulgation of Decree No. 28 of 1970 was notable, far reaching and a reversal of its earlier position on the constitutional supremacy of the Federal Military Government as expressed in the decision of the court in the Lakanmi case.[80] To confirm the lame duck position of the Supreme Court in relation to the Military Government, Adetokunbo Ademola Chief Justice said:

> With respect to the second part of Decree No. 8 of 1970, even if it be arguable and indeed argued that, that part assumed the possibility of a court assuming jurisdiction with respect to one or the other of the matter envisaged on the ground of manifest excess or incompetence or other type of invalidity (and we make no pronouncement on this point), that part declares (and this is the word used and presumably deliberately so used) and such pronouncement in exercise of such assumed jurisdiction and having the tendencies therein described to be null and void.[81]

In order not to infringe on the power and prestige claims of the Federal Military Government, the Supreme Court under Adetokunbo Ademola preferred judicial abdication of its functions as the apex court in cases involving judicial review of actions taken and orders given under a Decree. Military rule compelled supremacy to shift from the constitution to the lawmaker, that is, the Supreme Military Council.

In the aftermath of the Lakanmi case, the Supreme Court became neutralistic thereby making its relationship with the executive difficult to understand and explain. For Adetokunbo

Ademola, it was only a question of time to leave judicial service. The Federal Military Government was not prepared to relax its hold on the machinery of government in Nigeria. A successor could not be immediately found, as all the Supreme Court Justices below Adetokunbo Ademola were considered fiercely loyal to their Chief Justice and shared the same judicial outlook with him. The fear was that the Supreme Court did not reflect the new direction in the country just as it could not adequately appreciate the national interest of the country as defined and conceptualized by the military government. While it was still shopping for a capable successor to Adetokunbo Ademola as Chief Justice, the Federal Military Government promulgated the Chief Justice of Nigeria (Extension of Period of Office) Decree 1971 (Otherwise known as Decree No. 2 of 1971). The Decree provided that, "Not withstanding section 113 (1) of the constitution as amended, any person holding the office of Chief Justice of Nigeria on 30th January 1971 shall continue to hold that office until his successor has been appointed and has entered on the duties of the office."[82]

Probably as a mark of recognition of the diligent and sustained judicial service of Adetokunbo Ademola on the bench in Nigeria, The Legal Practitioners (Amendment) Decree 1971 was promulgated. Importantly, Decree No. 54 of 1971 slightly amended the Legal Practitioners Act of 1962 by inserting some new sections. The first new section created a body of Legal Practitioners of the highest distinction in the legal profession in Nigeria to be known as "the Body of Benchers". The body was to be responsible for the formal call to the Bar of persons seeking to become legal practitioners in Nigeria. It was to be made up of:

(a) The Chief Justice of Nigeria
(b) The Attorney General of the Federation
(c) The Chairman of the Council of Legal Education
(d) The Chief Justices of all the States of the Federation
(e) The Attorneys-General of all the States of the Federation
(f) The President of the Nigerian Bar Association and

(g) 2 members of the Nigerian Bar Association of not less than 15 years post call standing who shall be nominated by the Association.[ce]

Although the Decree provided that a Bencher shall vacate his office as a Bencher if he ceased to be the holder of any office by virtue of which he was appointed a Bencher, subsection 3 provided further than the Chief Justice of Nigeria shall hold office as such a Bencher for life.[84] And so it was for Adetokunbo Ademola who retired as the Chief Justice of Nigeria on 1972 and was succeeded by Dr. T.O. Elias the Attorney General of the Federation and renown academic.[85]

Notes

1. Literature on the civil war include but not limited to the following works: Wale Ademoyega , *Why We Struck* (Ibadan: Evans Brothers, 1981), N.U.Akpan, *The Struggle for Secession 1966-1990: A Personal Account of The Nigerian Civil War*, (London, Frank Cass, 1977), O. Balogun , *The Tragic Years: Nigeria in Crisis 1960-1970*, (Benin City: Ethiope, 1973) Z.A.Carvenka, *A History of The Nigerian Civil War, 1967-1979*, (Ibadan: Onibonoje Press, 1972), F. Forsyth, *The Biafran Story*, (London: Cox And Wimann Ltd.., 1969), Joe Garba, *Revolution In Nigeria Another View*, (London: African Books Ltd., 1982), R. Niven, *The War for Nigerian Unity,* (London: Evans Publishers, 1980), Arthur Nwankwo, & S. Ifejika, *The Making of a Nation: Biafra* (London: Hurst & Co., 1969) and John De St Jorre, *The Nigerian Civil War*, (London: Hodder & Stoughton,1972).
2. For a discussion of the ideological persuasion of the major coup plotters, see Oyeweso (ed.), *Perspectives on the Nigerian Civil War* (Lagos: Campus Press Limited, 1992) pp. 19-33.
3. Wale Ademoyega, *Why We Struck* (Ibadan: Evans Educational Publishers, 1978, p. 15.
4. Trevor Clark, *The Right Honourable Gentlemen...*p. 800.
5. *Ibid.*
6. Government Notice No. 147 of 26 January 1966.
7. Government Notice No. 148 of 26, January 1966.

8. *Ibid.*
9. Trevor Clark, *The Right Honourable...* p. 801.
10. B.O. Nwabueze, *A Constitutional History of Nigeria* (Lagos: Longman Group Limited, 1982), p. 206.
11. *Ibid.*
12. *Ibid.*
13. Constitution (Suspension and Modification) Decree No. 1, 1966 Schedule 2 section 1.
14. Schedule 2 section 12. Section 11 (1) (a-d) specified the composition of the Advisory Judicial Committee, which included, The Chief Justice of Nigeria as Chairman, the Chief Justices of Northern Nigeria, Eastern Nigeria, Western Nigeria, Mid Western Nigeria and the Chief Justice of Lagos. It also included the Grand Khadi of the Sharia court of Appeal and the Attorney General of the Federation. The solicitor General was to act as the Secretary for the Advisory Judicial Committee.
15. Constitution (Amendment) Decree No. 5 of 1972 amended this provision to the effect that the Chief Justice of the Federation was to be appointed and could be dismissed by the Head of State alone.
16. (1967) N.M.L.R 12, p. 163.
17. *Ibid.*, pp. 164-165.
18. Being a conservative elder statesman and judge reared in the English tradition of parliamentary supremacy, Adetokunbo Ademola was abhorrent of any action that could disrupt the fragile stability of the Nigerian State especially after the recent political and military upheavals.
19. *Boro Isaac J.A. & Ors. v. The Republic* (1967) M.N.L.R p. 163.
20. *Ibid.*, p. 167.
21. *Ibid.*
22. *Ibid.*, p. 166.
23. For details, see D.J. Muffett, *Let Truth be Told: The Coups D 'etat of 1966* (Zaria: Hudahuda Publishing House, 1982).
24. (1968) N.M.L.R p. 253.
25. W.N.L.N. No. 19 of 1967.
26. Section 3 (4) of Decree No. 1 of 1966.
27. *N.K. Adamolekun v. The Council of the University of Ibadan* (1968) N.M.L.R., p. 260.

28. *Ibid.*
29. *Ibid.*
30. Abiola Ojo, "Public Law, the Military Government and the Supreme Court" in A.B. Kasumu (Ed.), *The Supreme Court of Nigeria 1956-1970* (Ibadan: Heinemann Educational Books Ltd), p. 96.
31. (1968) N.M.L.R., p. 259.
32. *Ibid.*, p. 260.
33. An edict could in fact not modify a decree or the provisions of the Constitution. The Constitution allowed a right of appeal up to the Supreme Court.
34. *Lakanmi E O and Kikelomo Ola. v. Attorney General Western State & Ors.* (1971) 1 U.I. L.R. 201.
35. Supplement to Western Nigeria Gazette Extra-ordinary No. 17 vol. 16, of 14 April 1967.
36. Ibid.
37. Western State Information Service, "Somolu Assets Investigation Tribunal (Ibadan: Government Printer, 1967), p. 54.
38. Ibid.
39. "Somolu Assets Investigation Tribunal".... p. 55.
40. Contained in the Order published as Supplement to the Western State of Nigeria Gazette Extra Ordinary December 1, 1967 as «The Public Officers and other Persons (Forfeiture of Assets) Order, 1867, Schedule first column.
41. Lakanmi Case of High Court Ibadan Suit No. M/45/67 Unreported.
42. (1) No. 37 of 1968: The Investigation of Assets Public Officers and other Persons (Amendment) Decree 1968.

    (2) No. 43 of 1968. The Investigation of Assets (Public Officers, and other Personnel) (Amendment Decree 1968).

    (3) No. 45 of 1968 The Forfeiture of Assets etc. (Validation).
43. (1971) U. I. L. R. p. 201.
44. Ibid.
45. Ibid.
46. Ibid.
47. D.O. Aihe and P.A. Oluyede, *Cases and Materials on Constitutional Law in Nigeria*.... p. 65.

48. (1962) W.N. L.R. 185.
49. Ademola Popoola, "Some Aspects of Constitutional Adjudication in Nigeria" Ph.D. (Law) Obafemi Awolowo University, Ile-Ife, 1994 pp. 671-672.
50. Ibid.
51. Abiola Ojo, "The search for a Grundnorm in Nigeria" *J.C.L.* p. 239.
52. *New Nigerian* 12 May 1970.
53. (1971) U.I.L.R. p. 201.
54. *Odofin Bello* v. *The State* (1967) N.M.L.R. 1.
55. Chief Adeyi was the Treasurer of the NNDP in the Western Region.
56. *Odofin Bello v. The State* (1967) N.M.L.R. 1.
57. *Ibid.*
58. See the daily proceedings of the Somolu Tribunal for verbatim report of the charges preferred against E.O. Lakanmi and his specious defense. Report of the Somolu Tribunal of Investigation Report of 8, 9 & 11 August 1968.
59. *Nigerian Daily Times* May 1970.
60. B.N. Cardozo, *The Nature of the Judicial Process* (New Haven: Yale University Press, 1960), p. 168.
61. *Ibid.*
62. Walter Murphy, "Judicial Values" *Encyclopedia Britannica,* vol. 19. 315.
63. *Ibid.*
64. Oliver Wendell Holmes, *The Common Law* (Cambridge Massachusetts: Cambridge University Press, 1963), p. 5.
65. For Abiola Ojo, the *Lakanmi Case* involved a selection of values. Abiola Ojo, "Public Law the Military Government and the Supreme Court" in a A.B. Kasumu (ed.) *The Supreme Court of Nigeria...* p. 66.
66. Laws of the Western State of Nigeria.
67. L.K. Jakande, *The Ordeal of Chief Obafemi Awolowo....*
68. Obafemi Awolowo, *My March Through Prison...* p 213.
69. Trevor Clark, *Right Honourable Gentlemen...* P.620.
70. Abiola Ojo, "The search for a Grundnorm in Nigeria The Lakanmi Case" *Journal of Contemporary Law* III, 1 1972 p. 23a..

71. This was in so far as the Edict was not inconsistent with a Decree.
72. Decree No. 28 of 1970.
73. Kayode Eso, "Is there a Nigerian Grundnorm?" University of Benin Convocation Lecture, 1985, pp. 12-13.
74. *Ibid.*, p.73.
75. *Denloye*, v. *Medical and Dental Practitioners Disciplinary Tribunal*. Supreme Court of Nigeria Sc. 91/1968.
76. *Ibid.*
77. *Ibid.*
78. *Chief Adebiyi Adejumo* v. *H.E. Mobolaji O. Johnson,* Military Governor, Lagos State SC. 158/70 (Unreported). p. 11.
79. Abiola Ojo; "Thee Search for a Grundnorm in Nigeria: The Lakanmi Case" *Nigeria Journal of Contemporary Law*, pp. 239-40.
80. *Ibid.*
81. Supreme Court of Nigeria Suit No. 158/70.
82. Chief Justice of Nigeria (Extension of Period of Office) Decree 1971. Supplement of Official Gazette No. 5 vol. 58 February 4 1971.
83. The Legal Practitioners (Amendment) Decree 1971. Supplement to Official Gazette No. 60 vol. 58 December 1971.
84. Section 1(3).
85. For detailed discussion of the life, legal exploits and contributions of Elias to law in Nigeria, See Fatayi Kuti, *Elias: A Man of His Time* (Benin City: Patrac Ltd., 1991).

Conclusion

The Jurisprudence of Sir Adetokunbo Ademola

> While constitutional exercise of power by the executive and legislative branches is subject to judicial restraints, the only check on our own exercise of power is our own sense of self-restraint. For the removal of unwise laws from the statute hooks, appeal lies not to the courts but to the ballot and to the processes off democratic government.
>
> Harlan Fiske Stone in *United States v. Butler* 297 U.S. I 78, 88 (1936).

Our examination of the judicial career of Sir Adetokunbo Ademola which covered an unbroken period of thirty three years concludes that the subject developed a judicial philosophy which failed to provide a uniform and consistent guide for the relationship between the executive and the judiciary without an adverse effect on the independence of the judiciary as a separate arm of government. It has also been shown that the judicial attitudes of Sir Adetokunbo Ademola depended, more or less, on the nature and character of the government in power at the given time. Being a biographical study, and to avoid the pit fall of unnecessary repetitions, the judicial attitudes of Sir Adetokunbo as they related to the courts and the executive were examined under four major concerns which invariably coincided with the major phases of his stewardship on the bench.

At the beginning of his career, and under colonial rule when the post of a magistrate was practically that of a career officer in the civil service, Adetokunbo Ademola was understandably concerned with the need to use the lower court as an effective agency of legal control. The various ordinances relating to the courts and the judicial reforms that were introduced defined the judicial duties of officers and at the sane time influenced their judicial performance. The lower court system helped to maintain the legal and social systems that were constructed to enhance colonial administration and exploitation.

Under colonial rule, the judiciary remained a part of the elaborate colonial civil service and there was hardly a need to establish a system of justice that would seem to be independent of the executive.[1] Judicial independence was never contemplated partly because the colonial apparatus in Nigeria was not considered autonomous and independent of the British home government. The judiciary therefore operated on the basis of being a part of the machinery of British administration in colonial Nigeria without any existence of its own. The executive headed by the governor made all judicial appointments. In theory, the governor acted on the instructions of the Secretary of State for the Colonies in London, but in reality the Colonial Office never made any judicial appointment without the input of the governor. In colonial Nigeria, judges and magistrates held offices during Her Majesty's pleasure.[2] The implication of this is that they could be removed from office at will and for any reasons. The independence of the judiciary under colonial rule was further assaulted by an administrative procedure or practice that required that judges and magistrates be reported upon by the Chief Justice. As rightly observed by Roberts Wray, the practice was "in principle out of harmony with judicial independence."[3]

It could therefore be understood why Adetokunbo Ademola's magistracy was characterized by the need to protect the interest of Britain in Nigeria. As noted above, his educational and professional background in English legal traditions, the cordial relationship between his uncle, Sir Adeyemo Alakija, and his father Sir Ademola II the Alake of Egbaland on the one hand and influential British officials and politicians on the other, compelled the young magistrate to develop a collaborative and supportive judicial orientation. It would seem that by 1939, Adetokunbo Ademola was convinced of the civilizing mission of Britain in Nigeria. He probably did not understand the political economy of colonialism and the role the judiciary could play in bringing about a more humane administration.

The Oliver Lytelton's constitution of 1954 regionalized the judiciary and in spite of the avowed opposition of Adetokunbo Ademola to judicial decentralization, he was appointed the first Chief Justice of the Western Region. The historical and political circumstances of the Western Region during this time were probably in part, responsible for the development of a new judicial outlook in Adetokunbo Ademola. As Chief Justice, he distinguished between the interests of' the state and that of the political party that formed government in the Western Region. While he would not frustrate the policies of the A.G. led government, he was equally alert to defend the opposition party against possible abuse of privilege. His concern seemed to be the need to protect the interest of opposition so that it serve as check on the possible abuse of power by politicians in power in the Western Region. We have led evidence to show that he became too personally involved in opposition to the interest of the party in government. By so doing, he unwittingly exposed the judiciary he headed to denigrating and uncharitable remarks of those who believed that the Chief Justice was brazenly partisan in both judicial and private capacities.

When Adetokunbo Ademola was appointed Chief Justice of the Federation in 1958, the centrepiece of his policy was the strengthening of the powers and leverage of the central government so that it could arrest drifts toward decentralization. Adetokunbo Ademola became an advocate of unrestricted centralization, as he was convinced of the need for federal supremacy in order to have an effective state system. Reading the Westminster script, Adetokunbo Ademola believed that excessive and compulsive opposition to the programmes, policies, and intentions of the central government by the Action Group was detrimental to progressive and accelerated development of the Nigerian State.

It was believed that the quality, quantity, and vehemence of the opposition put up by the Action group would invariably make the country ungovernable. The Supreme Court under the leadership of Adetokunbo Ademola became involved in the efforts to silence opposition in order to avoid what Adetokunbo Ademola preferred to call a "slip into anarchy".

Military rule in Nigeria has been variously commented upon in terms of reasons for intervention, contributions to national unity and integration, and with respect to the militarization of all the institutions of state. As noted elsewhere, the military in 1966 was ill prepared and ill equipped intellectually and by training to manage the affairs of state. In this regard, some of the policies and laws that were introduced in pursuit of ill-conceived objectives became sometimes contradictory, counter productive, and a negative blot on the national psyche.[4] The pseudo puritanism of the military led to the promulgation of laws that affected individual liberties, freedom, and the right to property. Adetokunbo Ademola became concerned of the need to protect individual rights against state excesses as contained in *ad hominem* laws that, in most cases, had retrospective effect. The Supreme Court in a few cases that came before it had to review some instances of excessive exercise of power by the military. A high water mark was attained in the *Lakanmi case*. In spite of the gallantry and activism displayed by the court to emphasize the concept of judicial independence and uphold the principle of separation of powers, the circumstances of the case, the general climate of opinion, and perhaps most importantly, the weak theoretical and intellectual foundations of the judgement swept the rug off the feet of the Supreme Court. The book has examined these concerns vis a vis the extent Adetokunbo Ademola demonstrated consistency in principle while giving effect to these concerns as reflected in his judicial performance.

In 1963, the Supreme Court became the apex court for all Nigerian cases. The decision to stop further appeals to the Privy Council was taken to establish the "fact of Nigeria's sovereignty". Beyond this however, it would seem that the Nigerian government was more concerned with the need to vest the determination of political matters finally in the Supreme Court of Nigeria which was then headed by a collaborative, supportive and predictable Chief Justice. As noted above, the decision of the Privy Council in the *Adegbenro v. Akintola*[5] irked the Prime Minister seriously. The new status of the Supreme Court provided opportunity for Adetokunbo Ademola to lead the court and to provide it with an institutional identity. This identity became variously described depending upon the angle of the prism the observer was. While it may be difficult to describe Adetokunbo Ademola as a great judge, we cannot overlook his exemplary leadership of the Supreme Court. In the legal profession, judges of appellate courts hold pre-eminent positions in terms of status, prestige, and influence.[6] By reason of his position, Adetokunbo Ademola had a rare opportunity to exercise leadership through his judicial and quasi-judicial activities and involvements. He was a diligent Chief Justice who over the years, developed and attained clarity in writing. He believed that clarity of a judge's writing was a key element in leadership since the lower courts and legal practitioners were bound to study the opinions of the Supreme Court. To him every sentence, phrase and footnote in court opinions carried significant weight in the legal community. In a number of important cases, he took pains to set the arguments straight in unambiguous style based on simple logical reasoning. However, unlike Oliver Wendell Holmes, he did not believe that arguments within historical context could be of any assistance in constructing the intent of the constitution. A careful review of landmark judgments in other judicial traditions has shown that by placing law in its historical context, opinions of justices are "informative and insightful beyond mere exposition of legal principles."[7]

Adetokunbo Ademola provided leadership to the legal profession in Nigeria by his involvement in activities broadly related to the development of the profession in Nigeria. He attended conferences and seminars on law within and outside the country and in some cases, presented papers for discussion. His commitment to the administration of justice cannot be easily faulted. He played a leading role in the establishment of the Council of Legal Education, the Nigerian Law School[8] and the institution of the Body of Benchers of which he became the first President. In the words of F.R.A. Williams, Fakayode and Olatawura, Adetokunbo Ademola was a positive influence on the legal profession because of his firm belief in the fraternity of learned brothers. The most eloquent testimony of Adetokunbo Ademola's leadership effectiveness was consensus building among the justices of the Supreme Court. He had the uncanny ability of securing the concurrence of the justices on many occasions to the extent that, except on very few occasions, the Supreme Court under him spoke with one voice. As rightly submitted by Sherman Finesliver, 'controversial and innovative decisions carry more weight and better stand the test of time when a unanimous or near unanimously court joins the decision'.[9] This fact is better illustrated in the *Lakanmi case,* which was unanimously determined in spite of the overwhelming and intimidating presence of the military in government.[10] The ability of the Chief Justice to secure unanimity of his brethren on the bench added to the credibility and relevance of the court in Nigeria. There is no evidence that the Chief Justice employed any unorthodox means to ensure unanimity in the Supreme Court. There is much sense in Lewis Powell's observation that splintered decisions often provide 'insufficient guidance to lower courts'.[11] In deed, the failure of an appellate court to agree on a rationale for a decision is capable of inviting continuous attack on court decisions and case re-examination.

In spite of his longevity, status, and influence on the bench as Chief Justice, Western Region (1954 - 1958) and the Supreme Court (1958 - 1972), Adetokunbo Ademola did no establish a definite and recognizable judicial tradition in Nigeria. Adetokunbo Ademola possessed qualities of leadership, had appropriate professional educational background and could communicate effectively. He was equally diligent, industrious and hardworking but failed to meet the high stringent requirements of attaining the status of being described as a great judge. A careful review of the numerous judgments of Ademola would reveal that he was not as academic as one would have expected of a judge of his status, experience and exposure. He wrote very little as some of his judgments have been described as skeletal and scanty. He was obviously a smart judge who could not be influenced by impressive performance of brilliant counsel. He developed a capacity to assimilate, modify or reject tendentious arguments of even persuasive counsel who were more oratorical than legal.

Adetokunbo Ademola possessed an able and agile mind, but somehow lacked craftsmanship and technique in writing. His talent seemed to be an analytical mind and remarkable competence in judicial administration. One major criticism of the jurisprudence of Adetokunbo Ademola is his failure to demonstrate judicial neutrality of which Lord Denning became so well known. By training he could not be said to have been well grounded in the principles of constitutional adjudication. This deficiency, no doubt was responsible in part for his failure to develop a solid understanding of the proper judicial role of the Chief Justice of Nigeria under a written constitution. Despite the flash of activism that was demonstrated in the *Lakanmi case,* Adetokunbo Ademola was an apostle of judicial self-restraint. The performance of the Supreme Court in constitutional cases between 1960 and 1965 created and sustained the impression of political bias. The Supreme Court seemed to be aiding the politicians in power at the centre in the persecution and the attempts to annihilate all oppositions and in the re-writing of the constitution. Adetokunbo Ademola believed that the constitution could only succeed if the politicians approached it with tolerance, and the judges interpreted it with prudence and restraint.

Evidently, the political role of the Chief Justice circumscribed and limited his ability to hold and apply consistent principles. He could neither develop a rounded judicial philosophy nor retain a sense of promoting the higher values of using the agency of the Supreme Court to promote service to humanity through law. Here, judicial consistency is not synonymous with reluctance to re-evaluate *stare decisis* in order to correct past injustice and make the law responsive to contemporary definition of social reality and social values. It could be said that Adetokunbo Ademola was better pre disposed to the principles of expediency in espousing the law and interpreting the constitution, especially as they affect inter-government relationship. The Supreme Court under Adetokunbo Ademola knew that the national question was how to weld together the different ethnic groups with their different languages and culture. The court did not however, rise to the occasion of obliterating primordial cleavages amongst sub nationalities in Nigeria.

Adetokunbo Ademola could not establish a definite and recognizable judicial tradition in Nigeria in spite of his towering judicial stature. This inability could be ascribed to institutional and personal limitations on the part of the State and the Chief Justice respectively. In the first instance, the nature, dynamics, and volatility of Nigeria's political system exposed judicial personalities to too much involvement in partisan politics. The political role of Adetokunbo Ademola within the divisive context of the zero sum game politics of the First Republic brought the judiciary into the thick set of political mud slinging. The Chief Justice failed to appreciate the fact that constitutional decisions should be genuinely principled in the sense that they must be based on sound reasoning which in most cases would be as obvious and as convincing. In the words of Wechsler, such reasons must be in respect to all the issues in the case, reason that in their generality and their neutrality transcend any immediate result that is involved.[12] Nwabueze has even maintained that a constitutional decision should not be based on expediency but upon reason commanding a generality and neutrality of application. It would seem that the Chief Justice did not see the peculiar purpose of constitutional adjudication in resolving the problems of inter regional and partisan conflicts and crises in a plural society. The Supreme Court failed to play the role of a national arbiter and consequently its decision did not enjoy the acceptance and confidence of the critical public. The decisions of the Supreme Court in many of the constitutional cases reviewed did not serve the best interest of the Nigerian State as they failed woefully to stabilize political activities and solve the national question by reducing to the minimum, instances of suspicion, hostility and rivalry among the ethnic groups. Adetokunbo Ademola's reluctance to adopt more radical judicial attitude became noticeable when he used the occasion of conference on the problems of federalism in Nigeria to answer the critics of his conservative judicial orientation and attitude. He believed that much had been said about the liberal method of interpretation, but that, it must however be remembered that conditions were different from one country to another. In his words, 'whilst therefore judicial interpretations in Nigeria may not necessarily follow those of other countries, it was to be hoped that courts in Nigeria would evolve their own distinct jurisprudence.'

This distinct jurisprudence did not however evolve as prophesied by Adetokunbo Ademola. Military rule and the subsequent militarization of all the institutions of state and their processes ushered in a period of stress and strain for the judiciary especially the Supreme Court. Apart from the mistrust in some quarters based on the alleged partisanship of some of the decisions of the Supreme Court, the introduction and the use of decrees by the military opened up the flanks of the Supreme Court to attack by critics. The court had to contend with decrees ousting its jurisdiction entirely and some others violating the fundamental human rights of citizens. Again, the nature and character of military rule did not allow for the existence of an independent judiciary. The command and authority structure of the military organization became visible in the administration and governance of the Nigerian State. Although the judiciary, the public service, the armed forces, and the police continued as before, military dictatorship circumscribed the powers of the court. The procedure for the appointment of judges of the superior courts was deliberately altered. The Chief Justice of the Federation was to be appointed and could be dismissed from office by the Head of State and Commander-in-Chief of the Armed Forces without reference to any other body. The Supreme Court became too cautious and thereby open to condemnation as lacking a proper appreciation of the pervasive values of the Nigerian society.[13]

The heavy workload of the Supreme Court was another major limitation on the establishment of a definite and recognizable judicial tradition by Adetokunbo Ademola. The Supreme Court felt the strain of the heavy workload especially on the judicial performance of its justices. The Chief Justice once had cause to comment that the workload was capable of stifling the performance of the justices when he said:

> At the rate at which the justices of the Supreme Court are working not much should be expected from them. Three justices are sitting all the time during the week. At the same time, they must squeeze in time to write judgments of the cases already heard. And again contemporaneously, they must also read the record of appeal to be heard in the week following and delve into their personal research of the authorities likely to be employed in argument. It seems impossible and it all boils down to the issue of the workload on the Supreme Court.[14]

Workload of the Supreme Court

YEAR	CIVIL	CRIMINAL	TOTAL
1958	71	63	134
1959	64	156	220
1960	86	75	161
1966	*122*	90	212
1967	69	58	127
1968	75	32	107
1969	7 8	45	123
1970	80	45	130

Source: A.B. Kasumu (ed.), *The Supreme Court of Nigeria, 1956 – 1970* (Ibadan: Heinemann Books Nig. Ltd., 1977), pp. 36- 37.

Obviously, the heavy workload of the Supreme Court encouraged what could be described as skeletal judgments and the tendency of the justices to restrict themselves narrowly to the issues before them instead of utilizing the opportunity as a final court to clarify the law, particularly in cases where there were no precedents. Evidently, these disenabling situations made it convenient for the Supreme Court to shirk its responsibility as the apex judicial authority in making definite pronouncement one way or the other on important legal issue that could have given the court a definite judicial image and a tradition.

A trenchant review of the socio-economic and intellectual background of Adetokunbo Ademola, the changing political character of the Nigerian State, and the institutional limitations imposed by the system, would confirm Mayer's trite submission that "no legal system, no matter how logical its design or how elegant its procedure, can rise higher than the personnel who administer it."[15]

Notes

1. *'Terrell v. Secretary of State for the Colonies* (1953), 3 W.L.R. 331 See also B. O. Nwabueze, *Judicialism in Commonwealth Africa* (London: C. Hurst & Company 1977), p. 266.
2. *Ibid.*
3. Roberts Way "The Independence of the Judiciary in Commonwealth Countries" in *Changing Law in Developing Countries* (ed.) Anderson, 1963, pp. 67-68.
4. Toyin, Falola, A. Ajayi, A. Alao and T. Babawale, *The Military Factory in Nigeria, 1966-1985* (New York: Edwin Mellen Press, 1992), pp. 69-72.
5. *Adegbenro v. Akintola & Aderemi* (1962), 1 ALL NLR. 465.
6. Sherman G. Finesilver "Leadership on the United States Supreme Court: Justice who have made A Difference" in W.D. Fedenson and N.W. Provizer, *Great Justices of the U.S. Supreme Court,* p. 350.
7. *lbid.*
8. Adetokunbo Ademola personally donated the parcel of land on which the Law School, Victoria Island, Lagos was eventually built in 1962.

9. Sherman Finesilver, "Leadership on the United States Supreme Court..." p. 357.
10. Adetokunbo Ademola sat with Justices G.B.A. Coker, Ian Lewis, Charles Olusoji Madarikan and Sir Udo Udoma.
11. Justice Lewis Powell, .1.R. "Stare Decisis and Judicial Restraint", Speech Before the Association of the Bar of the City of New York (October 17, 1989), in 'Vital Speeches of the Day November 15, 1989", at p. 80.
12. Herbert Wechsler "Towards Neutral Principles in Constitutional Law" in *Selected Essays on Constitutional Law* (Association of American Law Schools 1963), p. 475, reprinted from *Harvard Law Review*, 73 (1959), p.1.
13. B.0. Nwabueze, *Judicialism in Commonwealth Africa...* p. 145.
14. NLQ vol. 6 (1973), p. 393.
15. L Meyers, *The American Legal System* (New York: Harper & Row, 1955), p. 369.

Bibliography

PRIMARY SOURCES

Reported and Unreported Judicial Decisions

Abudu Aliwo v. *Oseni Oregbesan*
Supreme Court Ibadan S/N 1/68/1952
6 November 1953. (Unreported)

Adegoke Adelabu and L. Ade Bello v. *Inspector General of Police*
High Court of Justice Ibadan.
22 November 1955 WRNLR 1955-56 pp 6-12

Akerele v. *Inspector General of Police*
Federal Supreme Court Ibadan
7 January 1955 NLR vol xxi pp 37-38.

Akinola Allen v. *I . B.A. Adegoke (Representing Iba Oluyole Family), Mawad*
Bello Adedibu, Tella Ashipa
High Court of Justice Ibadan SN.1 1/172/55
1 4 August 1957 (Unreported)

Ali Adekunle and two others in re: Stanley Bazuaye v. *Inspector General of Police*
High Court of Justice Ibadan
27 July 1955 WRNLR 1955-56 pp 16-17

Amachree and Others v. *Newton*
Federal Supreme Court Port Harcourt P/74? 1950
7th May 1951 NLR vol xx, pp. 13-15, 1954.

Bright v. *E.D. Lines Ltd and General Manager, Nigerian Railway.*
Supreme Court Port Harcourt P31/1952
3 October 1952 NLR vol. xx, pp 79-80, 1954.

Gafaru Akanni (Tajani v. *J.A. Sijuade*
High Court of Justice Ibadan SN 1/93/1956
7 July 1956 (Unreported)

Gbolade Johnson v. 1. *Abigail Ebun Johnson, David Olu Olufunmilayo Johnson, Olufemi Johnson, Adekunle Johnson, Akintunde Johnson, Sukaratu Babatunde Ogun*
High Court of Justice Ibadan SN 1/300/55
29 November 1956 (Unreported)

Horvat v. *Police*
Supreme Court Port Harcourt P/23A/1952
21 June 1952 N.L.R. vol x, pp. 52-54, 1954.

Ibadan District Council v. *Ishola Mosadogun, Afolabi Ajagbe, Oyeleke Ayinla Agboola Akande & Jimoh Odutola*
High Court of Justice Ibadan
25 July WRNLR 1955-56, pp. 22-27

M.I. *Igbintola (judgement creditor)* v. *Muili Ishola (Judgement Debtor) in re: Raliatu Busari and 3 other claimants*
Supreme Court Ibadan S/N 1/137/1953
30 March 1954. (Unreported)

Inspector General of Police v. *Anozie*
Supreme Court, Ibadan.
16 July 1954 N.L.R. vol. xxi, pp. 29-30, 1957.

Inspector General of Police v. *Olatunji*
Supreme Court Ibadan 12 May 1955 NLR vol. xxi, pp. 52-53.

Inspector General of Police v. Ganiyu Oyeneye
High Court of Justice Ibadan No. 1/35CA/55
12 October 1955 WRNLR 1955-56, pp. 4-5

Isaac Otunuga and Others v. *Salami Adelaja*
High Court of Justice Ibadan SN 1/54/54
5 February 1957 (Unreported)

Jacob Oyedokun v. *J.A. Odutola & Co.*
Supreme Court Ibadan S/N 1/135/1953
29 March 1954 (Unreported)

John Holt & Co (Liverpool Ltd.) Judgement Creditor v. *Yinusa Goodluck (Judgement Debtor) in re: Tijani Okufadi [Claimant]*
High Court of Justice Ibadan SN 1/26/1956
20 December 1956. (Unreported)

Joshua Fowowe v. Ajimoko (Haastrup) Owa of Ilesha
High Court of Justice Ibadan
30 May 1956 WRNLR 1955-56, pp. 103-104

Khalil & Dibbo Transport Ltd. v. Gabriel Oyewumi
Supreme Court Ibadan S/N 1/139/1953
16 December 1953 (Unreported)

Lawani Tewogbade, Ladosu Adigun, Salami Alalade, Jacob Ogundijo, Salami Kayode (for themselves and other members of the Elemo Chieftaincy Family of Ikirun) *v. Chief Lawani Adeyemi Akinrun of Ikirun, Chief Raji Oyeniyi, Odofin of Ikirun, Raji Abioye of Ikirun*
High Court of Justice Ibadan SN 1/99/54
7 June 1956 (Unreported)

Mustafa Ayinde Laniyun v. *A.G. Ijala, Suleman Ajadi*
Supreme Court Ibadan S/N 1/588/53
29 March 1954 (Unreported)

Naim Khalil Zard v. *Michael Joseph Saliba*
High Court of Justice Ibadan
23 March 1956 WRNLR 1955-56, pp. 63-65

J.B. Okafor v. *Messrs Richard Costain Ltd.*
Supreme Court Ibadan S/N/122/1953
16 December 1953 (Unreported)

Oyebanji Ajadi & Family v. *Seriki of Ibadan &Principal Wesley College Ibadan*
High Court of Justice Ibadan SN 1/75/55
5 February 1957 (Unreported)

Olajide Babalola & 6 Ors. v. *Hannah Magbabeola & Anor.*
Supreme Court Ibadan S/N 1/23/1952
29 March 1954 (Unreported)

The Queen v. *Emmanuel Jegede, Rufai Odutola. Turuku Shonubi. Odu Ogun,Idowu Dada, Abudu Aluko*
High Court of Justice Ibadan
17 October 1955 WRNLR 1955-56, pp. 33-37

The Queen v. Joseph Kesinro
High Court of Justice Ibadan
15 March -1956 WRNLR 1955-56, pp. 56-57

The Queen v. *The Minister of Education Western Region Ex Parte Emmanuel S. Akappe, Applicant*
High Court of Justice Ibadan SN 1/20/57
20 March 1957 (Unreported)

Re: Marcus O Ajaero
Supreme Court Port Harcourt P/21A/1952
23 September 1952 N.L.R. vol. xx, pp. 77-75, 1954.

Regina v. Ilorin Native Court Ex Parte Jomoh Aremu & Ors. Applicants
Supreme Court Ibadan Suit No. M/2/1953
31 August 1953. NLR vol. xx, pp 144-146, 1954.

Regina v, *The Resident of Oyo Province, His Excellency the Governor of Nigeria Ex Parte Tiamiyu Adebayo Adeniran (Aremo of Oyo),* [Applicant].
Supreme Court Ibadan S/No. 45/1953.
6 November 1953 (Unreported)

Regina v. *The Resident of Ibadan Province Ex parte Sanusi Oyegbesan, (Applicant)*
Supreme Court Ibadan S/NM 45/1953
7 December 1953 (Unreported]

Regina v. Ladokun (Bashorun of ()yo) & 6 Ors., Ex Parte Adeleke Balogun and 10 Others.
Supreme Court Ibadan S/N/l /129/1953.
10 February 1954. (Unreported)

Regina v. *The Ibadan Judicial Council re: A.R. Salami Applicant.*
Supreme Court Ibadan S/N/1/36/53
30 March 1954 (Unreported)

Regina v. Diyaolu
High Court of Justice Ibadan
29 September 1955 WRNLR 1955-56, pp. 30-31

Robert O Oshinfekun v Yinusa Lana High Court of Justice Ibadan
2 May 1956 WRNLR 1955-56, pp. 93-94.

Rosa Nwosu v. *Babalola Kuteyi_& Ojo Adcbedu*
Supreme Court Ibadan S/N /1/33/1953
12 April 1954.

A.R. Salami v. Joseph Nahman
High Court of Justice Ibadan
2 November 1955 WRNLR 1955-56. pp. 18-19.

Sunmola Alaga v. *Lasisi Amao & Lamide Ayinde*
Supreme Court Ibadan (Unreported)
15 December 1953.

T.A. Doherty & H.A.A. Doherty (Surviving Executors of the Estate of J.H. Doherty (Deceased) v. *Nigerian Properties Company Ltd., & Michael Courie Aboud.*
High Court of Justice Ibadan S/N. 1/3/55
7 March 1957 (Unreported)

Viatonu v. Odutayo and Kuyoro Consolidated with Kuvoro v. Viatonu
Supreme Court Lagos LS 271/149 & LS 216/49
25 September 1950, N.L.R. vol. xix, pp.119-121, 1954.

Waluid Shaar v. *Anthony Younan*
Supreme Court Ibadan S/N 1/35/1953
29 March 1954 (Unreported)

Yesufu Adegbindin (For and on behalf of his family)
v. *Adegoke, Mustapha Alhaji, Lasisi Alhaji, Raji Adesokan*
High Court of Justice, Ibadan S/N. 1/58/56
17 July 1957 (Unreported).

SECONDARY SOURCES

Selected Articles

Adei C.Y.U. "Limits in the Application of English Law", *Nigeria* vol. 3 1 & 2, 1968. pp 11-21 .

Aguda ;A.T., "The Definition of Crime in Nigeria", *The Nigerian Bar Journal* ix, 1, 1963.

______ "Judicial Attitude to Certain Fundamental Issues under the Constitution", *Nigerian Bar Journal* xi, 1973.

Aihe, D.O. "An Evaluation of the Role of the Judiciary in the Working of the Nigerian Constitution since 1960", *Quarterly Journal of Administration* v, 1971.

______ Fundamental Rights and the Military Regime: What did the Courts Say?" *Journal of African Law*, ii, 1970.

Ajayi F.A., "The Interaction of English Law With Customary Law in Western Nigeria, *Journal of African Law,* iv, 1, 1960, and in iv, 2, 1960.

Akande, I. "The Problem of Locus Standi in Judicial Review" *Nigerian Current Law Review* January 1982.

Akanki, O. "Reflections on Some Recent Constitutional Issues," *Nigerian Law Journal* 3, 1961.

Beidelman, T.O. "The Influence of English Law on West Africa" *Journal of African Law* x, 1,1961.

Benson, LO.S. "Lawyers and Our Society" *The Nigerian Bar Journal*, 12, 197.1.

Blasi, V. "The Court as an Instrument of Change" *Dialogue* 67,1985.

Brett Sir Lionel, "*Stare Decisis* in Nigeria: Some Random Thoughts", *Nigerian Bar Journal*, vi, 1965.

Cottrell, J. "Ultra Vires is Alive and Living in Nigeria", *Nigerian Journal of Contemporary Law* iii, 1, 1972.

Dabiri A.F.O. "Local Attorneys as Pioneers of the Legal Judicial Preceden,s", Modern *Law Review* 18, 1955.

Elias, T.0., "Colonial Courts and the Doctrine of Judicial Precedents", *Modern Law Review* 18, 1955.

______"The Independence of the Colonial Judiciary, *Juridical Review* I (New Series), 1956.

______"The New Constitution of Nigeria and the Protection of Human Rights and Fundamental Freedoms", *Journal of the International Commission of Jurists* ii, 2, 1959-60.

______ "Legal Education in Nigeria". *Journal of African Law*. xi, 2. 1962.

______"A Report on African Legal Studies in the United Kingdom", *Journal of African Law,* v, 3, 1961,

Eweluka.`D.1.0. "Declaratory Judgments in Nigerian Public Law" *Nigerian Law Journal,* viii, 1974.

______ "Proceedings by and Against the Slate in Nigeria" *Nigerian Bar Journal* xi, 1973.

______ "The Doctrine of Covering the Field" *Nigerian Juridical Review*, 11, 1977.

______ "The Constitutional Aspects of the Military Take Over in Nigeria" *Nigerian Law Journal* 11, 6, 1967.

Ezcjiofor, G. "Nigerian Judicial Structure and the Distribution of Judicial Competence" *Nigerian Bar* Journal, xi, 1973.

Grove, D.L.V. "The Sentinels of Liberty? The Nigerian Judiciary and Fundamental Rights", *Journal of African Law,* 152, 1963.

Guobadia, A. "Constitutional Adjudication *Locus Standi*: Recent Trends in Nigerian Courts" *The Nigerian Juridical Review*, iii, 1978.

Hollanbds, D.C. "Human Rights in Nigeria", *Current Legal Problems,* xv, 1962.

Ijalaye, D.A. "Doing Justice in Nigerian Courts" *Nigerian Lawyers Quarterly*, v, 1-4.

______ "Contempt of Court in Nigeria: A Re-evaluation" *The Nigerian Bar Journal"*, xi, 1973.

Jegede, M.I.. "The Position of the Head of a Family in Relation to Family *Nigerian Bar Journal* vii, 1966.

Karibi-Whyte. A.G. "Some Problems of Conspiracy in Nigeria Criminal Law" *Nigerian Bar Journal* ix, 1971.

______ "Federal Military Government (Supremacy and Enforcement of Powers) Decree 1970". *Nigerian Journal of Contemporary Law* i, 2, 1970.

Levasseur, G., "Justice and State Security" *Journal of the International Commission of Jurists*, v, 2, 1964.

Lloyd, P.C. "Some Notes on the Yoruba Rules of Succession and on Family Property" *Journal of African Law* iii, 1959.

Nwabueze, B.0. , Nigerian Appeals to the Privy Council" *Nigerian Bar Journal,* iv, 1, 1963.

Obilade. A.O., Revolutionarv Regimes and the Pre-existing Laws in Nigeria" *Nigerian Bar Journal,* xx, l, 1985

OIuyede. P.A. "Judicial Approach to Customary Law *Nigeria Lawyers Quarterly,* iii, I S 2, 1965.

Ojo Abiola, "The Search for a Grundnorm in Nigeria: The Lakanmi Case", *Nigerian Journal of Contemporary Law,* iii, 1972.

______ "Habeas Corpus in Nigeria: Some Views on the Scope of" *Nigerian Journal of Contemporary Law,* i, 1, 1970.

______ "The Role of the Supreme Court in the Resolution of Power Conflict Between the Federal and Regional Governments under the Constitution of the First Republic" *Nigeria Law Journal* viii, 1974,

Olaogun. B.A. "Contempt of Court" *Nigerian Bar Journal,* vii, 1966.

Olawoyin, G.A. "The Effects of Repugnancy Clause on the Validity of Customary Law" *Nigerian Bar Journal,* x, 1972.

Read, J.S. "Constitutions on the Move: Constitutional and Political Developments in 1958", *Journal of African Law,* 1, iii, 1, 1959.

______ "Criminal Law in the Africa of Today and Tomorrow" *Journal of African Law* vii, 1. 1963.

Roberts Wray Kenneth "The Adaptation of Imported Law in Africa" *Journal of African Law,* iv, 2. 1960,

Sagay, Itse "State Rights to Prescribe Grounds for Appeal to the Supreme Court" *Nigerian Bar Journal,* vii, 1966.

CONFERENCE PROCEEDINGS

1. All Nigeria Judges Conference, Ilorin, Kwara State. 8-16 March. 1982.

Agbaje, A,G.O., "Fundamental Rights Provision of the Constitution."

Ardo, M.B., "The Place of the Judiciary in the Constitution"

Craig" E.B. "Control of the Funds and Staff of the Judiciary"

Eso, K., "The Problems of Interpretation and of Application of the Provisions of the Constitution."

Fatayi-Williams, A., "Appointment of Justices or Judges to Head Commissions or Tribunals of Inquiry."

General Reports of Panel Discussions and Resolution "Appointment of Justices or Judges to Head Commissions or Tribunals of Inquiry."

General Reports of Panel Discussions and Resolution on the Subject of the Control of the Funds and the Staff of the Judiciary.

Idigbe, I., "Fundamental Rights Provisions of the Constitution."

Karibi-Whyte, A.G., "The Problems of Interpretation and of Application of the Provisions of the Constitution: Commentary."

Kawu, S., "Control of the Funds and Staff of the Judiciary: Commentary."

Mohammed, U., "Appointment of Justices or Judges to Head Commissions or Tribunals of Inquiry: Commentary."

Nnaemeka-Agu, P., "The Problems of Interpretation and of Application of the Provisions of the Constitution: Commentary."

Obi-Okoye, A., "Appointment of Justices or Judges to Head Commissions or Tribunals of Inquiry."

Orojo, O., "Control of the Funds and Staff of the Judiciary."

2. All Nigeria Judges Conference, Abuja. 4-10 September 1988.

Bello, M., "Opening Address."

Ardo, M.B., "Administration of the Judiciary."

Eso, K., "The Courts as Guardian of the Constitution."

Karibi-Whyte, A.G.,, "Politics of the Judiciary: Commentary."

Nnaemeka-Agu, P., "Politics of the Judiciary in the Second Republic: Commentary."

Nnamani, A., "Abuse of Judicial Process."

Nassir, M., "Politics of the Judiciary in the Second Republic."

Ogundare, M.E., "Politics of the Judiciary in the Second Republic: Comments."

Omo, U., "The Courts as Guardian of the Constitution,"

Oputa, C.A., "The Place of the Judiciary in the Third Republic: Commentary."

3. 1990 Judicial Lectures, Enugu

Agbaje, A. M., "Contempt of Court and Discourtesy."

Akanbi, M.A., "Constitutional Structure and the Position of the Judiciary: Fundamental Rights."

Aniagolu, A.N., "Contempt of Court and Discourtesy."

Anogu, F., "Interim Order and Perpetual Injunctions."

Karibi-Whyte, A.G., "Considerations and Preliminary Objections: Locus StandiScope of."

Nassir, N.J., "The Judiciary Under the Constitution".

Nwokedi, P.K., "Stay of Proceedings and Execution"

Ogundare, J.D., "Judicial Ethics with Particular Reference to Discipline within the Judiciary including Comportment of Judges."

Oputa, C., "Judicial Ethics: Law, Justice and the Judiciary."

Obaseki, A.0., "Constitutional Structure and the Position of the Judiciary: Interpretative Jurisdiction of the Courts and Interpretation of other Statutes."

4. Conference of the Attorneys-General. Abuja. 11- 13 October 1988.

Fabunmi, H.B., "How Independent is the Independence of the Judiciary." Haruna, I..B.M. "Administration of Justice in a Military Era."

Orojo, O., "Code of Conduct for Judges."

Aguda, T. A, "Locus Standi and Constitutional Adjudication."

Akande. J.O., "The Role of Judicial Precedent in Constitutional Adjudication. A Comparative American and Nigerian Experience

Eweluka, D.O., "Judicial Enforcement of Constitutional Guarantee of Human Rights."

Graham-Douglas, N.B., "Principles and Expediency in Constitutional Adjudication.'

Kolawole, 0., 'Justiciability of Constitutional Adjudication."

Nwabueze, B.0., "Comparative Analysis of the Principles of the Nigerian and U.S.A. Constitutions."

5. Seminar on Constitutional Adjudication: A Comparative American and Nigerian Experience (Organized by the Nigerian Institute of Advanced Legal Studies in Collaboration with the Institute of Judicial Administration of the New York University. 12-18 September 1982).

Orojo, O., "Development of the Constitution through Judicial Interpretation."

Howard D.. "Stare Decisis" (First Presented at a Seminar for Federal Appellate Judges Sponsored by the Federal Judicial Center (U.S.A,) May 1975.

6. National Conference on Law Development and Administration in Nigeria 21-25 September 1987.

Aminu, M., "The Observance of the Rule of Law and Fundamental Rights."

Nnaemeka-Agu, P., Independence of the Judiciary with particular Reference to Appointment, Removal and Discipline."

Nwabueze, B., "The Observance of the Rule of Law and Fundamental Human Rights."

Oloko, O., "Independence of the Judiciary."

Oputa, C., "1ndependence of the Judiciary with particular Reference to Appointment, Removal and Discipline."

Ojo, Abiola., "The Observance of the Rule of Law and Fundamental Rights: Commentary."

Yakubu, Musa., "Independence of the Judiciary."

7. Proceedings and Papers of the Sixth Commonwealth Law Conference, Lagos. Nigeria 17-23 August 1980

Graham-Douglas. N. B., "Judicial Process Today: Constitutional Interpretation."

McAustin, J., "Judicial Precedent in the Commonwealth."

8. Proceedings of the 20th Annual Conference of the Nigerian Association of' Law Teachers. Maiduguri 16-19 August 1982.

Chand, H., "Riddles of the 1979 Constitution: Some Interpretational Challenges."

Oretuyi, S., "The Exercise of the Impeachment Power under the Constitution of the Federal Republic, 1979."

Yakubu. M., "The Judiciary, under the Presidential System."

9. Proceedings of the 26th Annual Conference of Nigerian Association of Law Teachers. Port-Harcourt, 28 March 1988.

Obaseki, A., "The Judicial Impression of the Property: Any need for Reform' (Key-note Address).

Adigun, 0 & Utuama, A., "A Decade of Land Reform in Nigeria - The Land Use Act 1978 in Perspective."

10. 28th Annual Conference of the Nigerian Association of Law Teachers lbadan. 1-4 May 1980.

Adikankwu, S. & Akigbe, *M.,* "Judicial Activism in the Third Republic."

Owasanoye, B.& Kosoko, "Enforcement of Judicial Decisions in Nigeria."

11. Record of Proceedings of a Seminar on Constitutional Problems of Federalism in Nigeria Lagos 8-15 August 1960 under the auspices of the Ford Foundations of America.

Brett, L., "The Role of the Judiciary in a Federal Constitution with particular Reference to Nigeria."

De Winton M., "Fundamental Rights in Nigeria."

Taylor, C.,: "Emergent Federalism in Nigeria."

BOOKS

Abraham, H.J., *The Judicial Process* (Oxford: Oxford University Press,

Adamolekun, Ladipo, *Politics and Administration in Nigeria* (lbadan: Spectrum Books Ltd., 1986).

Adedeji Adebayo, ed., *Nigerian Administration and its Policy Setting* (London: Hutchinson Educational Books, 1968).

Adewoye, Omoniyi, *The Judicial System in Southern Nigeria: Law and Justice in a Dependency* (London: Longman Group Ltd., 1977).

Agbede, I.0., *Hon. Dr. T. Akinola Aguda: The Man, His Works, and Society.* (Lagos: Nigerian Institute of Advanced Legal Studies 1956).

Aguda, A., *Flashback* (Ibadan: Spectrum Books Ltd. 1982).

______. *The Judiciary in the Government of Nigeria.* (1badan: Horn Press, 1983).

______. *The Challenge of the Nigerian Nation.* (Ibadan: Heinemann, 1985).

______. *The Judicial Process and the Third Republic* (Akure: E. & A Publishers, 1992)

Aihe, D.O. and Oluyede, P.O. *Cases and Materials on Constitutional Law in Nigeria* (London: Oxford University Press 1979).

Ake, Claude, *A Political Economy of Africa* (London: Longman Group Limited, 1981).

Akinrinola, R, *Salute to Courage: The Study of Justice Yaya Jinadu* (Lagos: Nigerian Law Publications Ltd. 1989).

Akinyemi, A.B, *et al* (eds.) *Readings in Federalism* (Lagos: NIIA, 1979).

Allott, A.N. (ed.), *Judicial and Legal Systems in Africa* (London Butterworths African Law Series, 1962).

Awa, A. *Portrait of Service: Biography of Hon. Justice Abai lkweche* (Enugu: Vivians & Vivians Publishers Ltd., 1989).

Awa, E.O. *Federal Government in Nigeria* (Berkeley and Los Angeles: University of California).

Awogu, F. O., Civil *Proceedings By and Against the State in Nigeria* (Onitsha: Pacific College Press, 1981).

Awolowo. O, *Path to Nigerian Freedom* (London: Faber & Faber, 1947).

______.*The People's Republic* (Ibadan: Oxford University Press).

Ayandele, E.A., The *Educated Elite in the Nigerian Society* (Ibadan: Ibadan University Press, 1974).

Badenheimer Edgar, *Jurisprudence: The Philosophy And Method of Law* (Cambridge Massachusetts: Harvard University Press, 1962).

Begho, M.A. *The Dog Bite Magistrate: His Struggles: An Autobiography* (Lagos: The Daily Times of Nigeria. Ltd., 1985).

Bell, John, *Policy Arguments in Judicial Decisions* {Oxford: Oxford University Press, 1983).

Braitwaite, T., *The Jurisprudence of the Living Oracle* (Benin City: Ethiope Publishing Co., 1987).

Clark Trevor, *A Right Honourable Gentleman: Sir Abubakar Tafawa Balewa* (Zaria: Hadahuda Press, 1992).

Coker, Folarin, *Sir Adetokunbo Ademola: A Biography* (Lagos: Daily Times of Nigeria Ltd. 1976).

Coleman, J.S. *Nigeria: Background to Nationalism* (Berkeley: University of California Press, 1963).

Cox Archbald, *The Role of the Supreme Court in American Government* (Oxford: Oxford University Press, 1976).

de Smith, S.A., *Judicial Review of Administrative Action* (London: Stevens & Sons Limited, 1973).

Denning Alfred, *The Discipline of Law* (London: Butterworths, 1979).

______. *The Due Process of Law* (London: Butterworths, 1980).

______. *The Closing Chapter* (London: Butterworths, 1982).

______. *What is Next in the Law* (London: Butterworths, 1982).

Elias, T.O. *Law and Social Change in Nigeria* (Ibadan: Evans Brothers Nigeria Publishers Ltd.).

______. Judicial Process in the Newer Commonwealth (Lagos: University of Lagos Press, 1990).

______. *Groundwork of Nigerian Law* (London: Routledge & Kegan Paul, 1954)

Esiemokhai, F.O. *The Colonial Heritage In Nigeria* (Akure: Fagbamigbe Publishers Ltd. 1986).

Eso, Kavode, *Thoughts on Law and Jurisprudence* (Lagos: M.1. Professional Publishers Ltd.)

Falola, Toyin (ed.) *Britain and Nigeria: Exploitation or Development* (London: Zed Books Ltd. 1987).

Falola, O, Ajayi A, Alao A, Babawale B, *The Military Factor in Nigeria 1966-1985* (Lewiston: Edwin Mellen Press, 1994)

Frank, Jerome, *Courts on Trial: Myth and Reality in American Justice* (New York: Athenaeum Publishers, 1970).

Hedges, R.Y. *Introduction to Criminal Law of Nigeria: Excluding the Northern Region* (London: Sweet and Maxwell, 1962).

Iluyomade B.O.& Eka, B., *Cases and Materials on Administrative Law in Nigeria* (Ile-Ife: University of Ife Press, 1980).

Karibi-Whyte, A, *The Relevance of the Judiciary in the Polity in Historical Perspective* (Lagos: Nigeria Institute of Advanced Legal Studies, 1987).

Kasumu. A. B, *The Supreme Court of Nigeria* (Ibadan: Heinemann Educational Books Nigeria Limited. 1977).

Kuti. A.F.D, Elias: *A Man of His Time* (Lagos: Patrae Ltd., 1991).

Lugard, E.D, *The Dual Mandate in British Tropical Africa* (London: 1922).

Murphy, Walter & Pritchett, C.U, *Courts, Judges, and Politics: An Introduction to the Judicial Process.* (New York: Random House, 1979).

Newbury, C.W, *British Policy Towards West Africa: Selected Documents* 1875-1914 (Oxford: CIarendon Press. 1971).

Nnoli, O, *Ethnic Politics in Nigeria* (Enugu: Fourth Dimension Publication, 1977).

Nwabueze, B.O. *Machinery of Justice in Nigeria* (London: Butterworths African Law Series, 1963).

______. *Judicialism in Commonwealth Africa* (London: C. Hurst and Company, 1977).

______. *Constitutional History of Nigeria* (Ibadan: Longman Nigeria Limited, 1982).

Nwogogu F.I. (ed.), *Current Legal Problems in Nigeria: Proceedings of the Anambra State Law Conference* (Enugu: Anambra State Government Printer, 1986).

Obasanjo, O. and Mabogunje, A., *Elements of Democracy* (Abeokuta: African Leadership Forum Publications, 1992).

Obilade. A.O. *The Nigerian Legal System* (London: Sweet and Maxwell, 1970).

Obilade, A.O. & Braxton G.J., *Due Process of Law* (Lagos: U S IS 1994).

Odumosu, L.O. *The Nigerian Constitution* (London: Sweet & Maxwell, 1963).

Ogunba Oyin, *Governance and the Electoral Process: Nigeria and the United States of America* (Lagos: American Studies Association of Nigeria, *1997*)

Ojo Abiola, *Constitutional Law and Military Rule in Nigeria* (Ibadan: Evans Brothers (Nig.) Publishers' Ltd., 1988).

Ojo J.D, *The Development of the Executive Under the Nigerian Constitution* (Ibadan: University Press Limited, 1985).

Ozekhome, Mike *A.A., The Nigerian Law of Locus Standi* (Lagos: *Mikzek Law* Publications Ltd., 1988).

Olaniyan R.A. (ed.), *Federalism in a Changing World* (Ile-Ife: Obafemi Awolowo University Press, 1992)

Pederson,W.D. Provizer, N.W, (eds.) *Great Justices of the U.S. Supreme Court: Ratings & Case Studies* (New York: Peter Lang Publishing Inc., 1993}

Sagay I. E . *Legacy for Posterity: The Work of the Supreme Court, 1980-1955* (Lagos: Nigeria Law Publications Ltd. 1988).

Sklar, R., *Nigerian Political Parties* (Princeton: University Press, 1963).

Smith, I.O, & Alade, I.A., *Taslim Olawale Elias* (Lagos: Lagos State University, 1991).

Thompson, Adewale, *Reminiscences at the Bar* (Ibadan: Bookcraft Ltd. & Associated Book Makers Nigeria Ltd., 1991).

Tamuno, T.N. *The Evolution of the Nigerian State: The Southern Phase 1898 – 1914* (London: Longmann Group Limited, 1972).

Udo-Inyang, D.S., *The Man-Sir Udo Udoma* (Calabar: Wusen Press Ltd., 1985).

Ume, F.E.O., *The Courts and Administration of Law In Nigeria.* (Enugu: Fourth Dimension Publishing Company Limited, 1989).

Umoh, P.U., *Precedents In Nigerian Courts* (Enugu: Fourth Dimension Publishing Company Limited, 1984),

White Edward, *The American Judicial Tradition: Profiles of Leading American Judges (*New York: Oxford University Press, 1976).

Williams Fatai Atanda, *Faces, Cases, and Places* (London: Butterworths, *1983).*

GOVERNMENT PUBLICATIONS

Fitzgerald et al, Report of the Commission of Enquiry into Disorders in the Eastern Provinces of Nigeria, December 1949. (London: I IM5, (PC) 256, 1950),

Phillipson, Sir Sidney et al. The Nigerianization of the Civil Service: A Review of Policy and Machinery (Lagos: Government Printer, 1952).

Robinson:, G.G., Report of the Commission of Inquiry into the Okrika-Kalabari Dispute (Enugu: Government Press, 1950)

Kingdon, Sir Donald, Report on a Tour of the Courts of the Protectorate of Nigeria (Lagos: Government Printer, 1940).

Price, H.L, Land Tenure in the Yoruba Provinces MN/X31, An Appraisal of the Development of Western Nigeria 1955-1960 (Ibadan: Government Press, 1961).

Rankine, Sir John, The Speech Delivered at the Opening of the First Session of the Western Region Legislature on October 5, 1954. (Ibadan: Government Press, 1955).

Review of the Constitution and Regional Recommendations (Lagos: Government Printer, 1919).

Recommendations of the Western Regional Conference on the Review of the Constitution. (lbadan: Advent Press, 1949).

Minutes of the Proceedings of the Western Regional Conference on the Revision of the Constitution. (Abeokuta: Egba Native Authority Printer, 1949).

Record of the Proceedings of the Nigerian Constitution held in London in July and August 1953. (Lagos: Government Printer, 1954).

Report by the Conference on the Nigerian Constitution (Lagos: Government Printer, 1953).

Record of the Proceedings of the Resumed Conference on the Nigerian Constitution (Lagos: Government Printer, 1954).

Nigerian Constitutional Conference, London, August 1953.

A Minority Report by the Action Group. (London: F.J. Everett and Co., 1953).

Courts and Native Authority Legislation in Force on September 1, *1934.*

Trials of Criminal Cases in the Provincial Courts.

Colonial Regulations: Being the Regulations for Her Majesty's Colonial Service (Public Officers).

Regulations Governing King's College, Lagos.

Debates of the Western House of Assembly 1947-1962.

Annual Report of the Ministry of Justice *1960-65.*

Supplements to Western Regional Government Gazettes 1954-63.

Colonial Nigeria and Federal Staff List 1919-1963.

High Court Sessions, Oyo Province 1955-1957.

Index